Thornwald

A Testament of the Sadler Legacy

Laura L. Strickler

Book designed by author

Edited by author and Jan Sheaffer

Printed and bound by Wert Bookbinding

Copyright © 2012 by Laura L. Strickler

ALL RIGHTS RESERVED

No part of this book may be reproduced or transmitted in any form or by any means whatsoever without express written permission from the author.

ISBN: 978-1-4675-3512-0

Table of Contents

Acknowledgements V

Introduction.. VII

Chapter 1: The Sadler Family... 9

Chapter 2: "Like Father, Like Son".. 15

Chapter 3: The Bosler Family.. 18

Chapter 4: "Sadler-Bosler"... 22

Chapter 5: Years at Cottage Hill.. 24

Chapter 6: Dr. and Mrs. Horace Sadler... 26

Chapter 7: The Residence of L.S. Sadler.. 32

Chapter 8: "Thornwold"... 54

Chapter 9: Additions to the Thornwald Estate...................................... 108

Chapter 10: Living in High Society.. 114

Chapter 11: A Black Cloud Looms Over Thornwald............................ 120

Chapter 12: A Man of Distinction.. 124

Chapter 13: The Inheritance.. 138

Chapter 14: The Final Years of Justice Sylvester Sadler..................... 142

Chapter 15: The Final Years at Thornwald... 146

Chapter 16: The End of an Era.. 154

Chapter 17: The Sale of the Sadler Heirlooms..................................... 172

Chapter 18: Homewood……………………………………………………….. 184

Chapter 19: Thornwald Park……………………………………………….. 214

Chapter 20: The Demise of Thornwald……………………………………. 216

Chapter 21: The Great Conflagration……………………………………… 222

Chapter 22: A Second Chance……………………………………………… 240

From the Author……………………………………………………………… 244

Appendix: Thornwald Chronology…………………………………………. 248

Endnotes …………………………………………………………………….. 252

Select Bibliography………………………………………………………... 277

Select Index………………………………………………………………… 281

Courtesy of Homewood Retirement Centers

Acknowledgments

For the past three years, I spent several hours at the local Cumberland County Historical Society researching the history of the Sadler family and the Thornwald Mansion. However, during the course of writing this book there was a number of times when the task seemed a bit overwhelming. During those difficult times, there were a number of people in my life, who kept me moving on.

I would like to first thank my Lord and Savior Jesus Christ, for giving me the opportunity of a lifetime in writing this book. I would also like to thank my husband, Scott, along with my parents, Mr. and Mrs. Joseph Panza for supporting me along the way and giving me advice when I needed it the most. I would also like to thank Jan Sheaffer, for taking the time to look over my manuscript and making corrections where it was necessary.

During the course of my research, I spent a great deal of time at both the local Cumberland County Historical Society and the Dickinson College Archives and Special Collections. I would like to thank the staff of both institutions, for providing me with the materials that I needed for my research and answering any questions that I had. I would also like to thank the Borough of Carlisle and the Department of Parks and Recreation for giving me additional information on the Thornwald Mansion along with providing the materials that I needed for my research.

While I did spend a majority of my time at the Cumberland County Historical Society, I did not find everything I needed for my research, and therefore it was necessary to interview people to get additional information regarding the history of Thornwald. I would like to take the time to thank those individuals, which included Harold North, Lester Wallace, and Ronald Shearer. I would also like to thank those individuals who gave me additional information regarding Albion Point, which included Anne Kramer Hoffer and John Fowler III.

I would like to say a special thank you to Henry Line, for allowing me to use a portion of his manuscript for this book. Prior to reading his experiences with Dr. and Mrs. Horace Sadler during their final years at Thornwald, I knew very little about the distinguished couple other than that they had inherited the estate in 1923. Therefore, I am thankful that he took the time to write about his memories of Thornwald and his friendship with Dr. Sadler because it gave me an inside look at their lives which otherwise I may have omitted from this book.

I would also like to thank Rkia Hall, for giving my husband and me, the opportunity of a lifetime in taking part in the rebuilding of Thornwald. In doing so, I was able to get a better sense of how the mansion was constructed along with the materials that were used, such as the English tile. I would also like to extend a special thank you to Mrs. Hall, in rebuilding Thornwald from the inside out, and for continuing on even when it seemed like it was impossible. Due to her perseverance and determination, she has brought back a Carlisle landmark that was on the verge of being demolished.

In the course of putting this book together, I intended to include a number of photographs along with photographs and blueprints of the Thornwald Mansion. Therefore, it was necessary to obtain a number of photographs from the Cumberland County Historical Society, the Library of Congress, the Pennsylvania Archives, and Dickinson College Archives and Special Collections.

A majority of the photographs used in this book along with the blueprints came from the local Cumberland County Historical Society. I would like to say a special thank you to Mike Getter, and Assistant Librarian, Rob Schwartz, for scanning the photographs and Photo Curator, Richard Tritt, for creating the captions. I would also like to thank Librarian, Cara Holtry, for copying and scanning a number of blueprints for this book.

I would also like to thank all those who contributed photographs for this book including the Borough of Carlisle, Cordier Auctions, Marshall Dixon, John Fowler III, Rkia Hall, Charles Heinze, Andrew Henry, Historical Society of the Cocalico Valley, Homewood Retirement Centers, Hurley Auctions, Allison Keating, Lew Martin, Penn State University Dickinson School of Law, Bob Rowe, and Thornwald Home.

The Mountain Springs Hotel as it appeared prior to demolition in August 2004.

Courtesy of the Historical Society of the Cocalico Valley, Ephrata, Pa.

The Thornwald Mansion as it appeared in the fall of 2006.

Photo by author

Introduction

Prior to moving to Carlisle in the fall of 2006, I had a love for both old homes and architecture. As a child, I enjoyed the Mountain Springs Hotel in Ephrata, Pa. The hotel was gigantic in size, although at the time it was abandon and in need of repair. However, despite its condition I was in awe every time we drove by the hotel. I could not help but feel it must have been a prestigious hotel back in the day

The hotel dated back to 1848, and over the years a number of prominent statesmen stayed at the hotel including, Presidents James Buchanan, Abraham Lincoln and Ulysses S. Grant. Then in 2004, the hotel was demolished to make way for a Hampton Inn hotel and an Applebee's restaurant. However, today a section of the old hotel still stands and is now used as office space.[1]

Years later in 2006, I moved to Carlisle and took a job at the nearby Thornwald Home, although at the time I did not realize how it received such a name. However, at the start of my shift one day I saw a large brick building through the trees inside Thornwald Park. At first glance, I thought it was an office building, but upon asking one of my co-workers, they informed me that it was in fact an abandon mansion. Days later, I took a walk inside Thornwald Park to get a closer glimpse of the mansion and was awestruck at how beautiful it really was. At the time, I did not know the history behind it until the following year when it succumbed to a horrific fire.

The fire occurred on the morning of August 21, 2007. Upon hearing the news of the fire, I was devastated. Immediately, my mind raced back to the Mountain Springs Hotel, which I still held dear in my heart and how it too faced a tragic end when it was demolished some years ago. I now could not help but wonder what would be the fate of the mansion?

A few days after the fire, I began to write about the mansion although at the time I had done little research. Then three years later, in August 2009, I made my first trip to the Cumberland County Historical Society. There I found numerous newspaper articles pertaining to the mansion including the blueprints. Over the next several months and into the following year, I spent several hours looking at microfilm and researching not only the history behind the mansion, but also learning about the distinguished members of the Sadler family who for nearly forty years had called it their home.

When Lewis Sadler set out to create Thornwald in 1909, he did not envision a stick built home ,but instead he set out to construct a home that could withstand the test of time by being "constructed of steel, stone, and brick" similar to the castles in Europe which stood for centuries.[2] In turn, he built what could be referred to as a monument, since if it were not for him few would have known little about the family other than their ties to the Carlisle Hospital and the Dickinson Law School. Today, Thornwald stands as a monument symbolic of the Sadler family, a lasting testament of their impact on the town of Carlisle, and the states of Pennsylvania and New Jersey.

In an effort to give an accurate history of the Sadler family along with the history of Thornwald, I relied mostly on historical documents, newspapers, and books of the time. In regards to the layout of the mansion, I relied on the blueprints drawn in 1909 and those drawn in 1959, along with the observations that I had made of the interior of the mansion within the last two years.

The first two chapters look at the history behind one of Carlisle's most distinguished families, the Sadlers. The chapters look at the early years of Judge Wilbur Fisk Sadler along with the early education of his four sons, Wilbur Jr., Lewis, Sylvester and Horace. The next few chapters look at the events that led up to the construction of Thornwald, from Lewis Sadler's marriage to the wealthy, Miss. Mary Bosler, in June 1902 to the construction of Albion Point in 1908.

A great portion of the book gives an inside look at the construction of Thornwald, along with giving a glimpse of what the mansion looked like upon completion in 1911 and the additions that were made to the estate during the next few years. The next few chapters take a look at the lives of Mr. and Mrs. Lewis Sadler, during the time that they lived at Thornwald, along with the members of the Sadler family, who later called the mansion their home. The remaining chapters give an inside look at of how the mansion appeared at the time of Dr. Sadler's death in 1953, along with tracing the history of Thornwald up until November 2010. Also included, are photographs of how the exterior of the mansion appears today, just five years after the fire.

Above: Portrait of Lewis Sterrett Sadler by Marceau, Philadelphia.

Cumberland County Historical Society, Carlisle, Pa.

Left: Wilbur Fisk Sadler

Cumberland County Historical Society, Carlisle, Pa.

Chapter 1

The Sadler Family

Lewis Sterrett Sadler, the visionary behind Thornwald, was born in Carlisle on March 3, 1874 to Wilbur Fisk and Sarah Ellen Sterrett Sadler. He was the second eldest of the family next to his brother, Wilbur Fisk Sadler Jr., who was born on November 4, 1871. For a number of years prior to his birth, his father was among the leading attorneys in all of Carlisle.[1]

Wilbur Fisk Sadler was born on October 14, 1840, to Joshua and Harriett Stehley Sadler just outside of York Springs, Adams County, where Richard Sadler, of England, first settled in 1740.[2] He was the fourth child and eldest son of Mr. and Mrs. Joshua Sadler, both his siblings, Richard and Mary, died at an early age. Unlike his brother, John, who later went on to pursue the lumber industry, Wilbur went on to pursue a higher education. He was the first member of his extended family to go onto college, with the exception of his cousin, John Durbin Sadler, who attended Dickinson College. Wilbur Sadler attended the Dickinson Seminary in Williamsport, which today is Lycoming College, where he studied law under Mr. Morrison, and is where he graduated in 1863.[3]

During this time, the Civil War was already in full swing across the eastern United States, and in June of 1863, Pennsylvania was bracing itself for the Confederates who were making their way north towards Harrisburg. Immediately, Sadler joined the 181st Regiment of the Pennsylvania Volunteer Emergency Calvary under the command of Colonel John E Wynkoop where he served for six months. However, this was not the first time that he was mustered into service. In 1862, he was stationed in Franklin County during the Battle of Antietam.[4]

Upon returning home, he practiced law in Carlisle, under the mentorship of Alexander Brady Sharpe and James Marion Weakley.[5] By the following year, he was admitted to the bar and established a law office inside the Volunteer Building in downtown Carlisle by September 1865.[6] The following year, he left the family home in Penn Township, and bought a house located at 64 South West Street in Carlisle. However, he was not alone. Joining him, was his widowed mother, who shortly afterwards passed away in 1868.[7]

During this time he continued to practice out of his law office along South Hanover Street, where he continued to handle cases that dealt with "defaulted mortgage[s]".[8] Later, in December 1868, he partnered with his former mentor and neighbor, James Marion Weakley. Together they operated the law firm of Weakley and Sadler, which was located at 16 South Hanover Street until 1871.[9]

Outside the law firm, he served as secretary of the Cumberland County law library and chairman of the Republican committee.[10] In 1868, he ran for state senator, although he was not elected. During this time, he also served as a member of the town council, a director of the First National Bank, a member of the Cumberland County Agricultural Society, and a secretary of an insurance company. In later years, he served as a director and president of Farmers Bank.[11]

By the close of 1870, he had lived nearly five years in Carlisle. However, at thirty years of age he was still a bachelor, although it would not be long until he was a married man. Nearly two weeks later, in January of the following year, he married Miss Sarah Ellen Sterrett of Carlisle. "Sadie", as she was known by her close friends and relatives, was born in Huntington County, Pennsylvania on September 8, 1841 to Rev. David and Mary Woods Sterrett. At an early age, she attended the nearby public school and was a former graduate of the Lawrenceville Seminary in New Jersey. On January 19, 1871, the couple was united in marriage at the Sterrett residence along High Street in Carlisle.[12]

Afterwards, the newlyweds moved into a magnificent mansion located on the southwest corner of North College and Louther Streets. Prior to marrying Miss Sterrett, Sadler already owned a few properties in Carlisle including a house situated on the corner of the Mooreland Estate and a home located on North

The Sadler home along North College Street. Copied from a real photo postcard, c. 1930

Cumberland County Historical Society, Carlisle, Pa.

Hanover Street near the Carlisle Deposit Bank. However, neither one was an ideal home for the newlyweds, and instead, they moved into their newly built home located along North College Street.[13]

Prior to the wedding, Sadler had purchased the lot of ground in October 1867 from Mr. and Mrs. George Pettinas for $6,500.[14] There he erected a three story, brick Italianate villa fit with dormer windows, a wraparound porch, and a brick stable located in the rear of the property. The home was located in front of the estate of W.L. Haller and beside the home of T. Paxton. Also, along the same block on North College Street was the home of Miller and C. Staymen along with the Beetem & Brothers coal yard & warehouse, which sat on the corner of North College and High Streets. Years later, Sadler's rival, Judge Edward Biddle would have his home constructed on the site of the former coal yard.[15]

Located opposite of the Sadler residence was Dickinson College, which at the time only contained two buildings along with the preparatory school that sat directly across the street from Old West.[16] Later, the Sadlers would be known for their contributions to the college along with Wilbur Sadler playing a key role in jump-starting Judge John Reed's law school in 1890.

Upon settling into their new home, the newlyweds did not wait long to have a family of their own. Nearly two months after they were married, Sarah was already pregnant with their first child. On November 4, 1871, she gave birth to their first son, whom they named Wilbur Fisk Sadler Jr., and three years later Lewis Sterrett Sadler was born on March 3, 1874, although he was not the last son of Mr. and Mrs. Wilbur Fisk Sadler. A few years later, Sarah gave birth to two more sons, Sylvester Baker Sadler, who was born on September 29, 1876, followed by Horace Trickett Sadler, who was born two years later on February 2, 1879.[17]

During this time, in 1874, their father had served as district attorney of Carlisle all the while maintaining business at his law office that was now located along West Main Street.[18] For some time prior to 1871, he worked out of the law firm of Weakley and Sadler along South Hanover Street with his former law partner, James Marion Weakley. However, the law firm was only in operation for a short time, and later he left the firm to open a new law firm with his friend and former Dickinson College professor, William Trickett.[19]

Early on, Sadler was well acquainted with Trickett since they had boarded at Egolf's boarding house prior to his marriage to Miss Sterrett in 1871.[20] Throughout the next few years, they operated their law office out of 11 West Main Street in Carlisle before moving across the street to 8 West Main Street by the 1890's.[21]

By now, Sadler was among the leading lawyers of Carlisle. In addition, he now ranked high in Republican politics ever since his nomination for state senator in 1868.[22] In 1874, he made his first attempt at running for judge of Cumberland County, but was "defeated" by Democrat Martin C. Herman.[23] However, it would not be the last time that he would run against Herman.

Ten years later in 1884, Sadler once again ran against him for county judge, although he faced strong criticism from the Democratic *American Volunteer*. Early on, the paper despised him and stirred up rumors regarding his fraudulent means of securing votes once saying: "Will Sadler's self-respect permit him to gain a seat which he knows he can only gain by purchasing with money corrupt and hiring traders, who in turn will corrupt and buy weak, and vacillating voters at the polls in November".[24]

Although the *Volunteer* criticized him, *The Evening Sentinel* told of Democrats in Penn Township, where he had spent his childhood, who had swung their votes in favor of him therefore giving him 76 Democratic votes. By November of that year, he defeated former Judge Herman as judge of Cumberland County by nearly 1,000 votes.[25] During the next ten years, he governed the county courthouse, all the while his four sons were just beginning their education at the Dickinson Preparatory School.

William Trickett, photo taken in 1919 by Guth & Hensel, Carlisle.

Cumberland County Historical Society, Carlisle, Pa.

A political cartoon depicting a man who voted for Wilbur Fisk Sadler.

American Volunteer
19 November 1884

A view of the Dickinson College campus as it appeared in 1895. In the center of the photograph, behind the trees and to the right of the townhouses, is the Sadler residence along North College Street.

Archives and Special Collections, Dickinson College, Carlisle, Pa.

All four of the Sadler children attended the nearby public school prior to 1888. In that year, Lewis, along with his brother Wilbur, were the first of their family to enter the nearby Dickinson Preparatory School.[26] The school was a two-story limestone structure, which was located along High Street across the road from Old West. During their first year at the school, their father took an active role in their education by becoming a member of the board of trustees and remained on the board throughout their years at Dickinson.[27]

Throughout the next two years, the children learned the fundamentals of reading Latin and Greek, along with mathematics and history. By the following year in 1889, Sylvester joined his siblings at the preparatory school while Wilbur Jr. became the first of his siblings to enroll into classes at Dickinson College.[28] All three of the children attended the Dickinson Preparatory School and Dickinson College with the exception of Horace. The reasons are unknown why Horace never attended classes at Dickinson, along with his siblings, since both the preparatory school and the college were within a short walking distance from the family home. Instead, he attended classes at the Chambersburg Academy in Franklin County.[29]

In 1890, Lewis Sadler joined his brother Wilbur at Dickinson College where his brother had become a member of the Theta Delta Chi fraternity. However, by the following year Wilbur left Dickinson and afterwards moved to Harrisburg.

During his time in Harrisburg, Wilbur lived along Front Street and worked at the lumber mill of Moser, Sadler, and Musselman, which was located at the corner of 7th, and Briggs Streets.[30] Prior to this time, Henry Moser operated the lumber mill and by 1890, his father, Wilbur Fisk Sadler, partnered with Moser and F.B. Musselman to form the lumber mill of Moser, Sadler, and Musselman.[31] In 1894, his father turned the business over to him, and afterwards he collaborated with Joseph Kaufman. Together they operated the mill until two years later when Wilbur left to pursue building street railways in northern Schuylkill County.[32]

Judge Wilbur Fisk Sadler surrounded by his four sons: Wilbur Jr., seated left, Sylvester, standing left, Horace, standing right, and Lewis, sitting right. The photograph may have been taken sometime after June 26, 1902, when Lewis Sadler was married, hence him wearing a light colored suite, instead of black like the rest of his family.
Photo by John N. Choate

Cumberland County Historical Society, Carlisle, Pa.

    Although Wilbur may have found success outside of Dickinson College, Sylvester and Lewis were walking in the footsteps of their father in their pursuit of law. By the following year, in 1892, Lewis left Dickinson College to attend classes at Yale University. There he enrolled as a sophomore in the academic department of Yale College.[33]

    Yale University was in the heart of suburban New Haven, Connecticut, which had a staggering population of 81,298 compared to the town of Carlisle that contained only a population of 7,620 in 1890.[34] The university offered a wealth of courses, which included basic academics, to studies in theology and the arts. In addition, the university also offered courses in philosophy, law, and medicine, which were different from the few courses that were offered at Dickinson College.[35]

    During his first year at Yale College, he lived at 205 Crown Street although by the following year he moved to 1010 Chapel Street where he shared a room with his brother, Sylvester.[36] During their time at Yale, Lewis and Sylvester roomed together and served as each other's best friend. Together they attended the required classes that were part of Yale's academic program and outside of their schoolwork; they both were active members of Yale's University Club and Psi Upsilon.[37]

    Throughout 1893, the two continued to attend classes at Yale until 1894. That year, Lewis returned home to Carlisle while Sylvester remained at the college for the next four years rooming alone inside Vanderbilt Hall.[38] However, in January 1895, Sylvester returned home along with his brother Wilbur, to attend the first funeral to occur at their home along North College Street.

Their mother, Mrs. Sarah Ellen Sterrett Sadler, had acquired pneumonia following a walk that she had taken with her sister Annie Sterrett, and afterwards was bedridden. For nearly a week, she laid in bed in hopes of recovering from her illness. However, on January 10, 1895, she passed away at fifty-four years of age.[39]

That day the *Carlisle Herald* announced the death of Mrs. Sadler as a "death of a most estimable woman".[40] Just two days later, family and friends of the Sadlers gathered at their home along North College Street to pay their condolences. According to *The Evening Sentinel* "the funeral was one of the largest ever witnessed in this place" and even the Sadler residence was filled beyond capacity.[41] Afterwards, interment took place at the Ashland Cemetery in Carlisle.

Following the death of their mother, Wilbur Jr. left Carlisle to return to work at the lumber mill in Harrisburg and by the following year, he was in Schuylkill County working along with a group of men in constructing street railways. Two years later, in 1898, he moved to Trenton, New Jersey where he furthered his career in building street railways. During his time in New Jersey, he was involved in the construction of the Trenton, Lawrenceville and Princeton Railroad, the Yardley, Morrisville and Trenton Street Railway, along with the Philadelphia, Bristol and Trenton Street Railway. A few years later, he became president of the Broad Street National Bank and in 1907 served as president of the Trenton Chamber of Commerce. Just like his father was to Carlisle, he too was among the notable citizens of Trenton, New Jersey. Two years later in 1909, he was elected Adjutant General of New Jersey under Governor John Franklin Fort.[42]

Wilbur Jr. was not the only member of his family to leave Carlisle. A few years later, Horace, too, left to enroll into a "military school" located just outside of Philadelphia. Afterwards, he went on to study dentistry at the University of Pennsylvania where he graduated in June 1901.[43]

As for Lewis and Sylvester, they remained close ties with their father. In the summer of 1895, Lewis enrolled in the Dickinson Law School's summer school along with his brother, Sylvester, where their father had played an influential role in the reestablishment of the law school.[44]

Chapter 2

"Like Father, Like Son"

Emory Chapel, the home of the Dickinson Law School from 1890-1918, was located on the corner of Pomfret and South West Streets. Photo by A.A. Line

Cumberland County Historical Society, Carlisle, Pa

By late 1889, during his first term as Judge of Cumberland County, Wilbur Fisk Sadler confronted his good friend and law partner, William Trickett, and President of Dickinson College, George Edward Reed, concerning reestablishing Judge John Reed's law school. For nearly fifteen years Reed had run the law school out of his home from 1835-1850.[1]

By the following year, on January 8, 1890, the future law school became a reality at a meeting held in Philadelphia of the board of trustees of Dickinson College.[2] The board appointed William Trickett as dean and George Edward Reed as president of the reestablished law school. Thereafter, the board selected Emory Chapel, as the site for the school, which was located not far from Dickinson College at the corner of South West and Pomfret Streets. During the next few months, the chapel underwent renovations by William C. Allison to make it fit for classes by the fall of that year.[3]

Months later, in October 1890, a number of men turned out to attend the opening ceremony of the reestablished Dickinson Law School. Among the men present that day, was Judge Wilbur Fisk Sadler, who gave an opening speech. Later, he too would join the law school faculty as a professor of criminal law along with his former law partner, James Marion Weakley, who served as professor of the law of pleading.[4]

The Dickinson Law School class of 1896, taken in front of the Sadler home. Lewis Sadler is pictured in the back row, sixth from left.

Cumberland County Historical Society, Carlisle, Pa.

In the summer of 1895, Lewis Sadler attended the law school's summer school along with his brother, Sylvester, who currently was still a student at Yale.[5] By the fall of that year, he entered the junior class of the law school where he was unanimously elected class president.[6] His class numbered fifty-two students, nine of whom were from Carlisle including William Boyd, Ray Zug, J. Harris Curan, Edwin F. Brightbill, Herman Berg Jr., John M. Rhey, William W. Fletcher and Frank Bosler.[7]

During his junior year at the law school, Sadler served as vice president of the Athletic Association and was a member of the Allison Law Society where his father was an "honorary member" along with James Marion Weakley, Edward Biddle, William Trickett and other notable attorneys of Carlisle.[8] Three years later in 1898, Sylvester, too, would become a member of the society.[9]

On the evening of June 8, 1896, Lewis Sadler along with the forty-five members of his class received their bachelor of law degree inside Emory Chapel. Afterwards, the class posed for a photograph in front of the Sadler residence along North College Street.[10]

After graduation, Sadler was admitted to the bar and then went to work as an attorney for the Carlisle Borough Council, a position that he held for one year.[11] Thereafter, he worked out of his father's law firm of Sadler and Sadler, which was now located at 8 West Main Street in Carlisle.[12] Prior to him entering the law firm the office was home to his father along with James W. Eckels, William Trickett, and Thomas E. Vale.[13] However, upon Sadler entering the law firm, Eckels and Vale left leaving the firm to Lewis and his father along with William Trickett. In later years, Trickett would live on the first floor next to the Sadler law office and would remain closely connected with the law firm until his death in 1928.[14]

During this time, in 1896 his brother, Sylvester, graduated from Yale and received his Bachelor of Arts degree along with an honors in history.[15] Shortly afterwards, he enrolled in the Dickinson Law School. There, he too, became president of his junior class and formed a close bond with his professor and dean of the law school, William Trickett.

Trickett was the professor of law at the school and was also the author of several books on law, which included but not limited to *Law of Liens in Pennsylvania* (1882), *Law of Limitations* (1888) and *Law of Highways (1895)*.[16] The following year, Sylvester worked closely with him in collecting court cases and preparing the index for yet another one of his books on law entitled, *The Law of Boroughs in Pennsylvania,* published in 1898.[17]

The Dickinson Law School graduating class of 1898, taken in front of the Sadler home. Sylvester Sadler is pictured in the back row, third from left. Photo by A. A. Line

Cumberland County Historical Society, Carlisle, Pa

    In June of that year, Sylvester graduated from the law school. However, unlike his brother's graduation that occurred just two years prior, Sylvester received the highest honors of his graduation class. He delivered the "class oration" on June 11, 1898 inside Bosler Hall in front of his fellow classmates. During his speech, he spoke on equal justice for all, saying, "law is the perfection of reason and in its action, the machinery should be so well adjusted that even handed justice will be meted out to all without fear or favor". In addition, that day, Sylvester received a volume set of "encyclopedias on pleading and practice" that were provided by Edward Thompson and given by Ex-Judge Charles Barnett for his winning essay on "Orphan's Court Sales in Pennsylvania". Furthermore, Barnett praised Sadler for the "originality" of his essay. Upon graduation, he became a professor of the law of bailment at the law school working alongside both his father and William Trickett.[18]
    The following year, in 1899, the family home along North College Street was in jeopardy. The home had gone up for sheriff sale in February of that year after their father had failed to pay a sum of $2,021.25. Fortunately, on the day of the sale both Lewis and Sylvester were able to buy back the house for $9,100. Thereafter, the Sadler home along North College Street remained in Lewis's name.[19]
    By the turn of the century, Sylvester was on his way towards becoming a notable attorney. In September 1900, he was present for the Martin Fry murder trial along with his father and District Attorney, William Alfred Kramer.[20] Lewis was not present for the trial, which was not at all surprising. He was not an established attorney like his brother, Sylvester, nor would he live up to high expectations of his father.
    Sylvester went on to become the shining star of the family next to his oldest brother, Wilbur Jr. Sylvester, walked in the footsteps of his father and William Trickett. In 1903, Sylvester wrote his first textbook on law entitled *Criminal and Penal Procedure in Pennsylvania*, which he dedicated to his good friend and mentor, William Trickett. His final book on law was published in 1904 and was a ten volume set entitled *Pennsylvania Supreme Court Cases, 1885-1889* often known as *Sadler's Cases*.[21]
    In 1904, he succeeded his father as professor of criminal law at the law school upon his father's election as judge of Cumberland County.[22] Throughout the next ten years, both Sylvester and his father governed the county courthouse and on a few occasions, Sylvester made a few appearances inside the Supreme Court in Philadelphia.[23] Although he had walked in his father's footsteps at becoming one of Carlisle's leading attorneys, he never married into one of the wealthiest families in all of Carlisle, the Boslers.

Chapter 3

The Bosler Family

View of Cottage Hill, the residence of James Williamson Bosler. Photo by A. A. Line

Cumberland County Historical Society, Carlisle, Pa

    Located on the opposite side of town just off the York Road was an Italianate mansion known as "Cottage Hill". Built in 1867, Cottage Hill was home to one of Carlisle's wealthiest couples, Mr. and Mrs. James Williamson Bosler.

    At the time, the Bosler residence was unlike any other in all of Carlisle. Besides the mansion, the residence contained the office of James W. Bosler along with a stable in the rear of the property all being surrounded by nearly a hundred acres of land. Even the grounds contained a landscape that was designed by the creators of New York's Central Park while located on the front lawn was a large fountain that often drew attention from passersby along the York Road. Overall, the Bosler residence stood as a testament of their wealth that had been acquired through James Bosler's many business ventures out west.[1]

James Williamson Bosler was born in Silver Spring, Cumberland County on April 4, 1833 to Abraham and Eliza Herman Bosler. At nineteen years of age, he entered Dickinson College, but left in his junior year to pursue other interests out west in Moultrie, Ohio where he became a schoolteacher. Afterwards, he moved to present day West Virginia where he studied law and was later admitted to the bar. However, unlike Wilbur Sadler who had a passion for law, Bosler did not and therefore he soon took a job as a clerk at a store in Wheeling. During his time in Wheeling, he developed an interest in business and soon returned to Columbiana County, Ohio where he bought a store. For a short time, he operated the store until it was destroyed by fire.[2] Afterwards, he moved farther west, this time to Sioux City, Iowa where he settled in 1855.[3]

Upon arriving in Sioux City, he partnered with real estate agent, Charles Hedges and together they established the "Sioux City Bank" under the name of Bosler and Hedges. Outside of banking, Bosler and Hedges were also involved in furnishing supplies for both the "Interior and War Departments of the Government on the North Missouri river" which furnished supplies to the near-by Indian reservations. During this time, he also took advantage of the open plains and got into the business of raising cattle which he was said to have "reaped golden profits from it".[4]

Outside of his many business ventures, he was responsible for having "erected both the public school building and jail of Sioux City" and even took an interest in politics. Once, he was nominated as a Democratic treasure for the state of Iowa although he was not elected. However, he later served a term on the Iowa State Legislature before returning home to Carlisle in 1866 with his wife, Helen Louise Beltzhoover Bosler, and their two-year old son, Charles.[5]

Charcoal-enhanced portrait of James W. Bosler by John N. Choate. This portrait was made c. 1885 and appears in the June 20, 1885 issue of *Frank Leslie's Illustrated Newspaper.*

Cumberland County Historical Society Carlisle, Pa.

Upon arriving in Carlisle, Bosler had constructed the stately Cottage Hill Mansion, which was completed in 1867. Two years later, on May 1, 1869, Helen gave birth to their second son, Frank Clinton Bosler, and afterwards Helen gave birth to three more children. Mary Eliza was born on January 8, 1872, followed by De Witt Clinton on April 25, 1873. Three years later, Helen Louisa Bosler was born on November 20, 1876. Out of the five children, only four survived. Charles died a year after Frank was born in December 1870 at just six years of age.[6]

During his time in Carlisle, Bosler too became one of the leading citizens of the town and was regarded as "one of the most active and efficient promoters of business enterprises". He was involved in the organization of the Carlisle Manufacturing Company, where he served as its first president along with a "director in the Carlisle Deposit Bank, a director of the Carlisle Gas & Water Company, and also owned extensive farm interests in different parts of the county". During this time, he also stayed interested in politics. In 1880, he attended the Republican National Convention along with his friend, U.S. Senator James G. Blaine.[7]

The Bosler Memorial Library at Dickinson College. *Postcard from author*

Throughout his final years, he continued to stay interested in politics and even continued his business affairs out west. On December 17, 1883 he died suddenly of "apoplexy" inside his office at Cottage Hill at just fifty years of age.[8] Upon his death he left behind an estate valued at a million dollars which was divided between his wife and two brothers, John Herman and Joseph Bosler.[9]

Prior to his death, he agreed to pledge "ten thousand dollars for the endowment of a Prof. McClintock chair" at the centenary anniversary of Dickinson College. However, upon his death the pledge was still not carried out and therefore it was up to his wife to carry out his wishes. Instead of pledging the ten thousand dollars, she instead pledged "seven-fold" the amount and had constructed in his honor Dickinson's first library known as the "James W. Bosler Memorial Hall", which was completed in 1886.[10]

Upon the death of her husband, Mrs. Helen Beltzhoover Bosler was now a single mother to her four children. Prior to his death, all three of the children with the exception of Helen, attended classes at the nearby public school.[11] A few years later, Helen accompanied her siblings to Chauncy-Hall in Massachusetts where they attended classes for a short time until 1888.[12] Upon returning home that year, both Frank and Dewitt Clinton entered the Dickinson Preparatory School where they attended classes with Lewis and Wilbur Sadler, Jr.[13] However, the Bosler brothers' were well acquainted with Lewis and Wilbur Sadler, since they had known them early on from attending the First Presbyterian Church in Carlisle.[14]

Afterwards, both Frank and Dewitt Clinton entered Dickinson College although they did not attend there long and afterwards left Dickinson for Harvard. Unlike the Sadlers, who favored Yale, the Boslers favored Harvard, and is where both Frank and Dewitt Clinton Bosler attended classes between 1890 -1897.[15] During Frank's first year at Harvard, he witnessed the sudden death of his mother, Mrs. Helen Bosler, who passed away on October 5, 1890.[16]

At the time of her death, Frank was only twenty-one years of age, while the remaining three children were all under the age of twenty with Helen being the youngest, at just fourteen years of age. Afterwards, Frank was named the sole heir to his mother's estate valued at $269,000 or six million, today.[17]

According to her will, she wished for her four children to remain at Cottage Hill as long as they wished. All personal property "consisting of stocks, bonds, mortgages and other securities" was to be divided between her son, Frank, and her daughter, Mary. In addition to her personal property, was a large sum of money that was to remain in trust until her youngest daughter, Helen, reached twenty-five years of age. However, in the event that the children would sell Cottage Hill, the trust would cease, and all money was to be paid in full. In addition, each of the children were to receive $100 per year due to their management of the trust, while Frank would receive $200 per year, for the settlement of the estate.[18]

Each of the children became wealthy at an early age, and by the turn of the century, they were the wealthiest children in all of Carlisle. While each of the children were to receive their share of the will, Frank Bosler was among the wealthiest member of the family, since in addition to his inheritance, he already owned "5,000 acres in Nebraska", which he had previously inherited from his father. On the large tract of ground, he created what was later known as the "model farming community of the State".[19] However, despite his large inheritance, he went on to pursue his law degree.

Just a few years later in 1895, Frank entered the Dickinson Law School where again he met up with Lewis Sadler.[20] The two became close friends during their time at the law school and graduated together the following year in 1896. Afterward, Bosler kept his ties with the law school just as Sylvester had done by serving as president of the law school's alumni association along with serving on the Board of Incorporators where Judge Wilbur Sadler was also among its members.[21] In later years, both Lewis and Sylvester, too, became members of the Board of Incorporators.[22]

Although Lewis Sadler had perhaps the closest friendship with the Boslers due to his years having attended school with both Frank and Dewitt Clinton, Sylvester, too, had become close friends with the Boslers. In February 1899, he accompanied Frank, Dewitt Clinton along with Mary and Helen Bosler to a birthday party in Reading.[23] However, despite their close friendship, only two members of the Sadler family would marry into the Bosler fortune.

Chapter 4

"Sadler-Bosler"

Mr. and Mrs. Lewis Sadler and wedding party on the grounds of Cottage Hill.

Cumberland County Historical Society, Carlisle, Pa

    Lewis Sadler was the first to marry into the wealthy Bosler family. He married Miss Mary Eliza Bosler in the summer of 1902. Mary Bosler, also known to some as "Minnie", was two years older than Lewis, and was the wealthiest daughter of the late Mr. and Mrs. James W. Bosler. In addition, she was a former graduate of the Peebles and Thompson School in New York along with a member of the Carlisle Country Club.[1]

    His marriage into the family that year would set him apart from his siblings, Sylvester and Wilbur Jr., who were now among the distinguished members of the family. Early on, Sylvester had risen to fame as a prominent lawyer in Carlisle while Wilbur gained his fame from building trolley lines across Eastern Pennsylvania. Now his marriage into the Bosler fortune would make him the wealthiest member of his family, and place him among the distinguished citizens of Carlisle.

    The news of the future Sadler-Bosler wedding was such big news, that their marriage announcement appeared in the *Los Angeles Times* on May 29, 1902 nearly two months prior to their big day.[2] On June 26, 1902, at six o'clock in the evening, the couple was married inside the Second Presbyterian Church in Carlisle.[3]

Their royal wedding was such big news in Carlisle that the following day *The Evening Sentinel* reiterated the entire details from the ceremony to the reception for those who were not in attendance for the grand occasion. Furthermore, the paper declared that their wedding was "one of the most fashionable weddings in Carlisle's history of a century and a half".[4]

The church was beautifully decorated for the occasion by Thorley of New York. Down the aisle were sixteen posts that made up eight partial arches. The posts were covered in marguerites, lilies, and palms while the alter was adorned with roses and peonies. Even the windowsills were not overlooked, and were adorned with palms, white phlox and lilies.[5]

That afternoon, special trains from the Reading, Pine Grove and Cumberland Valley Railways transported guests to the church. *The Evening Sentinel* estimated that there were over two hundred guests that evening that had come from as far away as New York and Virginia. Among the guests included many distinguished couples from around the area, such as Mr. and Mrs. J. C. Bucher from Boiling Springs, who resided in the former Ege Mansion, along with Moorhead C. Kennedy, Vice President of the Cumberland Valley Railroad, who was accompanied by his wife. On arrival, the guests took their seats inside the church as they gazed at the beautiful floral arrangements and listened to the harmonious melodies played by the organist and members of the Pittsburg Symphony.[6]

The bridal party was large in number and was elegantly dressed for the occasion. The bridesmaids consisted of Ruth Wallace, Mary Bear, Nellie Jackson, Emelin Knox Parker, and Eliza Herman Bosler all who wore "white over green satin with picture hats", which were adorned with flowers. As they walked down the right side of the church, they carried with them a large boutique of "pink roses". The matron and maid of honor consisted of Mrs. Frank M. Andrews, and the bride's sister, Helen Louisa Bosler, each dressed in "light green over liberty satin" and carrying with them a large boutique of roses. As for Miss Mary Eliza Bosler, she was the most exquisite bride in all of Carlisle that evening, wearing a dress made of "white point lace over satin entraine" and a veil adorned with flowers. In her hand, she carried a large boutique of flowers that were tied together with a large satin ribbon. That evening, her oldest brother, Frank C. Bosler, gave her away.[7]

As for Lewis Sadler, he was also among the best dressed that evening wearing a black "frock" coat, along with a pressed white shirt with a starched collar, and white gloves. His ushers also wore the same attire and consisted of his brothers, Wilbur and Horace. Among the ushers was also Frank M. Andrews, Dewitt Clinton Bosler, J.B. Kremer Jr., and Harrisburg mayor, Vance McCormick. Serving as Sadler's best man was his younger brother and best friend through law school, Sylvester Sadler.[8]

The ceremony was held in a "solemn and impressive manner" with "sweet strains of Ave Maria by Gounod" playing in the background. Rev. George Norcross presided over the services, and altogether it was a memorable occasion for both the couple and the guests who attended that day. Afterwards, they took a ride to Cottage Hill, where they indeed felt as if they had stepped into paradise.[9]

According to *The Evening Sentinel*, the reception was "the most brilliant social function in old Carlisle for many years". The fountain on the front lawn contained a number of colored lights that drew attention from passersby along the York Road. Even the rear lawn contained a number of electric lights and Japanese lanterns, which further illuminated the landscape. Also located on the lawn was a rustic building where members of the bridal party, along with Wilbur Fisk Sadler, greeted the many guests that arrived for the reception. Across from the building was a platform that was constructed for the reception to hold the twenty-seven piece Hassler's orchestra from Philadelphia. In addition, dotting the landscape were a number of tables, which were decorated with "fancy candelabras". Upon the guests being seated, they were treated to a delectable dinner, which was catered by Trauer of Germantown, Philadelphia.[10]

After the fine festivities and entertaining had ended for the evening, the couple left for the Bosler summer home, "Meadow Brook". There they remained until the next day, when they left on their honeymoon to the "far east".[11]

Chapter 5

Years at Cottage Hill

Cottage Hill, taken from a stereoview card

Cumberland County Historical Society, Carlisle, Pa.

    Upon returning home to Carlisle, the newlyweds did not settle into a home of their own nor settle into the Sadler home along North College Street, which Lewis had currently owned. Instead, they settled into Cottage Hill, which was then home to Mary's brother and sister, Frank and Helen Louisa Bosler.[1]
    Throughout the next nine years, the couple lived at Cottage Hill while Sadler remained working out of his father's law office along West High Street. Although he remained an attorney at the Sadler and Sadler law firm, outside of the law office he was living an entirely different life. Upon marrying Miss Mary Bosler in June of that year, his life took a turn in a different direction. Prior to their marriage, he had taken no interest in clubs or organizations since his years at the Dickinson Law School. Now he was among the "active members" of the Harrisburg Country Club where both his wife, Mary, and her sister, Helen, were also among its members.[2]
    During this time, he also became involved in the social clubs of Pennsylvania such as the Harrisburg Club and the Union League of Philadelphia, which was home to some of the notable dignitaries in Pennsylvania. Both Frank and Dewitt Clinton, along with Sadler's brother, Wilbur Jr., were among the members of both the Harrisburg Club and the Union League.[3] When he was not wining and dining among the wealthy, both Mr. and Mrs. Lewis Sadler often hosted gatherings at Rose Balcony, which was their place of entertaining prior to Thornwald.

Rose Balcony, the former summer home of Mr. and Mrs. Lewis Sadler.

Courtesy of Marshall Dixon

    Rose Balcony was located not far from Boiling Springs along the Yellow Breeches Creek. Prior to their marriage, Miss Mary Bosler had owned two tracts of ground in Monroe Township, which may have been the beginnings of their summer home.[4] Lewis Sadler inherited the ground upon marrying Miss Bosler in June 1902. Although, two years later, they enlarged their land holdings this time receiving a tract of land from Frank Bosler, who had inherited the "Allenberry farm" upon the death of his brother, DeWitt Clinton in December 1903.[5] Throughout the next few years the couple continued to buy surrounding ground further enlarging their summer home.

    During this time, they took the opportunity to entertain a number of distinguished guests and family members at their summer home. In June 1908, the *Evening Sentinel* announced that Mary Sadler had entertained the Ashcroft-Bosler wedding party at "Rose Balcony Farm".[6]

    A few days prior to entertaining the wedding party, Lewis Sadler had entertained a number of "distinguished" men who were in town for the Dickinson College commencement at their summer home. Among the men present was Governor Franklin Fort of New Jersey, Ex-Secretary Shaw, Vice-President of the Cumberland Valley Railroad Moorhead C. Kennedy, Alexander C. Chenoweth L.L.D of New York, and his father Wilbur Fisk Sadler.[7]

    The galas at Rose Balcony were only the beginning for Mr. and Mrs. Lewis Sadler. By the following year, in 1909, they would establish their own private estate located along the Walnut Bottom Road in Carlisle although Mrs. Sadler would continue to entertain a number of guests at Rose Balcony throughout the next few years.

    Cottage Hill was certainly a prestigious estate, and over the past seven years, the couple made many happy memories there with Mary's siblings, Frank and Helen Bosler. However, by 1908, Helen was getting ready to move out of Cottage Hill, and it was not long until the couple too would find a place of their own.

    The couple would have no trouble buying their first home, since they were mere millionaires. Upon the death of Mrs. Helen Bosler in 1890, she left a considerable amount of money to her four children, Frank, Mary, DeWitt Clinton, and Helen all of which was to be paid in full when her youngest daughter, Helen, turned twenty-five years of age. Therefore, as early as 1901, each of the children received their share from the will. In addition, when DeWitt Clinton died in 1903, he left $400,000 (2010: 9.5 million) to his siblings at the Farmers Trust Company in Carlisle.[8] With the combined inheritance, Mr. and Mrs. Lewis Sadler were in fact the wealthiest couple in all of Carlisle and had more than enough money to build the largest home in all of Carlisle, if not in Central Pennsylvania.

    Prior to the couple leaving Cottage Hill, Mary's sister, Helen, married Lewis's youngest brother, Dr. Horace Sadler in March 1909.

Chapter 6

Dr. and Mrs. Horace Sadler

Above left: Circa 1930 photograph of Mrs. Helen Bosler Sadler, photo by E.F. Foley of New York.
Above right: Dr. Horace Sadler, enlarged from the Sadler family photograph by John N. Choate.

Cumberland County Historical Society, Carlisle, Pa

    In March 1909, Dr. Horace Sadler became the last member of his family to marry into the Bosler fortune. However, in comparison to his older siblings Sylvester and Wilbur, he was an unlikely candidate for Miss Helen Louisa Bosler. Like his brother Lewis, he too, was two years younger than his future wife was. However, in comparison to his eldest brother, he was neither an attorney nor had ties to Dickinson.

    Instead, Dr. Sadler had majored in dentistry at the University of Pennsylvania, where he graduated in June 1901.[1] Following graduation, he lived the next few years away from home in Philadelphia until 1904, when he returned home to Carlisle. Upon his return, he moved back into the family home along North College Street, and afterwards established a dental office at 22 West High Street in Carlisle. However, his career as a dentist was short lived.[2] Years later, he was recalled to have "retired due to personal reasons" although he kept the title of "Dr." for the remainder of his life.[3]

    Not long after returning home to Carlisle, he fell head over heels for Mary's sister, Helen Louisa Bosler. On March 6, 1909, the couple was married at Cottage Hill. Both Mr. and Mrs. Lewis Sadler took part in the wedding. Lewis served as Horace's best man while Mary served as Helen's matron of honor. Both Horace and Helen only had three attendants each for their bridal party compared to the large number at Mr. and Mrs. Lewis Sadler's wedding in 1902.[4]

    In comparison to the lavish wedding in 1902, the couple did not issue any invitations, and therefore it was considered a "private" affair.[5] The ceremony took place on the grounds of Cottage Hill that day, which was decorated by Thorley of New York. Thorley was the same florist who had decorated the interior of the Second Presbyterian Church in 1902 for the first Sadler-Bosler wedding. Even Trainer of Philadelphia catered the meal for the wedding.[6]

Despite the size of their wedding, the gifts were extravagant. Both Mr. and Mrs. Lewis Sadler presented Helen with a "diamond necklace". Wilbur Fisk Sadler gave her a "chest of silver", while her brother Frank, presented her with a "diamond pin". After the wining and dining that evening, the newlyweds left the following day for Cuba.[7]

Upon returning home from their extensive honeymoon, the newlyweds did not settle into Cottage Hill as Mr. and Mrs. Lewis Sadler had done in 1902. Instead, they moved across the road from Cottage Hill into Albion Point.[8]

Albion Point

Albion Point, the home of Dr. and Mrs. Horace Sadler. Photo by A. A. Line

Cumberland County Historical Society, Carlisle, Pa

Albion Point derived its name from its location between the Trindle and York Roads along with its white appearance.[9] The mansion was Helen Bosler's own masterpiece, and certainly, it was a piece of work. The Ahl farmhouse, which at one time was located on the ground, took a year to renovate to make it into the ideal home that she had envisioned.

In April 1908, Helen Bosler purchased the Ahl farmhouse and sixteen acres of ground from her siblings, Frank and Mary Bosler for $15,500.[10] Just days after purchasing the property, *The Carlisle Daily Herald* announced that the farmhouse was to undergo "extensive alterations" which included the home being "reconstructed in pure Colonial style".[11] She did not hire a local architect to draw up the blueprints for her future estate, but instead had the blueprints drawn by Herring of New York.[12]

Before renovations could begin on the farmhouse, the house had to first be moved back from the road several feet. The process was altogether a "tedious" one, and was performed by John Eichleay Jr., & Co. from Pittsburgh. The house was to be moved in two phases with the "main portion" being moved back "thirty-five feet" and from there the "rear portion", consisting of the "mansard roof", was to be moved back an additional ten feet. The entire moving of the house was considered by *The Evening Sentinel* as "a scene not often witnessed in Carlisle", and it certainly was.[13]

By the following month, the paper announced that the moving was finished and that "great improvements would now be made", which included the construction of a ten-foot section that would join the two halves together. In charge of constructing the ten-foot section, was Harry G. Brown of Carlisle.[14] Throughout the next several months, and into 1909, the mansion underwent renovations to make it into the lavish home that she had envisioned.

Upon her marriage to Dr. Sadler in March 1909, the mansion was officially completed.[15] On the outside, the home looked much like the Ege Mansion in Boiling Springs, which the Ahl family had owned for a number of years.[16] However, Albion Point was a much larger rendition of the Ege Mansion. On the outside, four short columns supported the main entrance, where above was located a small walkout balcony. On either side of the front portion of the home, were also two large porticos, where the guests could sit and enjoy the beautiful gardens that were one of the highlights of Albion Point.

Similar to Cottage Hill, was the landscape of Albion Point, which was designed by "two engineers from New York".[17] The lawn contained an array of flowers, vines, and cedar trees. Prior to the completion of Albion Point, *The Evening Sentinel* remarked how the estate would be "one of the garden spots of Carlisle".[18]

In contrast to the Victorian interior of Cottage Hill, was the interior of Albion Point, which was furthermore reminiscent of the Ege Mansion in Boiling Springs. The interior was colonial in style and contained an immense amount of mahogany woodwork, from the doors and stairway, to the paneling that covered the rooms of the mansion, while the floors were covered in squares of "parquet".[19] The mansion also contained "eight fireplaces" along with a living room, dining room, paneled den, and a billiard room on the third floor.[20] In order to keep with the colonial feel of the mansion, the couple further furnished the mansion with period furniture that they had bought from New York City.[21]

By now, Albion Point and Cottage Hill were two of the most remarkable mansions along the York Road standing as symbols of the Bosler wealth. Many may have looked to Mr. and Mrs. Lewis Sadler to build along the York Road although the couple had other ideas in mind. Just a month after Helen Bosler left Cottage Hill, Lewis Sadler set out to purchase a tract of land, which would be the canvas from which the couple would create their own masterpiece, "Thornwold".[22]

Upon completion in 1909, Albion Point closely mirrored the Ege Mansion in Boiling Springs, which was owned by the Ahl family for many years.

Photo by author

The photographs on the preceding pages were taken in 1960, and depict what Albion Point looked like both inside and out during the time it was occupied by John B. Fowler, Jr. and family.

Photographs courtesy of John B. Fowler III

The main entrance

The grand staircase

The living room

The fireplace inside the living room

The dining room

{ 30 }

The garage

According to *Pictorial Carlisle*, the gazebo, pictured above, was used as a "trolley station" during the years that Dr. and Mrs. Horace Sadler owned the estate.

Chapter 7

The Residence of L.S. Sadler

Noble's Woods

Mr. and Mrs. Lewis Sadler did not choose to build their home on the Bosler ground beside Cottage Hill nor build their home in Harrisburg, which was the rumor in the *Carlisle Daily Herald*.[1] Instead, they chose to build on a wooden tract of ground that lay on the southwest side of town just below South College Street. The lot of ground was known for many years as Noble's woods and was located along the Walnut Bottom Road. Prior to 1909, Noble's woods contained 231 acres of woodland and meadows.[2]

For nearly fifty years, the Nobles were known for their massive land holdings around Carlisle that consisted not only of Noble's woods but also of additional lots of ground in and around Carlisle.[3] For a number of years William Noble had owned the ground that bordered the Walnut Bottom Road. In January 1898, he passed away leaving his residence along South Pitt Street to his nephew, Dr. Joseph Noble, who resided in China.[4] Later, in the fall of 1899, Dr. Noble bought Noble's woods, which consisted of 231 acres for $28,000.[5] For nearly ten years thereafter, Dr. Noble owned the ground until 1909, when in that year, Sadler became interested in the wooden tract along Walnut Bottom Road.

The ground was the ideal setting for their future estate, and therefore he wasted no time in contacting real estate agent, Charles Liggett, in February of that year, about purchasing a portion of the ground.[6] On April 28, 1909, just a month after Dr. and Mrs. Horace Sadler had moved into Albion Point, Dr. Noble sold a forty-six acre wooden parcel that consisted of Noble's woods and "Rocky Lot" for $17,500 to Mr. and Mrs. Lewis Sadler.[7]

The transfer of sale was unlike any other in Carlisle and it is no wonder that both *The Evening Sentinel* and the *Carlisle Daily Herald* covered the full story in the following days paper.[8] The sale was considered "one of the largest real estate deals that has been consummated in Carlisle for some time" and even involved the use of a "cablegram" in order to communicate to Dr. Noble, who was away in Hong Kong, China.[9]

That day, at three o'clock in the afternoon, Sadler became the sole owner of the forty-six acre lot.[10] By the following day, he was off to New York to follow up with Hill and Stout, who were in charge of drawing up the blueprints for the mansion.[11]

Dr. Joseph Noble

Cumberland County Historical Society, Carlisle, Pa

IMPORTANT REAL ESTATE TRANSFER

LEWIS S. SADLER, ESQ., BECOMES OWNER OF VALUABLE NOBLE TRACT---WILL BUILD FINE HOME

Some time ago it was rumored among real estate circles that Lewis S. Sadler, Esq., son of Judge W. F. Sadler, had bought a portion of the farm located immediately southwest of town, and owned by Dr. Joseph W. Noble, of Hong Kong, China, formerly of Carlisle. It was learned then, that Mr. Sadler was negotiating with Clarence M. Liggett, the real estate agent, for the land, the latter having held an option on it since February.

Deal Closed.

Yesterday afternoon, at three o'clock, the deal was closed, and Mr. Sadler became owner of the land. It is a very valuable tract, containing 46 acres and 44 perches. It is located on the southwestern edge of town, and will front on the Walnut Bottom road. It is bounded on the east by Noble lands, on the south by the lands of Joseph Stuart, and on the west by lands of the Woods heirs. It includes what has been known for many years as "Noble's Woods." The woodland will be left practically in its present state.

Fine Residence.

Mr. Sadler will erect on his newly acquired possessions a magnificent home, plans for which have been drawn by a New York architect. It will stand near the edges of the woodland and stand back some distance from the road.

Mr. W. M. Henderson, of Carlisle, represented Dr. Noble, but in the transactions from time to time concerning the sale of the valuable tract it was necessary to cablegram as a means of rapid communication.

A Big House.

The Architects, Hill & Stout, of New York, are famous for erecting large buildings. They just finished a big building at Rutgers' College, and a large fraternity house there. The house will be 150 feet long and 40 feet wide. It will stand back from the road 800 feet. Fine driveways, shrubbery, etc., will make of it one of the most beautiful and costly homes in this section of Pennsylvania. A fine garage and stables will be built in the rear of the house.

Messrs. Bingham and Moore, of Carlisle, did the surveying for Mr. Sadler.

THE REAL FACTS AND CONDITIONS TODAY IN MESSINA.

The appalling magnitude of the calamity in Sicily makes Lyman H. Howe's reproduction of Sicily before and after the earthquake, of supreme interest. In the Carlisle Opera House matinee and night, on Saturday, May 1st, will be shown the very scenes which but yesterday abounded with life and beauty. Then these same scenes are visited after the terrible catastrophe. The sudden transition from the busy, prosperous Messina of yesterday to Messina as it now is, makes Mr. Howe's pictures vitally interesting and vitally instructive. By first showing the real importance of the city and its splendid buildings, Mr. Howe enables every spectator to realize how utterly hopeless has been the destruction. Having shown the city as it was, the pictures then take the audience to the city as it is today. Sale of seats opens at Houston's, Thursday morning April 29th.

A SPRING SONG.

The trees unfurl their pennons green
In honor of the May;
And rills, their sedgy banks between,
Go dancing on their way.

The tiny rootlets in the mould
The pipe of Pan have heard—
In bosky dell, by copse and wold,
The pulse of life has stirred.

The love-bird trills on bush and tree
His madrigal divine,
From bough 'neath blossom canopy
Or fringe of solemn pine.

Through fleecy cloud the sunshine glints
The sweet south wind to woo;
And flowers repeat their rainbow tints
In rosaries of dew.

Love's glad Evangel greets my ear
From every warbling throat
And all its harmonies I hear
In each ecstatic note.

It brings back joy when hope seems dead
O, miracle sublime!
Gives comfort for a Presence fled,

The Evening Sentinel,
29 April 1909

REAL ESTATE SALE.

Lewis S. Sadler, Esq., Purchases Portion of the Dr. Joseph W. Noble Farm Southwest of Town.

One of the largest real estate deals that has been consummated in Carlisle for some time was closed yesterday afternoon when C. M. Liggett, the real estate agent, disposed of his option on part of the Dr. Joseph W. Noble farm adjoining the southwestern end of Carlisle. The portion sold consists of 46 acres and 48 perches. It includes the Rocky lot and Noble's woods in the rear. All lying southward from the Walnut Bottom road. The purchaser was Lewis S. Sadler, Esq., who will erect on the property a modern dwelling house, and we understand it will be one of the finest and most attractive residences in this vicinity. Mr. Sadler will probably dispose of the lot he purchased in Harrisburg some time ago and upon which he expected to erect a residence.

Carlisle Evening Herald,
29 April 1909

The photographs below, are of the land survey that was done by Parker M. Moore and Clarence A. Bingham on May 15, 1909 and later revised on September 1, 1909. Land survey located in the same folder as the blueprints of the Thornwald Mansion at the Cumberland County Historical Society in Carlisle, Pa.

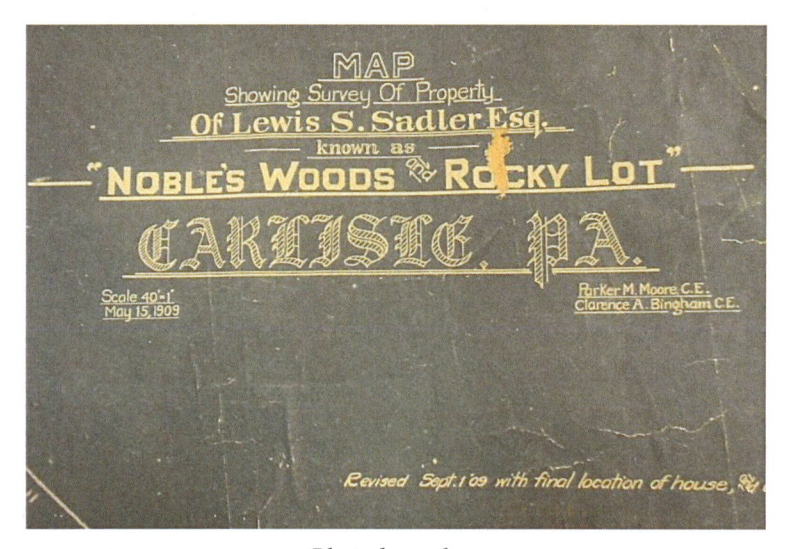

Photo by author

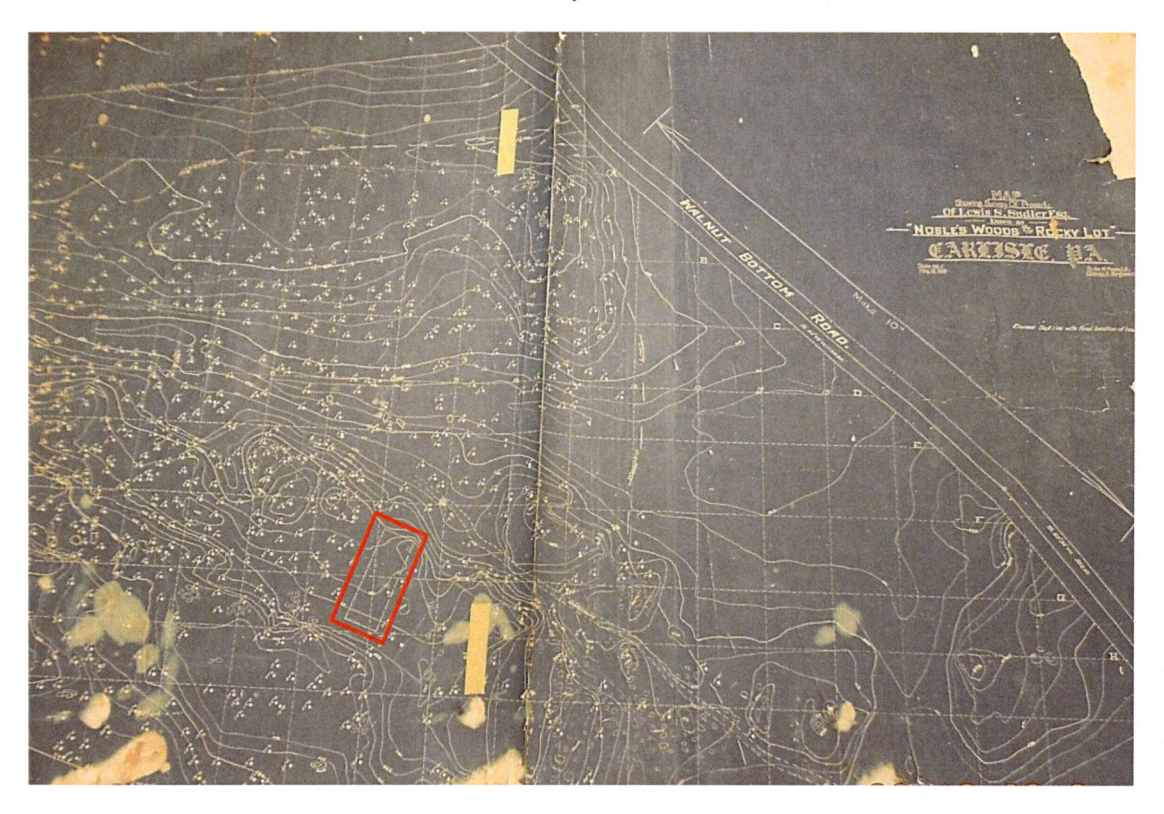

The red box indicates the location of the future Sadler residence while the many white dots indicate the numerous trees that were located on the grounds.

Photo by author

In the above photograph, the faint white rectangle indicates the previous location of the future Sadler residence, according to the survey done on May 15, 1909. However, after realizing that there was a large mass of limestone rock on the building site, the home was moved back several feet. Therefore, on September 1, 1909, Bingham and Moore revised the survey to show the present location of the residence indicated by the solid white rectangle.

Photo by author

The Plans Revealed

The day following the transfer of sale, on April 29, 1909, Carlisle citizens young and old read for the first time the full details in *The Evening Sentinel* of what was about to be constructed inside Noble's woods.

Mr. Sadler will erect on his newly acquired possessions a magnificent home, plans for which have been drawn by a New York architect. It will stand near the edges of the woodland and stand back some distance from the road.

The house will be 150 feet long and 40 feet wide. It will stand back from the road 800 feet. Fine driveways, shrubbery, etc. will make it one of the most beautiful homes in this section of Pennsylvania. A fine garage and stables will be built in the rear of the house.[12]

The Vision

What Mr. and Mrs. Lewis Sadler had envisioned was nothing like it in all of Carlisle or the state of Pennsylvania.

During their years at Cottage Hill, the couple often took extensive vacations to Europe where they spent several months at a time touring the United Kingdom.[13] Along their travels, they visited a number of homes and castles, including the Sutton House, located in Hackney, London, England, which was built by Lewis Sadler's great ancestor, Sir Ralph Sadler in 1535.[14]

In comparison to Albion Point, their home too would be colonial in style with emphasis on "Georgian and Palladian" architecture along with containing wide, spacious hallways and floors of parquetry.[15] However, while Albion Point boar resemblance to the Ege Mansion in Boiling Springs, their home would be modeled after the castles in England, which stood for centuries.

Sir Ralph Sadler was born in England in 1507. At an early age he was knighted, and later went on to serve as secretary of state for King Henry VIII in 1540. During this time, he was involved in several negotiations between England and Scotland and lived out of his home in Hackney. The home was a three-story, red brick Tudor, and contained an interior that was English in design along with containing walls paneled in oak, with a few of the rooms containing carved stone fireplaces.[16]

Therefore, when Lewis Sadler set out to construct their future residence, Sadler kept in mind his late ancestor's home and upon completion, a few of the rooms would bear resemblance to the Sutton House. Although the house did play a key role in the interior design of the mansion, the couple also read books on English architecture, such as Charles Latham's *In English Homes* that was later used as a reference for the "entrance gateway" which was constructed in 1912.[17]

While the interior was to be English in design, so was the layout of the many rooms in the mansion. Unlike those found in the average home at the turn of the century, their residence would contain a number of rooms that were designed for entertaining such as the library, reception room, dining room, billiard room, and rathskeller. Their residence would even contain rooms designated for servants', such as the servants' dining room, along with containing a separate servants' quarters on the third floor.

Altogether, their residence would be far from the average home in Carlisle, and therefore it is no wonder that throughout the next two years, the *Carlisle Herald* covered the ongoing construction of the mansion.

SADLER RESIDENCE COLONIAL STYLE

PLANS ARE NOW IN HANDS OF CONTRACTORS

New York Architects Have Designed for L. S. Sadler, Esq., a Spacious Mansion of Full Colonial Style—Contract for Excavation Awarded.

The plans for the new residence of Lewis S. Sadler, Esq., have arrived from New York city and are now in the hands of contractors for the preparation of bids.

This mansion is to be erected on the tract recently purchased by Mr. Sadler from Dr. Noble and will be one of the finest in the valley. The tract is situated on the southwestern edge of town, where West street connects with the Walnut Bottom road and is an ideal site for the mansion planned.

The residence will be full Colonial style, about 150 feet in length, with large pillars in the front reaching to a height of two stories. The mansion will be two stories and attic, with steep roof, dormer windows and old fashioned blinds at windows.

Thus is will be seen that the Colonial plan is being carried out in detail. The interior will be likewise Colonial in arrangement with wide halls, spacious rooms, dancing halls and all other perquisites which made the home of the olden tyme so attractive.

The plans were drawn by Hill and Stout, the noted New York architects of which firm the late Stanford White was formerly a member.

The contract for the excavations has already been awarded to W. S. Yarnell, of this place.

Carlisle Volunteer,
6 July 1909

The Blueprints

In charge of designing the blueprints for their future residence was Hill and Stout of New York, who were "famous for erecting large buildings".[18] Prior to this time, the company had constructed a large fraternity house at Rutgers University. Later in 1910, they would design the home for an eminent New York attorney, Albert B. Boardman, whose mansion was designed after the "Villa Medici" in Rome.[19] Certainly, the couple had chosen only the best architect to design their stately mansion in the woods.

By the following month, on May 15, 1909, Parker M. Moore & Clarence A. Bingham were out surveying the grounds for the future Sadler estate. According to the land survey, the mansion was to be constructed in the rear of the property surrounded by a number of walnut and oak trees that were already present on the grounds.[20]

During this time, Hill & Stout were busy at drawing up the blueprints for the foundation and the first floor, which were drawn on June 7, 1909.[21] However, it would be another month until work could begin on the residence.

On July 3, 1909, nearly two months since Sadler had purchased the ground, *The Evening Sentinel* announced that Winfield S. Yarnall, a prominent excavating contractor and who had previously done work on Albion Point, would soon begin excavating the grounds.[22]

Just three days after the paper had released the news of the excavation, the *Carlisle Volunteer* released an article pertaining to the mansion's blueprints, which had just arrived from New York. The front-page article read, "Sadler Residence Colonial Style", and for the first time the plans for the future Sadler residence was revealed. The paper considered the residence to be the "finest in the valley" and was to be "Colonial style".

Located in the front of the mansion, facing Walnut Bottom Road, was to be erected "large pillars" that would reach to the top of the second story along with an "attic with steep roof, dormer windows and old fashioned blinds at windows". As for the interior of the mansion, the paper described it as being "likewise Colonial in arrangement with wide halls, spacious rooms, dancing halls and all other perquisites which made the home the home of the olden tyme so attractive".[23]

North Elevation

Plan of the north elevation looking out towards Walnut Bottom Road drawn by Hill and Stout on June 7, 1909.

Cumberland County Historical Society, Carlisle, Pa

South Elevation

Plan of the south elevation facing present day I-81 drawn by Hill and Stout on June 7, 1909. Note the set of steps above that lead from the future ice box room. Upon completion of Thornwald in 1911, the steps were relocated on the left side of the mansion adjacent to the kitchen and the door on the icebox room was replaced with a window.

Cumberland County Historical Society, Carlisle, Pa

The Official Groundbreaking

Days passed, and anxious Carlisle citizens waited and wondered when would the ground be broken for the mansion? However, on July 17, 1909, on the front-page of the *Carlisle Volunteer,* Carlisle area citizens learned that Yarnall was now removing a few trees in preparation for the ground breaking that was to occur just three days later. On July 20, 1909, the *Carlisle Volunteer* announced that excavation of the grounds had begun and Yarnall would soon "put a large force of men and carts to work". In addition, that day the paper remarked how the mansion "[would] add materially to the attractiveness of that pretty district" furthermore, foretelling the "building boom" that would take place the following year along South College Street. [24]

"Work Started"

While the excavation of the grounds was officially in full swing, there was still no news of who was to construct the future Sadler residence. However, on September 9, 1909, the long wait for who was to construct the residence was officially over. According to the *Carlisle Daily Herald,* "Mr. Balcombe of the Thompson-Sterrett Construction Company" had received the contract for constructing their future home.[25] However, the company was not in the business of constructing large homes, but rather towering skyscrapers in metropolitan cities that reached several stories high.

According to *The New York Times*, Theodore Starrett was "one of the foremost developers of steel skyscraper type of construction and a leader in all lines of building".[26] The company had previously constructed the Robinson/Penn Building located in Philadelphia in 1902, which stood seventeen stories high. A year prior to the Robinson/Penn building, they had also constructed the Continental Trust Building in Baltimore, Maryland.[27]

Although Thompson-Starrett was in charge of constructing the mansion, there were also a number of Carlisle citizens who played their part in the construction. Harry Hertlzer, who operated a lumber manufacturing company along North Hanover Street, in Carlisle, cut a number of boards for the mansion. The Sheafer Brothers laid the brick and tile along with the help of a few Italians from New York City.[28] Later, Yarnall and Enos Stauffer, of Carlisle, would construct the long road that led to the mansion along with excavating the grounds for the lampposts, which would later be located on the front lawn.[29]

Throughout the next few months, the men were busy as bees, working day and night to get the job done before winter arrived. In September, the walls of the foundation were already starting to take shape. By the following month, the foundation was completed.[30]

By this time, the ongoing construction of the Sadler residence had become quite a curiosity for the Carlisle area papers, including the *Carlisle Herald*, which often kept its readers informed as to the ongoing construction of the mansion.

The Continental Trust Building, in Baltimore, Maryland was built in 1908 by Thompson & Starrett of New York.

Postcard from author

THAT MANSION IN THE FOREST

Foundations of L. S. Sadler Residence Finished

The new residence of L. S. Sadler, Esq., along the southern border of Carlisle, is to be a veritable mansion in the forest and is rapidly taking shape, although the work is hidden by the leaves of the trees and you would not observe the building operations in passing along the public highway.

The foundation walls are complete. The steel framework will be here by the 15th and then work upon the superstructure will be rushed. In the meantime the men are grading the driveway and putting in some outlying foundations and walls.

But there are public evidences of building operations. As you drive along the highway you see a deep trench lining the roadside and stretching across the hill to the woods beyond. It is the trench for the water mains, for the Carlisle water supply is being extended far beyond its former terminus in order to give this home an abundant supply of water. Then up in the woods can be seen a number of foresters at work trimming the forest trees, and whenever they find a sturdy oak or walnut which has commenced to decay, they scrape out the hollow places, fill in with plaster of Paris and paint it over, and thus save the tree.

For it is the purpose of Mr. and Mrs. Sadler to preserve the scene as natural as they found it. Not a tree in that woods is to be cut away (a few were removed to make room for the building and driveways), not a rock is to be removed, the bushes and wild flowers and plants are to remain even the weeds will not be disturbed. When the magnificent residence is completed, the occupants will have at front and rear door not widespreading lawns, but the little wild bush and vine and flower and weed, springing up among the rocks, as found in Pennsylvania wildwood.

The mansion is near the highest point of the grove—in a slight depression so that the top of the foundations is about on a level with the highest ground—and, when the building is completed and the leaves are off the trees, the mansion will occupy a commanding location, with knolls and rocks sloping down to the

Carlisle Herald
12 October 1909

On October 12, 1909, the paper released an article that appeared on the front page entitled, "That Mansion In The Forest: Foundations of L.S. Sadler Residence Finished". The article contained the first tidbits of information pertaining to the ongoing construction of the mansion along with the landscape of the grounds.

At this time, the mansion was "rapidly taking shape" and despite the several trees that surrounded the construction site there was already evidence that work was in progress. Passersby along Walnut Bottom Road could see "a deep trench lining the roadside and stretching across the hill to the woods beyond", which was later used for the Carlisle water mains that were said to be "extended far beyond their terminus". In addition, if one looked long enough they could even catch a glimpse of a forester trimming a few of the branches off the trees.[31]

The landscape of the Sadler residence was to consist of a "wild, natural scenery". According to the *Carlisle Herald*, "Not a tree in that woods is to be cut away (a few were removed to make room for the building and driveways), not a rock is to be removed, the bushes and wild flowers and plants are to remain even the weeds will not be disturbed".[32]

In order to preserve what remained, extreme measures were taken to keep the originality of the landscape, which included paying "$1,000" towards the preservation of the trees including patching a few of them.[33] Trees that were rotting from the inside out were repaired by a number of "foresters" who were at work scraping out the rotten areas in the tree and patching them with "plaster of Paris", later painting over the patched area with paint to make it appear as though the tree had never been touched.[34] Although the couple had went to extreme lengths towards preserving the landscape of Noble's woods, this was only the beginning of what lay ahead for the interior of the mansion that was to be done in great detail.

Located near the construction site was a small building that was built to house the blueprints during the construction. One day, a reporter from the *Carlisle Herald* got a glimpse of the blueprints while inside the makeshift building and further described the location of the residence along with the location of the driveway and walkways to its readers. The reporter noted the location of the many columns that would be constructed on the Sadler residence considering them "a leading feature" of colonial architecture.

While inside examining the blueprints that day, an individual who also was looking over the blueprints of the mansion at the same time remarked, "This will be the finest residence in this valley". In reply, Superintendent Balcom said, "It ought to be, for the cost will be about a quarter of a million". The price was steep, but the mansion was supposedly built to last, and was considered a "modern fire-proof building, constructed of steel, stone and brick".[35]

Built to Last

On the outside, the mansion was to be constructed of limestone, concrete and brick with the roof being covered in "Bangor slate".[36] The foundation was to be made of "Indiana limestone", while the tall Doric columns that supported the front portico and rear porte-cochere were to be made of concrete over a wood form.[37] Even the many rosettes, which would later be located under the front portico and the rear porte-cochere, were made of plaster over metal while the exterior walls of the mansion were to be constructed of triple brick.[38]

Above: A section of the slate roof, facing the rear lawn, as it appeared in October 2010.

Right: A photo depicting the three different sizes of slate that were used on the roof. The largest sheet of slate, pictured far right, was nearly two feet long and one foot wide.

Photos by author

On the inside were two layers of brick followed by a layer of exterior tapestry bricks that measured eighteen inches long, five inches wide, and two inches thick and furthermore, gave the mansion an "English" appearance. However, the bricks were not English, as presumed by Dr. Horace Sadler, who was interviewed by John Vernon Hertzler in 1952, but instead were made in America.[39] The bricks, which were branded with the name "Tapestry", were made by Fiske and Company of New York, who specialized in the manufacturing of tapestry brick.

One of the many "Tapestry" bricks used in the construction of Thornwald.

Photos by author

An enlarged photo of the type of bricks that were used in the construction of Thornwald.
Photo taken from *Tapestry Brick work,* a catalog published by Fiske & Company in 1909.

Despite the thick brick walls, even the interior was not overlooked. On the inside, the mansion was constructed similar to a skyscraper. Thick steel beams supported the brick walls, while steel reinforced concrete columns supported the concrete floor above.[40] The floors were "18-and-a-half inch thick poured [steel reinforced] concrete" and therefore was supported not only by the concrete pillars but also along with the double brick walls which ran from the basement to the second floor.[41] Four of the walls on the first floor, even ran up to the roof, further giving the mansion support along with the brick that was used for the many fireplaces in the mansion.[42] Overall, the mansion, indeed, was a "modern fireproof building", a theory that would be put to the test nearly a hundred years later.[43]

One of the many steel beams that held the mansion together.

Photo by author

The steel reinforced pillars that supported the concrete floor. These supports ran from the basement all the way up to the third floor. Upon completion of the mansion in 1911, the concrete pillars were covsered in oak wall paneling.

Photo by author

A section of the thick concrete floor, located above the main entrance.

Photo by author

"Work at Sadler Home"

By mid-October, the steel framework had arrived and now work was progressing at a fast rate.[44] No time was to be wasted since the winter months were fast approaching. Towards the last week in October 1909, the *Carlisle Herald* reported that the gas and water lines were being laid and thereafter the news ceased concerning the construction of the mansion.[45] However, although work may have ceased at the mansion, there was now men at work on the Sadler and Sadler law firm in Carlisle.

On November 22, 1909, the law office received a "2,750 lb. safe", which was raised by H.G. Rinehart and a large group of men. According to the *Carlisle Herald*, it was Lewis Sadler who was "fitting up" the room.[46]

By the start of the new year, construction on the mansion resumed. On January 7, 1910, the *Carlisle Herald* announced that the "concrete workers are employed at their labors and will soon have the job finished for the present". Once again, work was in progress on the mansion after the heavy winter had put a hold on construction.

For the next two months, the men worked on constructing the second story of the mansion, which was completed in March. On March 11, 1910, the *Carlisle Herald* released the news of the completion of the second story along with the news that the mansion may be ready by late spring. However, it would be another year until the mansion would be officially completed.

The "Building Boom"

During this time, the construction of the mansion was also playing a key role in the development of South College Street. Prior to the construction, the only homes that were located along South College Street included the Johnson Moore Estate known as "Mooreland", now the site of Dickinson College, along with nine dwellings that were located opposite of Mooreland and above West South Street.[47]

However, nearly a year after Sadler had purchased a portion of Noble's woods on May 2, 1910, the *Carlisle Evening Herald* announced that South College Street was about to see a "building boom of the best kind and latest style of residences". Furthermore, the paper declared that South College Street would be "one of the fastest growing fashionable sections of the town".

The homes that would later be constructed along South College Street would mirror the colonial architecture of Thornwald with a few being constructed of brick and bearing tall, white columns that reached to the second story and some even bearing dormer windows that peaked out from the rooftop.

In addition, South College Street was to be paved with brick, making it "one of the best and prettiest highways in the city" when completed.[48] However, by September of 1910, the Borough Council decided on creating a macadamized road instead, and in October, Lewis Sadler contributed "$1,000" towards the road construction.[49]

The former home of William H. Goodyear located at 270 South College Street in Carlisle.

Cumberland County Historical Society, Carlisle, Pa

The First Look Inside

Meanwhile, construction continued on the mansion, which was slowly nearing completion. Throughout the spring and summer months, the men continued working long hours at the mansion in hopes that it would be done in time for Christmas.

By August, the third story was completed and the roof installed. However, there was still more work to be done both inside and out. Prior to this time, the paper did not report on the construction of the mansion except for when Sadler first purchased the ground from Dr. Noble in April 1909. However, this time they gave Carlisle citizens what they had long anticipated for, which was the first glimpse of the inside of the mansion. Certainly, the citizens of Carlisle read of the ongoing construction, but to hear about what was behind the walls of the mansion was more newsworthy than one could have imagined.

On August 16, 1910, located on the sixth page of *The Evening Sentinel* was the article that read, "Facts Concerning the Magnificent Sadler Mansion", which gave readers young and old an inside look at the ongoing construction of the mansion along with the landscape of the grounds. Once again, the paper reiterated how the mansion was being constructed inside Noble's woods and how the nearly "1,300 trees" would remain "untouched". Although the news may have been old to some, there was new information concerning both the exterior and interior construction of the mansion.

During this time, a reporter from *The Evening Sentinel* had walked the grounds of the Sadler estate, observing the exterior of the mansion along with getting a never before seen look at the ongoing construction inside the mansion. In regards to the exterior of mansion, the reporter told Carlisle area citizens the following:

> The construction of the house is very extraordinary in point of architecture and materials used. It is nothing short of palatial in some features and there is nothing like it in this section of the country. Our readers can glean some idea of this house when they can imagine a Colonial structure 142 feet long, 52 feet wide, and 48 feet high, with front facing the north, and pillars on every side. The brick used are of the tapestry kind, and are eighteen inches in length. The base of the house is Indiana limestone, and the pillars, lintels, large flower beds, etc. are of Kingston trimming, which is white in color.[50]

By this time, the exterior was nearing completion, although the interior was still undergoing construction. The reporter, who had observed the exterior that day, later accompanied Superintendent Makin of the Thompson-Starrett Company, as he took him inside the mansion for a never before seen look at the ongoing construction.

At this time, the mansion was to have "forty rooms" upon its completion, although at the time of the tour there were far less. Upon stepping inside the mansion, the reporter noticed the double, wooden staircase along with a number of rooms, which were nearing completion on the first floor including the library, conservatory and kitchen. According to the reporter, the kitchen was "finer by far than any parlor in the town" and already contained walls covered in "white enamel brick", which was also used in the bathrooms of the mansion. In addition, the citizens of Carlisle were also informed that Mr. Sadler's office along with the ladies and men's dressing rooms would also be located on the first floor.[51]

While the first floor was designed for entertaining, the second floor was designated for Mr. and Mrs. Lewis Sadler's master bedrooms along with "sleeping apartments" and a "breakfast veranda".
Up on the third floor, the reporter saw the "gymnasium, pool and billiard rooms" which were already completed along with the "two large skylights" that were said to "admit an abundance of light".[52]

FACTS CONCERNING THE MAGNIFICENT SADLER MANSION

Although half a hundred men are working at the palatial home of Lewis S. Sadler, Esq., off the Walnut Bottom road, south west of town, the "house in the woods" (for such it veritably is,) will not be completed, in the opinion of Superintendent Makin, until Christmas. Some believe it will require a longer time. Superintendent Makin, of the contracting firm of the Sterrett-Thompson Company, New York, contractors for the house, courteously showed a Sentinel reporter through the house this morning, and while it is not nearly finished, a visit to the place will convey to anyone a pretty fair idea of what the magnificent structure will be like. We have referred to the building operations there from time to time, but a visit, and visit only is requisite to fully appreciate it.

Our readers are quite familiar with its location, in the heart or what was known for many years as "Noble's Woods". The house can scarcely be seen from the Walnut Bottom road. Large trees and shrubbery surround it on all sides, and the novel feature is that the 1300 trees, the shrubbery, etc., will not be touched. On the other hand about $1000. has been spent in the preservation of some of them. "They wouldn't saw off a limb of them", said Superintendent Makin. The work on road making is referred to in another column.

A Wonderful Structure

The construction of the house is very extraordinary in point of architecture and materials used. It is nothing short of palatial in some features and there is nothing like it in this section of the country. Our readers can glean some idea of the house when they can imagine a Colonial structure, 142 feet long, 63 feet wide, and 48 feet high; with the front facing the north, and pillars on every side. The brick used are of the tapestry kind, and are eighteen inches in length.

The base of the house is Indiana limestone, and the pillars, lintels, large flower beds, etc., are of Kingston trimming, which is white in color.

Forty Rooms

The house will have forty rooms. In the basement will be an ice manufacturing plant, a $5,000 Rathskeller, a hot water heating plant (all water will be heated by gas) a vacuum cleaner with a connection in each room, storage room, coal rooms, and a large compressed air tank to force the water to the third floor. There will be six and eight inch water mains but it will be necessary to force it to the third story.

Large Hallways—1st Floor

On the first and second floors are large, wide hallways, from which rooms are entered on either side. Near the main entrance are wide stairways on either side. To the far left is a conservatory, and the parlor and library will be very large. Mr. Sadler's office also will be on the first floor, besides private baths, and ladies and gentlemen's dressing rooms. There will be a breakfast room for the servants only.

Great Kitchen

Finer by far than many a parlor in the town will be the Sadler kitchen. It is not only large in dimensions, but its appointments are extraordinary. It is finished in white enamel brick, as are all of the bath rooms in the house.

The Second Story

On the second story are mainly sleeping apartments. Mr. Sadler and Mrs. Sadler will each have a suite of rooms. On this floor will be a breakfast room on a veranda.

Third Floor

On the third floor will be the apartments for the servants. It will have large trunk rooms and there will be rooms for guests. The trunk rooms are on either end of the house. In the center of the house, third floor are two large skylights which admit an abundance of light into the gymnasium, pool and billiard rooms. An elevator, an electric one, with push button runs from the basement to the third floor.

The house will have electric light and gas.

Electric lights will be placed on the road leading from the house northward at every 100 feet.

All of the wires about the house will be put under ground in a conduit from College street across the Walnut Bottom road on to the premises.

There will be about three quarters of a mile of special road making.

The tract about the house comprises 41 acres of land, very thickly wooded as above stated.

All of the radiators are encased in walls, etc., and those in bath rooms in tiling.

The architects are Hill & Stout, of New York, and the contractors the Thompson-Sterrett Co., of the same city.

The cost of the house is conservatively estimated at $250,000.00

The first glimpse inside the future Sadler residence.

*The Evening Sentinel,
16 August 1910*

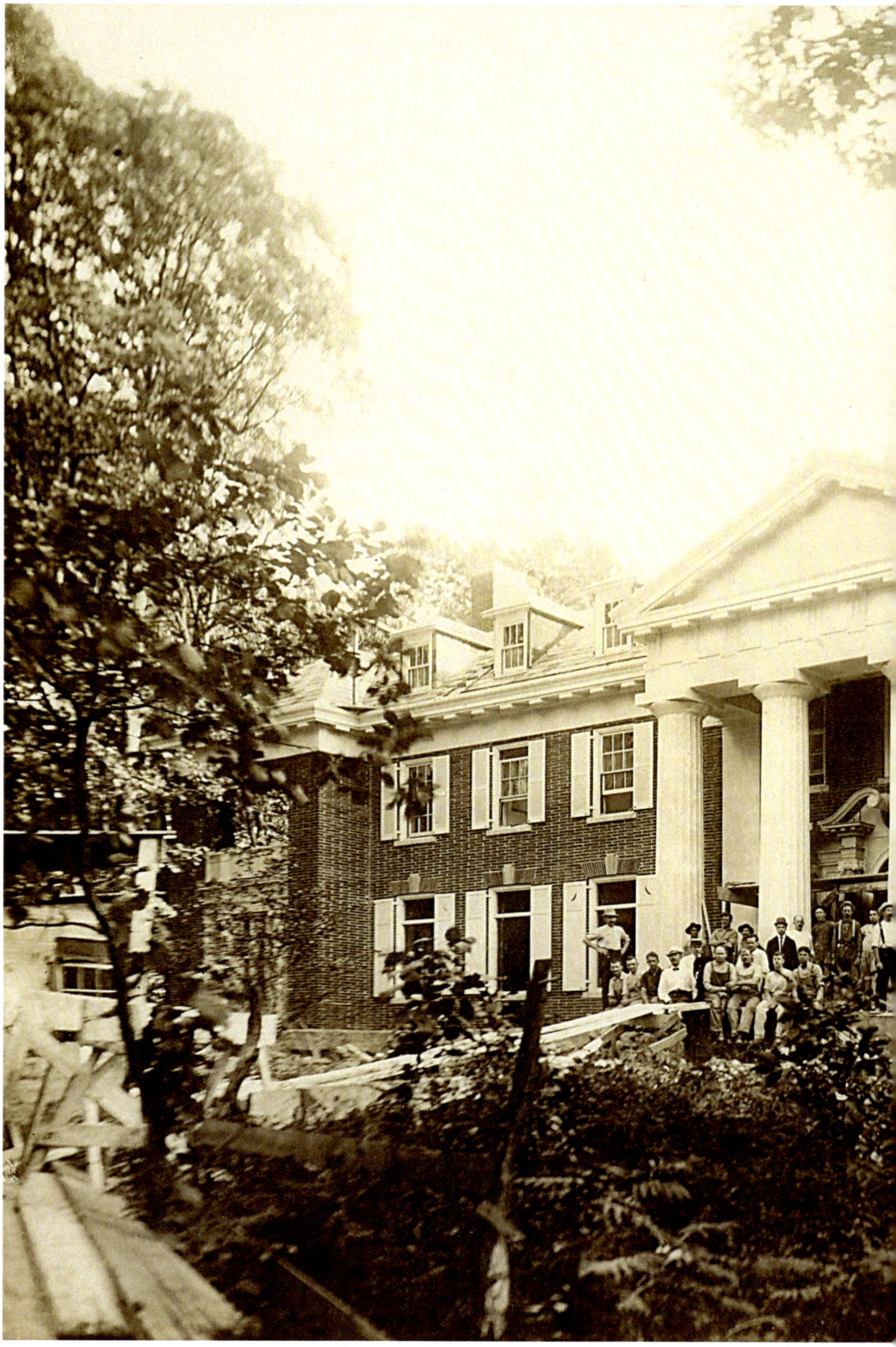

The construction crew poses for a photograph in front of the main entrance of Thornwald in late summer/early fall of 1910. The photograph is the first known photograph of the mansion, and is the earliest one taken of the exterior during construction.

Cumberland County Historical Society, Carlisle, Pa

TELFORD ROAD AT NEW HOME

Novel Driveway Construction to New Sadler Residence.

WINDING LENGTH 3300 FEET

First Is Foundation of Stones On Edge, Then Earth and Crushed Stone and Top Dressing—Durable And Dustless Passageway.

Contractor W. S. Yarnell has a number of men at work building what is known as a Telford road, and which will be the driveway into the handsome mansion being erected in what is known as Noble's Woods, in the southwestern section of town. The driveway will extend from the Walnut Bottom road at the intersection of College street, southward to the house. It will be very winding, encircling several small hills in its course to the house, and passing through a very picturesque and naturally beautiful tract of land. The entire length of the road will be 3,000 feet, and there will not be a straight stretch of over 200 feet in length.

The foundation of the road is built of stone six inches wide, about a foot long and a few inches thick, stood on the edge. A layer of earth is placed over this, then a layer of larger crushed stone, and then the top dressings are applied. After this is done and the surface thoroughly rolled, tarvia or some other good road surfacing will be applied, which will prevent dust.

The service road, which will be for delivery wagons passing to and from the house, will be shorter, and will be constructed in some such a manner as the other road. It will be to the west of the main driveway, and but about twelve feet wide, while the main passageway will be about sixteen feet in width. Enos Stouffer is superintending the work.

Carlisle Evening Herald,
15 August 1910

In addition, on the third floor the reporter was shown the elevator, which was said to be an "electric one, with push button", that ran from the basement all the way up to the third floor. As for the additional rooms, which would later occupy the third floor, these included "apartments for servants", along with additional guest rooms and two "large trunk rooms" which would be located at either end.[53]

As for the basement, it was to be unlike any other in all of Carlisle. According to *The Evening Sentinel* upon completion, the basement would contain "an ice manufacturing plant, a $5,000 Rathskellar, a gas hot water heating plant (all water will be heated by gas) a vacuum cleaner with a connection in each room, storage room, coal rooms, and a large compressed air tank to force the water to the third floor." In addition, the entire mansion would contain both electric and gas lighting and heated with the use of radiators. Since the radiators were large in size, and did not blend well with the colonial décor they were reported to be "encased in walls etc., and those in bath rooms in tiling".[54]

While the men continued to work on the mansion, there was another project fully underway. Already a number of men were at work on constructing the long road that would lead to the mansion from Walnut Bottom Road.

A day prior to *The Evening Sentinel* releasing the article pertaining to the layout of the mansion, the *Carlisle Evening Herald* released an article concerning the "Telford road" that was to be constructed on the grounds. According to the paper, the road was to be "3,000 feet" long and constructed by W.S. Yarnall and superintended by Enos Stauffer of Carlisle. Yarnall had previously done the excavation of the grounds, and now he was at work constructing the road that would lead to the Sadler residence.

Already, Yarnall had put a "number of men at work" on constructing the long road that was also to consist of a "service road", that would be located on the opposite side of the mansion. The service road was specially designed for "delivery wagons passing to and from the house".[55] Upon completion, the long road that wrapped its way around the mansion, was also adorned with a number of lampposts that lit up the grounds at night.[56]

The long road that led to the Sadler residence as it appeared in 1913. Note the lampposts located behind the gate, which lined the driveway. The lampposts also adorned the front and rear lawn of the residence.

Cumberland County Historical Society, Carlisle, Pa

Chapter 8

"Thornwold"

    The work on the magnificent Sadler residence continued throughout the next few months and into 1911. However, the Carlisle area papers did not give any details as to the ongoing construction of the mansion until May of that year. On May 5, 1911, the *Carlisle Evening Herald* announced that the mansion had just been completed and was called both a "show place" and "the finest in the valley" and certainly, it was.

    Just two days after the *Herald* released the news regarding the completion of the Sadler residence, the paper told of the couple's first guest inside their new home. On May 8, 1911, on the fourth page of the paper was a small article that read, "Governor at Thornewold". For the first time the name, "Thornwold" was used to identify the home of Mr. and Mrs. Lewis Sadler although it was spelled differently from present day "Thornwald". The name was English in meaning, and received such a name from the grove of "hawthorn" trees that were present at the entrance to the mansion.[1]

    According to the paper, "Governor Tener with a party of state officials motored to Carlisle yesterday and were the guests of L.S. Sadler at Thornewold".[2] That day the men were the first guests inside the mansion since its completion, and must have been in awe as Sadler gave them the grand tour of the residence, which was larger than the governor's own executive mansion in Harrisburg.

Pennsylvania Governor John Kinley Tener
Photo by J. Gutekunst, Philadelphia

Courtesy of the Library of Congress
LC-US762-54075

GOVERNOR AT THORNEWOLD
Governor Tener with a party of the State officials motored to Carlisle yesterday and were the guests of L. S. Sadler at Thornewold.

Carlisle Evening Herald, 8 May 1911

{ 54 }

The above photographs were taken in the winter of 1910, while the interior of the mansion was still under construction. Note the outbuilding, in the above photograph, which was located to the left of the main entrance. The outbuilding may have been the same one that housed the blueprints during the construction. In the photograph below, an outhouse can be seen hidden in the woods to the right of the rear entrance.

Cumberland County Historical Society, Carlisle, Pa.

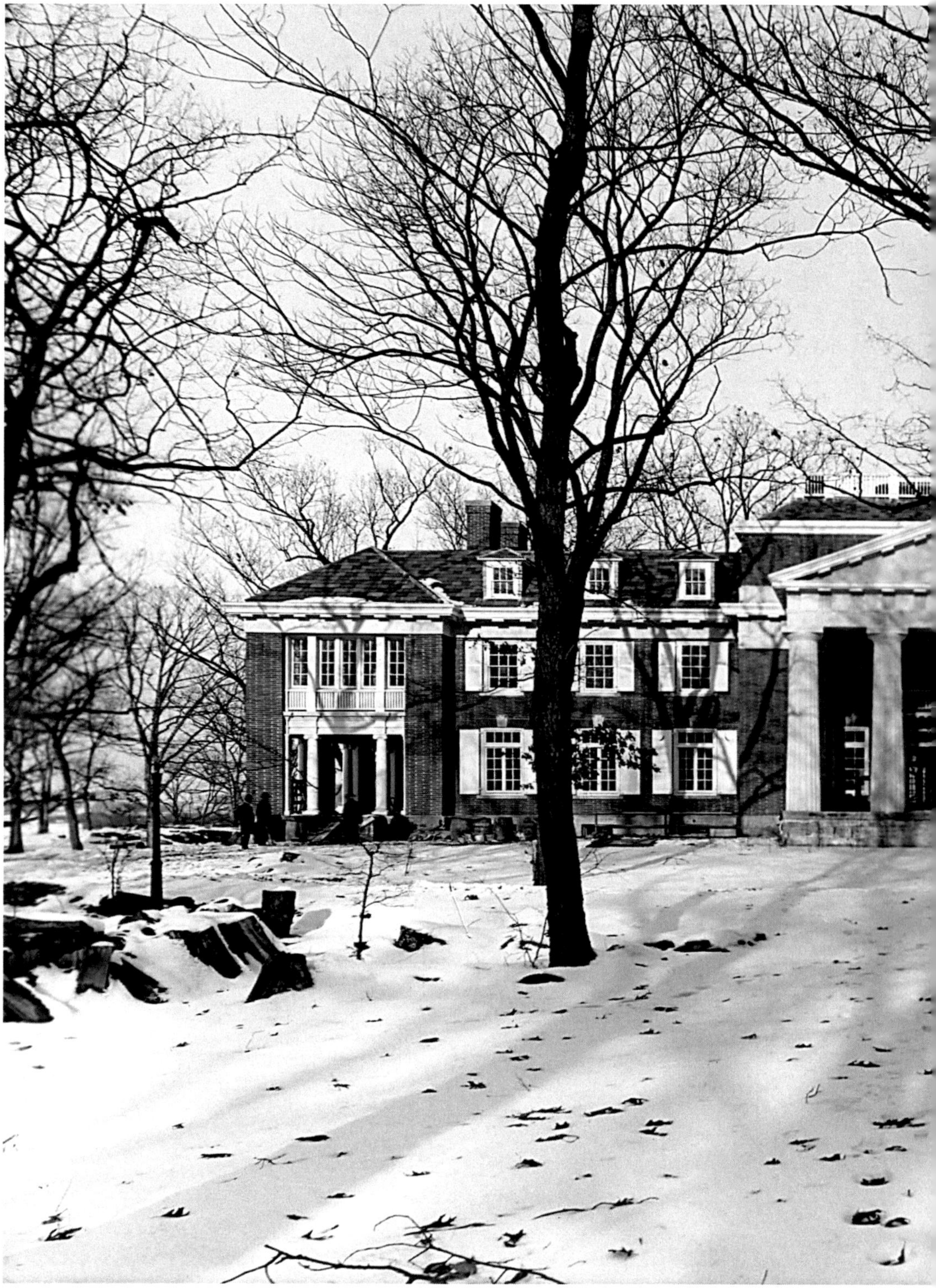

The first photograph of the rear entrance of Thornwald, was taken in the winter of 1910 by A. A. Line of Carlisle. At this time, the exterior was already completed, although over the next several months work continued on the interior of the mansion.
Upon completion, in May 1911, the rear lawn contained a number of lampposts along with a roundabout that was located directly in front of the porte-cochere.

Cumberland County Historical Society, Carlisle, Pa.

Main Entrance

The main entrance of Thornwald as it appeared in 1935. Besides the two lampposts, pictured in the photograph above, were another pair of lampposts that were placed further down the path that lead towards the Walnut Bottom Road.

Cumberland County Historical Society, Carlisle, Pa.

  On the outside, a formal garden was located on the front lawn, which contained four lampposts located on either side of a path that led up to the main entrance. The main entrance was elegant in design containing a tall portico that was supported by four Doric columns along with a four-foot limestone wall that hid the steps that led up to the front door from view. At the top of the stairs was a landing made of red quarry tile while under the portico was inset a number of rosettes that were made of plaster.
  Unlike the exterior tapestry bricks that served to give Thornwald its English appearance, the red quarry tile, was not made in the United States but was imported from North Wales. Besides being used in the landing in front of the main entrance, the tile was also used in a variety of areas throughout the mansion. From the landing located in front of the rear entrance and in between the two vestibules located inside the main hall, to the first floor conservatory and the two loggias located on either end of the second floor.

The main entrance of Thornwald as it appeared in April 1974. Photos by James Steinmetz

Courtesy of Thornwald Home

The steps leading up to the main entrance. Note the Ionic columns located on either side of the main entrance. The columns were also located on either side of the rear entrance.

Courtesy of Thornwald Home

A section of the red quarry tile floor. The highlighted photo, is the underside of one of the red quarry tiles, showing the inscription "N. Wales" located on the bottom.

Photos by author

Above: The rosettes under the front portico.

Right: A section of the main entrance showing the detail of the front doorway.

Courtesy of Thornwald Home

Loggia

    Located on the west side of the mansion was the loggia, which contained a red quarry tile floor and was equipped with a gas fireplace along with outdoor lighting. The loggia was conveniently located just off the library and could be accessed by either the two sets of French doors that were present on either side of the outdoor fireplace or the single set of steps that were located just off the rear driveway.

The fireplace inside the loggia. *Photo by author*

A view of the loggia looking towards the front lawn. The iron railing, pictured above, was added in the fall of 1953.

Photo by author

A section of the loggia, as it appeared in 2001, showing the French doors and quarry tile floor.

Courtesy of the Borough of Carlisle

Rear Entrance

Located in the rear of the mansion were two stairwells that led to the basement along with a towering porte-cochere. The porte-cochere was supported by six Doric columns and underneath hung "thirty"rosettes.[3] At night, the rosettes could be lit up along with those underneath the front portico although changing the bulbs was no small task and therefore involved the use of a long pole.[4]

Unlike the main entrance, which contained a set of steps that were concealed from view by a limestone wall, was the rear entrance, which contained landings made of red quarry tile along with a pair of massive stone flower boxes that were present on either side of the doorway. Due to the impressive features of the rear entrance, it is no wonder that many of times it was used as the main entrance since guests could be dropped off under the porte-cochere to escape any inclement weather.

The rear entrance as it appeared in 1973. Upon completion in 1911, the second floor contained two outdoor loggias, which by 1960 were enclosed.

Courtesy of Thornwald Home

A view of the loggia and rear entrance as it appeared in 1957.

Courtesy of Homewood Retirement Centers

The rosettes under the rear porte-cochere.

Courtesy of the Borough of Carlisle

The rear lawn as it appeared in the spring of 1974.

Courtesy of Thornwald Home

First Floor

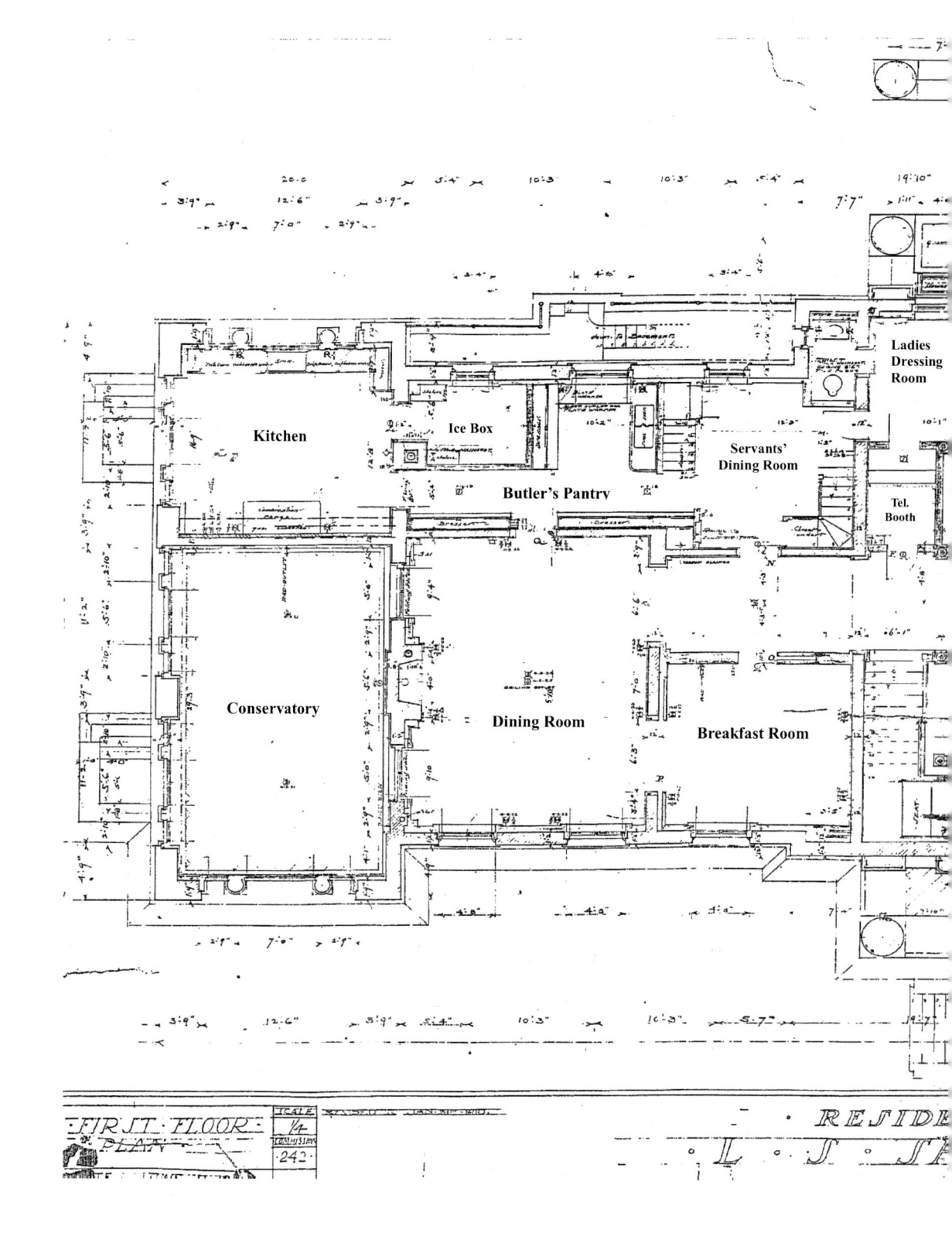

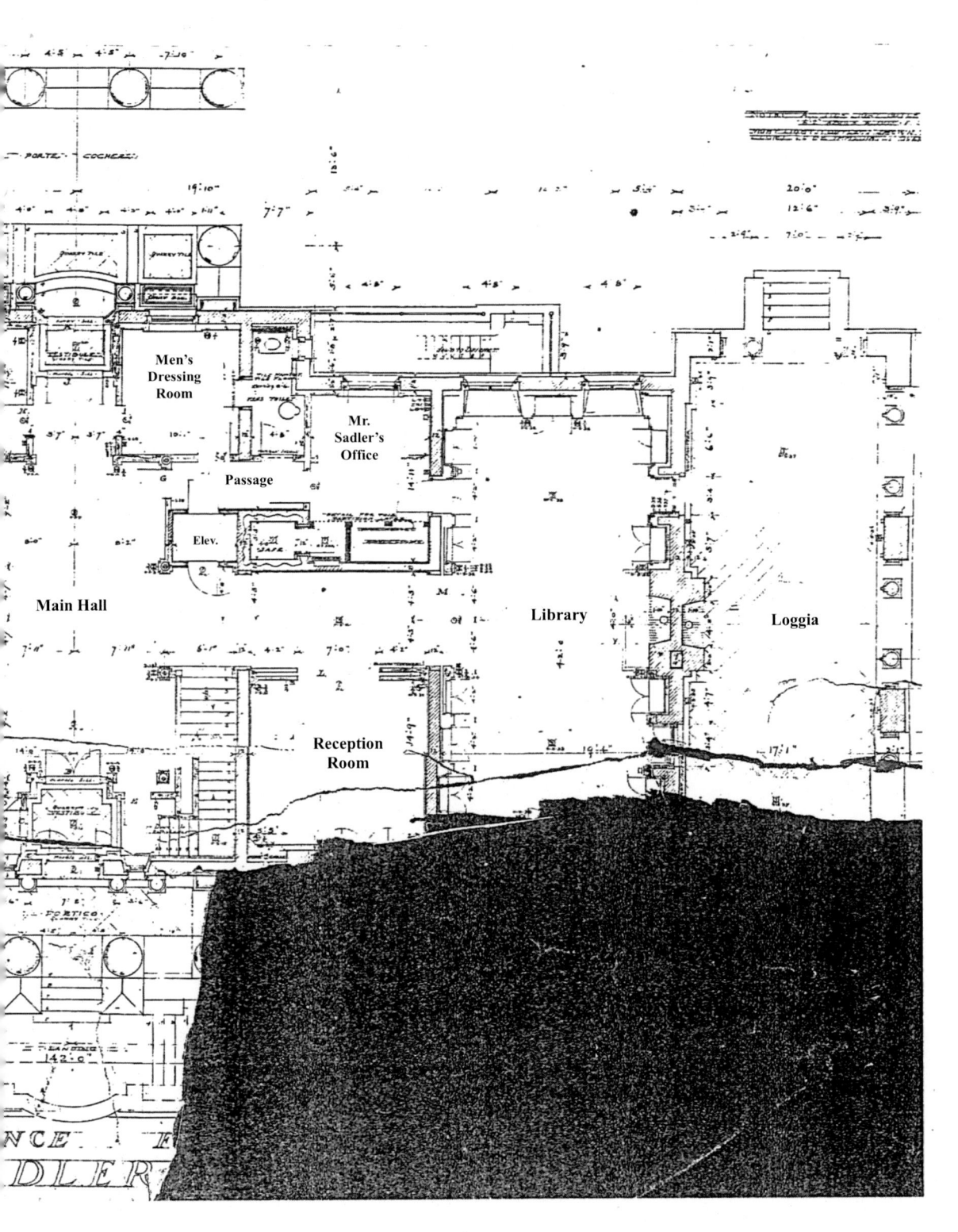

First floor blueprint drawn by Hill & Stout on June 7, 1909. Rooms relabeled for quality purposes.

Cumberland County Historical Society, Carlisle, Pa.

Main Hall

Upon entering the mansion, the main hall along with the wide hallway that branched off on either side was reminiscent of the couple's many trips to the United Kingdom, and therefore being English in design. The main hall contained walls and columns paneled in oak, a parquet floor, along with a carved plaster ceiling that was intersected by panels of wood. The square oak panels that covered the walls of the main hall were just one of the features that were similar to that found inside the Sutton House in London, England. [5]

To the left of the main entrance was a sitting room, and to the right, the entrance to the basement. Also located on either side of the main entrance, was the double grand staircase that contained a heavily carved bannister that was likewise, English in design.

Located at the bottom of the staircase and attached to the oak paneled columns, was a wall scone that resembled a torch. The scones were also present on the columns that were opposite of the double grand staircase along with present on both sides of the main and rear entrances.

The main hall looking from the rear entrance. Located on either side of the main entrance, were a pair of arched, leaded glass doors, similar in design to those of the main entrance (see page 210). The open door to the left, led to the basement while the small room to the right, was a sitting room. In later years, the room was remodeled into a bathroom.
Courtesy of A. Keating

One section of the double grand staircase as it appeared at Christmas time in 1973.
Courtesy of Thornwald Home

Close up view of the carved bannister that was English in design.
Courtesy of Thornwald Home

The stairs leading up to the second floor
Courtesy of Thornwald Home

Among the other features of the main hall was the telephone booth, elevator, and the ladies and men's dressing rooms. Both the telephone booth and the elevator were located across from the double grand staircase and located on opposite sides of the main hall. The elevator was a unique feature of the mansion, and was hidden in the oak wall paneling.[6]

Opposite of the main entrance, was the rear entrance, which was the location of the ladies and men's dressing rooms. Besides a dressing room, each of the rooms also contained a bathroom covered in white English tile wainscot and a floor made of white, octagon shaped tile. The tile that covered the bathroom walls was made by Minton & Hollins of England and was used in a few of the bathrooms of the mansion along with being used in the kitchen and icebox room.[7]

The rear entrance, which was the location of the ladies and men's dressing rooms.
Upon completion in 1911, both the main and rear entrances contained a vestibule that was closed off by a pair of leaded glass doors (see page 68) and contained a quarry tile floor. In the photograph above, the open door to the right of the rear entrance is the men's dressing room while to the left is the ladies dressing room.

Courtesy of A. Keating

A section of the servants' bathroom located in the basement, showing the English tile that was used in the bathrooms of the mansion.

Photo by author

{ 70 }

Breakfast and Dining Rooms

      Located to left of the main entrance, on the first floor, were the breakfast and dining rooms. Since there were few photographs taken of the breakfast room, it is unknown how it once appeared. However, according to Rkia Hall, who toured the mansion in 2001, the room appeared similar to the dining room, containing walls paneled in mahogany. The breakfast room also contained two sets of pocket doors, one at the entrance to the room along with a pair of doors that divided the breakfast room from the main dining room. The pocket doors were also present on the reception room and the library.

      Unlike the breakfast room, which was small in size, was the dining room. The dining room was similar in design to the one at Albion Point having a floor of parquetry and walls covered in mahogany wainscoting (see page 30). Above the mahogany wainscoting, was a panel of "green tapestry" that circled the top.[8] Located along the wall, was a red marble fireplace that was encased in a mahogany mantle that contained a "linen fold" pattern, the same pattern that was used in one of the rooms of the Sutton House.[9]

      Unlike most dining rooms, the room even contained two sets of French doors, which were fitted with a pair of iron grates. The grates could be pulled across to prevent anyone from entering the dining room from the conservatory and was just one of the unusual features of the mansion.

The dining room as it appeared in May 2001. The mantel shown in the photograph is not original to the mansion, and was added by the owner.

Courtesy of the Borough of Carlisle

Photo taken in the 1960's of the red marble fireplace inside the dining room. Note the "linen fold" pattern located above the fireplace. The same pattern covered the walls of one of the rooms of the Sutton House.

Courtesy of Thornwald Home

A modern day photo of the fireplace. Note the iron grates, located on either side of the fireplace, which were just one of the unusual features found inside the mansion.

Courtesy of A. Keating

Besides the iron grates in the dining room, there were also a pair of "iron shutters" that could be pulled down over the doors in the library that led to the outside loggia.[10] Among the other unusual features was the burglar alarm and intercom system along with a vacuum cleaner that had a connection to each room. The vacuum cleaner operated by pulling out an extension from the wall and then vacuuming the dust into a central bin.[11]

One of two iron shutters inside the library that could be pulled over the French doors that led to the outside loggia.

Photo by author

The original vacuum cleaner brush attachment found inside a wall in 2011.

Photo by author

Conservatory and Kitchen

Located just off the dining room was the conservatory, or commonly known as a greenhouse, which contained a red quarry tile floor along with an outside entrance. In addition, the conservatory also contained a "radiator outlet", which allowed for a variety of plants to be grown inside year round.[12]

Located beside the conservatory was the kitchen, which was herald by *The Evening Sentinel* in 1910 as "finer by far than many a parlor in the town".[13] Both the kitchen and the icebox room were covered in white English tile that was made by Minton & Hollins of England.[14] Such was the door in the conservatory, was also the door in the kitchen that led outside.

Upon entering the kitchen from the adjacent butler's pantry was a large gas "combination range" that sat between two wall outlets. On the opposite side of the kitchen, were a number of oak cupboards that sat underneath the zinc countertop. Located above the countertop, on opposite sides of the windows, was a large oak cupboard that contained a glass door.[15]

Also located in this room, was a walk-in icebox that contained a plastic floor along with two small shelves located on either side of the doorway.

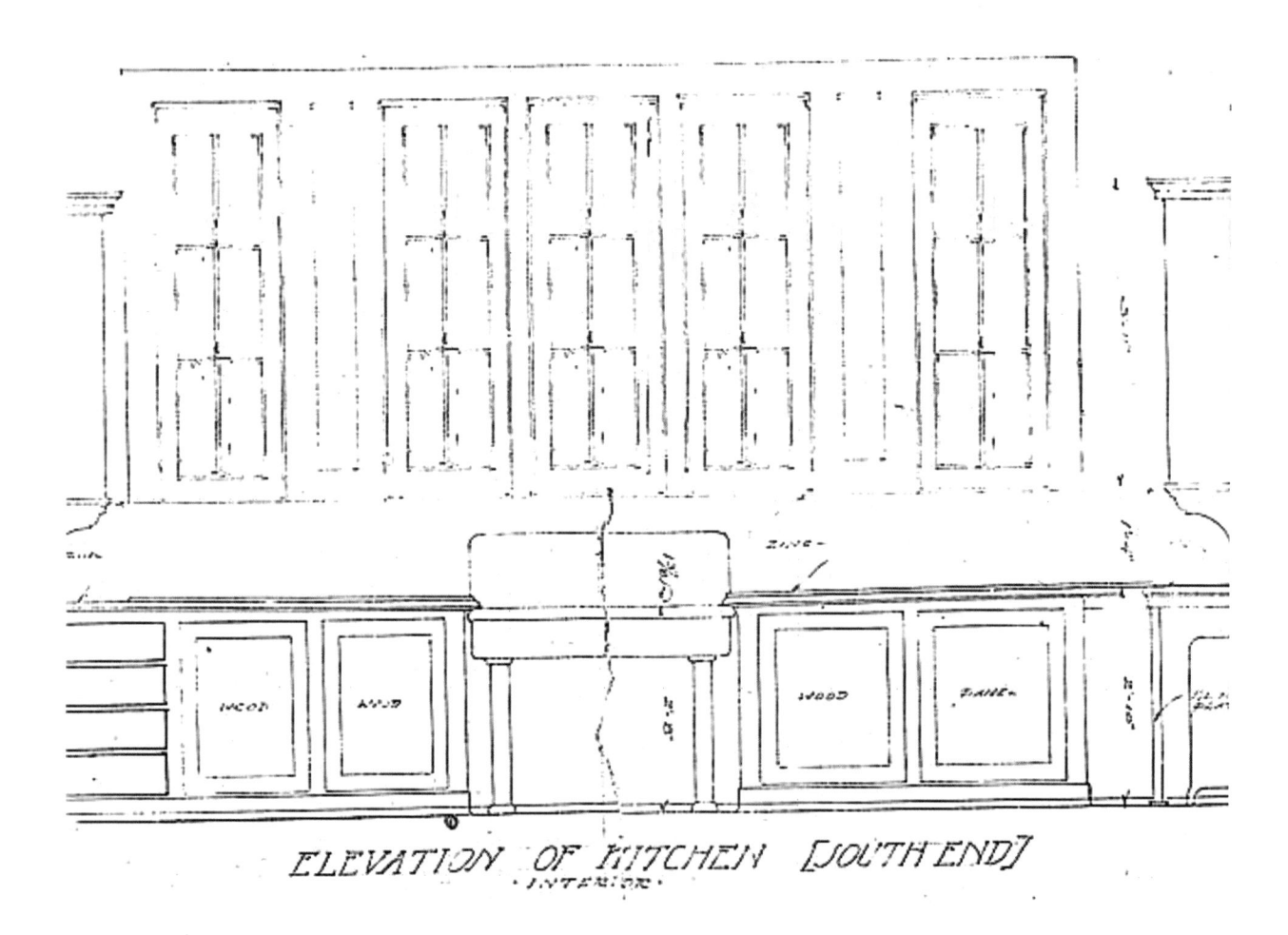

A detailed drawing of the kitchen drawn by Hill & Stout of New York.

Cumberland County Historical Society, Carlisle, Pa.

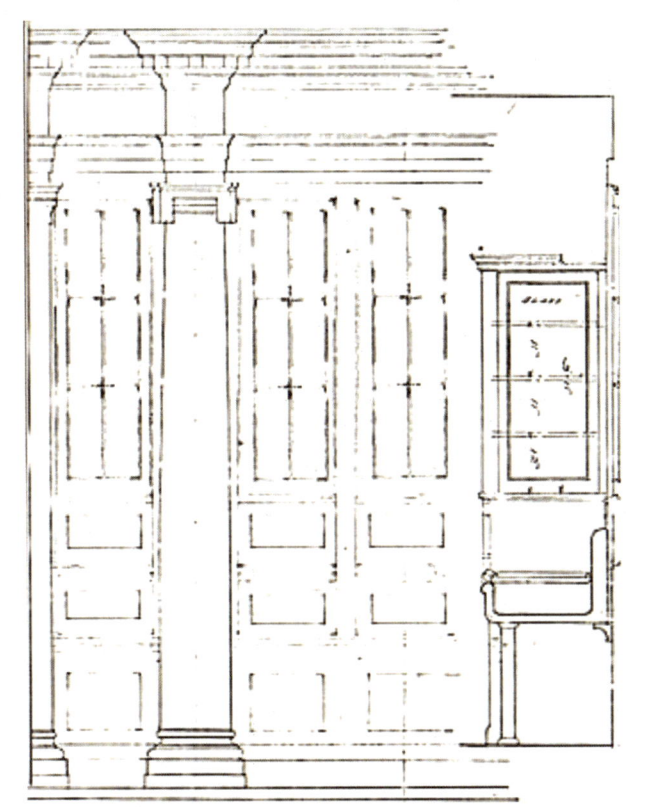

A side few of the kitchen showing the sink and the dimensions of one of the cabinets. Drawn by Hill & Stout of New York.

Cumberland County Historical Society, Carlisle, Pa.

A photograph showing a section of the English tile wainscoting in the kitchen. Note the round piece of metal, located on the wall, which was one of two wall outlets that were located on either side of the combination range.

Photo by author

Butler's Pantry and Servants' Dining Room

Located between the kitchen and the servants' dining room was the location of the butler's pantry. The pantry contained a number of "dressers", or cupboards, which were located on either side of the doorway that led into the dining room. Also located in this room was a double sink along with an electric plate warmer. The servants' dining room was located adjacent to the butler's pantry and contained a built-in cupboard, an electric panel, along with two sets of stairs; one that led to the basement and the other to the second floor.[16]

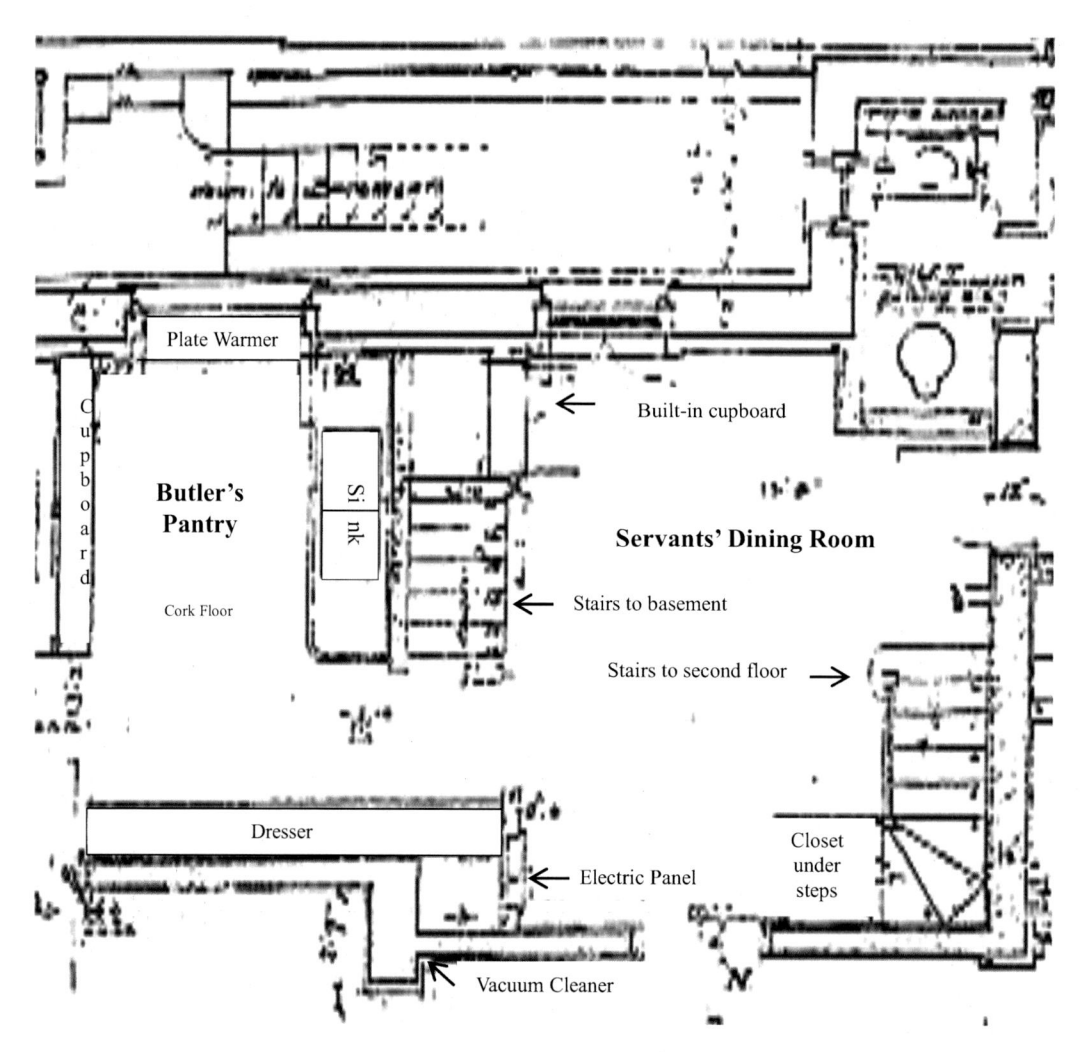

A section of the first floor blueprint drawn by Hill & Stout showing the butler's pantry and servants' dining room. Rooms retyped for quality purposes.

Cumberland County Historical Society, Carlisle, Pa.

The built-in oak cupboard located inside the servants' dining room was nearly two feet deep, and provided plenty of storage space for the servants' dishes and silverware.

Courtesy of Rkia Hall

The stairs that led from the servants' dining room to the basement.

Courtesy of A. Keating

Reception Room

      Located on the opposite side of the mansion was the reception room and library. These two rooms were perhaps the most used, especially when the couple entertained their many friends and special guests at Thornwald.

      The reception room contained a carved plaster ceiling and walls rich in woodwork.[17] Surrounding the room were "tapestry panels intersected by columns of inlaid wood" and a floor made of "parquetry".[18] The inlaid panel that separated the panels of tapestry was nearly six foot tall with the same pattern being repeated around the room (see page 219).

Photo taken in 2001 of an inlaid panel inside the reception room

Courtesy of the Borough of Carlisle

Shown below are three sections of the six-foot tall inlaid panel, which separated the panels of tapestry in the reception room.

Top | Middle | Bottom

Photos courtesy of Thornwald Home

Library & Office

The fireplace inside the library as it appeared in 1973. The fireplace was the focal point of the library, and may have been one of several pieces that were imported from the United Kingdom in April 1910.

Courtesy of Thornwald Home

    The reception room was quite small in comparison to the library, which was the largest room in the mansion next to the conservatory. Besides being used for entertaining, the library was also the location of the couple's extensive book collection.

    The library was reminiscent of that found in the English home, and contained walls paneled in oak, a carved plaster ceiling, a "richly carved" mantel and a stone fireplace. On April 7, 1910, during construction of the mansion, Mr. and Mrs. Lewis Sadler took an extensive vacation to "Europe". During this time, it is likely that they had purchased a number of pieces for the mansion, such as the stone fireplace in the library, from a castle in the United Kingdom that was on the verge of being demolished.[19]

    Located inside the library were twelve bookcases each containing a pair of leaded glass doors. One pair of bookcases, located on either side of the doorway that led into the library from the main hall, may have been used as a china cabinet, since the shelves inside the bookcases were not as wide as those found in the other bookcases in the room. In addition, each of the bookcases sat above a large drawer that allowed for additional storage of books. One of the bookcases, that was located between the two windows that faced the front lawn, even contained a built-in writing desk while another opened up to reveal a "secret room".[20]

    The room was Lewis Sadler's own private office. The office could either be accessed from the revolving bookcase or by the "passage" that was located behind the elevator in the main hall.[21] His office was even the location of a large walk-in safe, where they stored away their precious valuables.

The unsigned oil portrait of a seventeenth century gentleman that Mr. and Mrs. Lewis Sadler purchased from England. The painting hung above the fireplace in the library at Thornwald.

Cumberland County Historical Society, Museum Collection, Carlisle, Pa.

A section of the carved oak mantel

Courtesy of Thornwald Home

The library as it appeared in 1973. Note the books inside the bookcases, which at one time belonged to the Sadlers. In the above photograph, the bookcase located behind the sofa could swing open to allow entry into Mr. Sadler's office. In the photograph below, directly behind the couch, can be seen a section of the writing desk that was located inside the bookcase.

Photos courtesy of Thornwald Home

The bookcase that allowed entry into the office.

Courtesy of the Borough of Carlisle

Looking from the office into the library.

Courtesy of the Borough of Carlisle

Second Floor

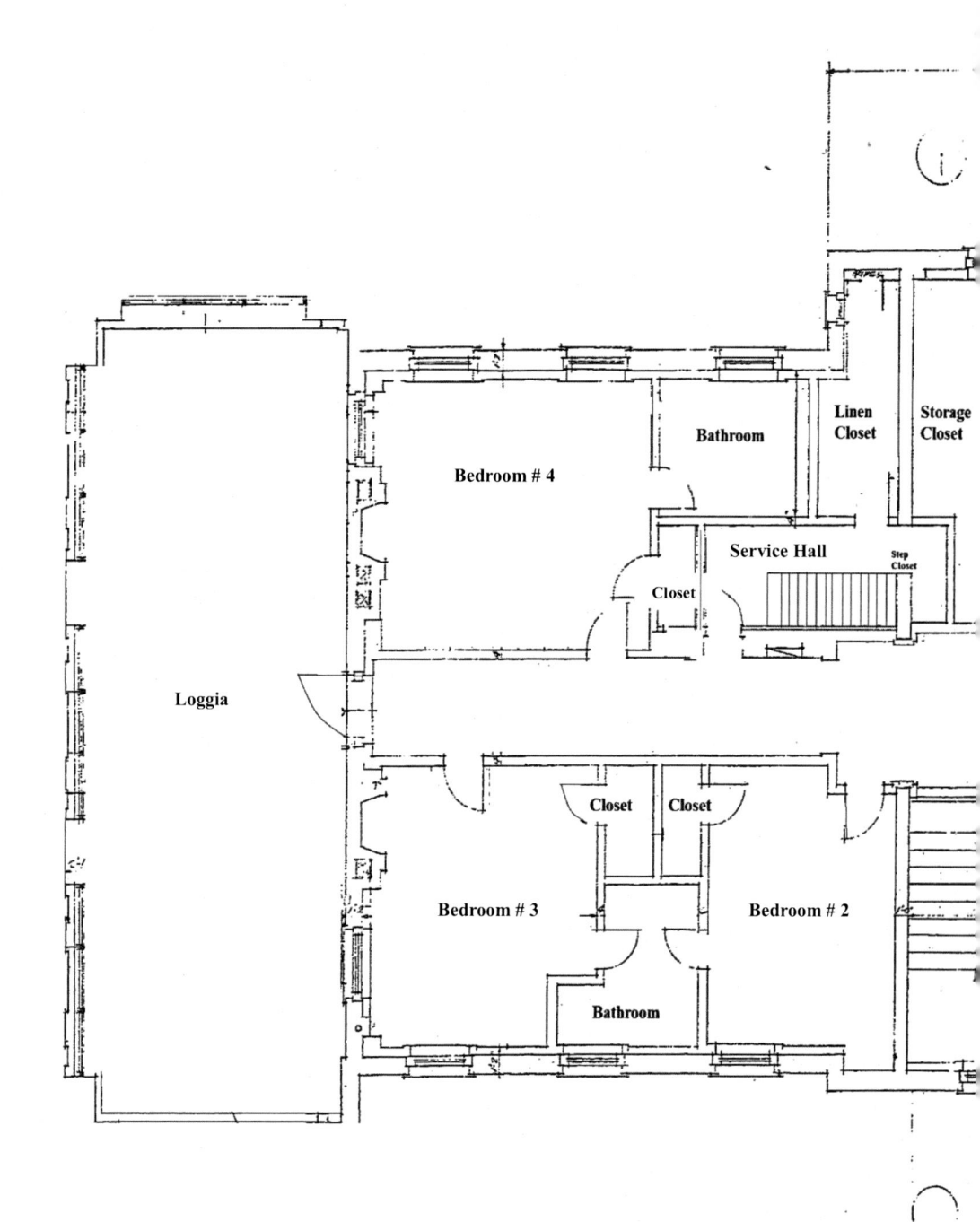

- Loggia
- Bedroom # 4
- Bathroom
- Linen Closet
- Storage Closet
- Closet
- Service Hall
- Step Closet
- Closet
- Closet
- Bedroom # 3
- Bedroom # 2
- Bathroom

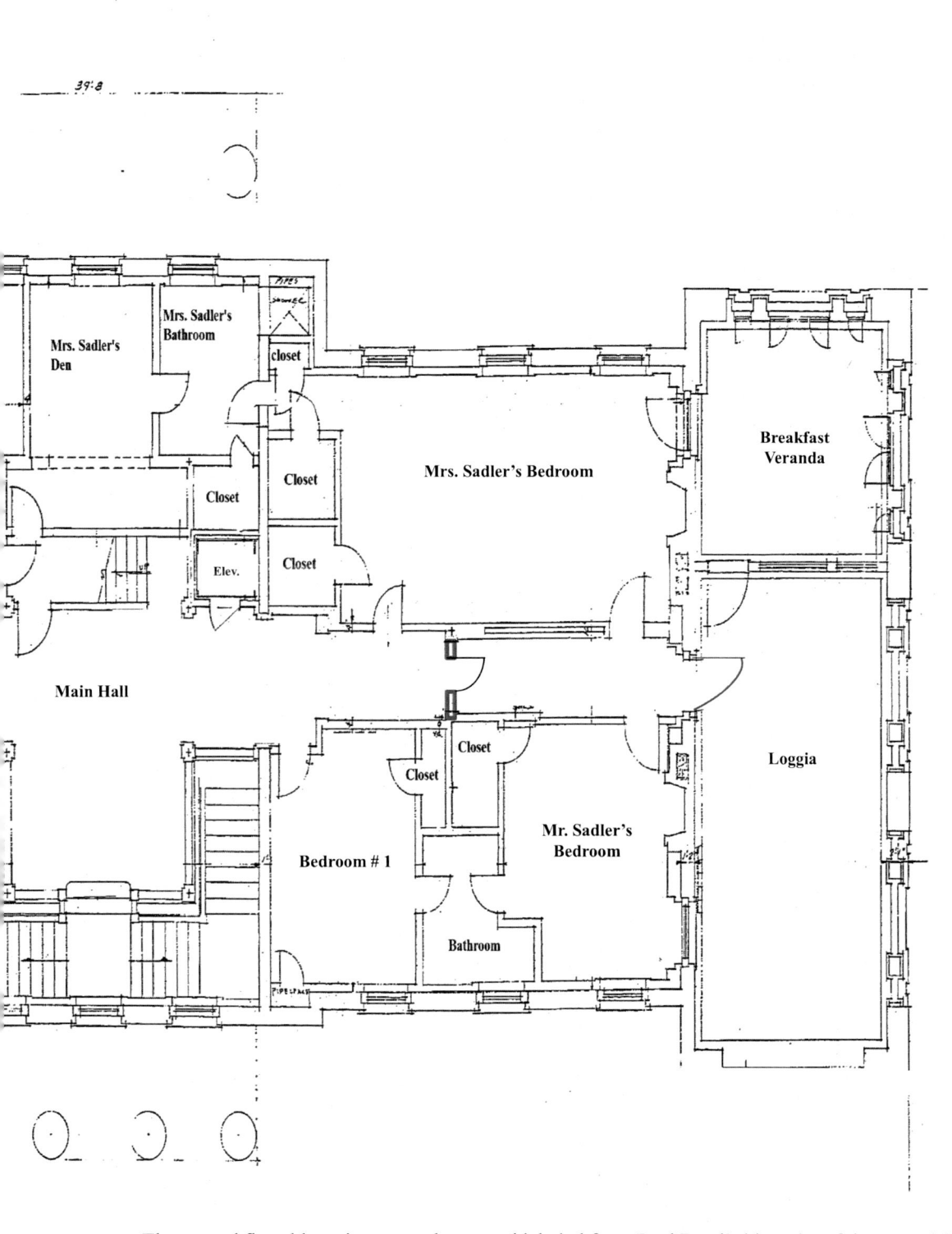

The second floor blueprint was redrawn and labeled from Paul Reed's blueprint of the second floor drawn in August 1959, which is located at the Cumberland County Historical Society in Carlisle, Pa.

West Wing

     Located on the second floor were a number of bedrooms along with Mr. and Mrs. Lewis Sadler's master bedrooms. While the first floor contained rooms with carved plaster ceilings and walls rich in woodwork, the second and third floors were simple in design. Due to the lack of photographs that were taken of the second and third floors, over the years, it is unknown how they once appeared. However, according to a photograph taken in 2001 of Mrs. Sadler's den, it is likely that a few of the rooms on the second floor, along with the third floor, were also paneled in wood.
     Located in the west wing were the couple's master bedrooms, breakfast veranda, loggia, and one single bedroom. As was the custom in the day, both husband and wife did not share the same bed, and therefore, they had separate bedrooms. Mrs. Sadler did not just have a bedroom, but a suite located above her husband's office. Her suite consisted of a large bedroom, a bathroom, and a den along with four closets. Her suite was also adjacent to the couple's breakfast veranda, which doubled as her sunroom.
     Her bedroom contained a fireplace along with two large walk-in closets and one small closet. The walk-in closet located just outside the bathroom, was the location of her wall safe. The safe was a unique feature in the couple's master bedrooms, and required "three keys to open, and each of the three compartments in them also required three keys".[22]
     As for her bathroom, it too, was also large in comparison to the other bathrooms of the mansion and was covered in English tile. Unlike the other bathrooms on the second floor, her bathroom not only contained a cast iron tub, but a shower lined with white English tile. Adjacent to her bathroom was her den, which contained a closet, and was covered in panels of wallpaper that were placed between sections of wood around the room.
     Across the hall from her bedroom was Mr. Sadler's master bedroom, which could also be accessed by the "solid mahogany door" in the hallway that divided the two bedrooms.[23] In comparison to her large suite, his bedroom also contained a fireplace although his closet was much smaller, and his bedroom contained a shared bathroom.
     The reason is unknown why he did not have his own private bath. Perhaps he intended his bachelor brother, Sylvester, to move into the adjacent bedroom upon completion of the mansion in 1911, although he did not and instead continued to live along North College Street. However, his brother, Wilbur Jr., of New Jersey, often stayed in the bedroom when he came to visit.

The three compartments that were located inside Mrs. Sadler's wall safe

Photo by author

A section of Mrs. Sadler's den as it appeared in May 2001.

Courtesy of the Borough of Carlisle

East Wing

While the master bedrooms were located in the west wing, the east wing contained three bedrooms along with an outdoor loggia. Since the couple never had any children, the bedrooms were used as guest bedrooms.

Both bedrooms three and four contained a fireplace while bedroom four had a private bathroom and bedrooms two and three shared a bathroom. In addition to the bedrooms, there were two large walk-in closets, one for storage and the other for linen along with a step closet that was located inside the service hall.

The service hall was located directly above the servants' dining room and contained two flights of stairs, one that led to the dining room below and the other to the servants' quarters on the third floor.

The fireplace inside bedroom number four. Both fireplaces in bedrooms three and four contained the same mantel, pictured above. According to a manufacturer's label found on the back of the mantel in 2011, the mantel was made by William H. Jackson of New York.

Courtesy of A. Keating

A section of the linen closet. The built-in cabinets located on the opposite wall were of the same design.

Photo by author

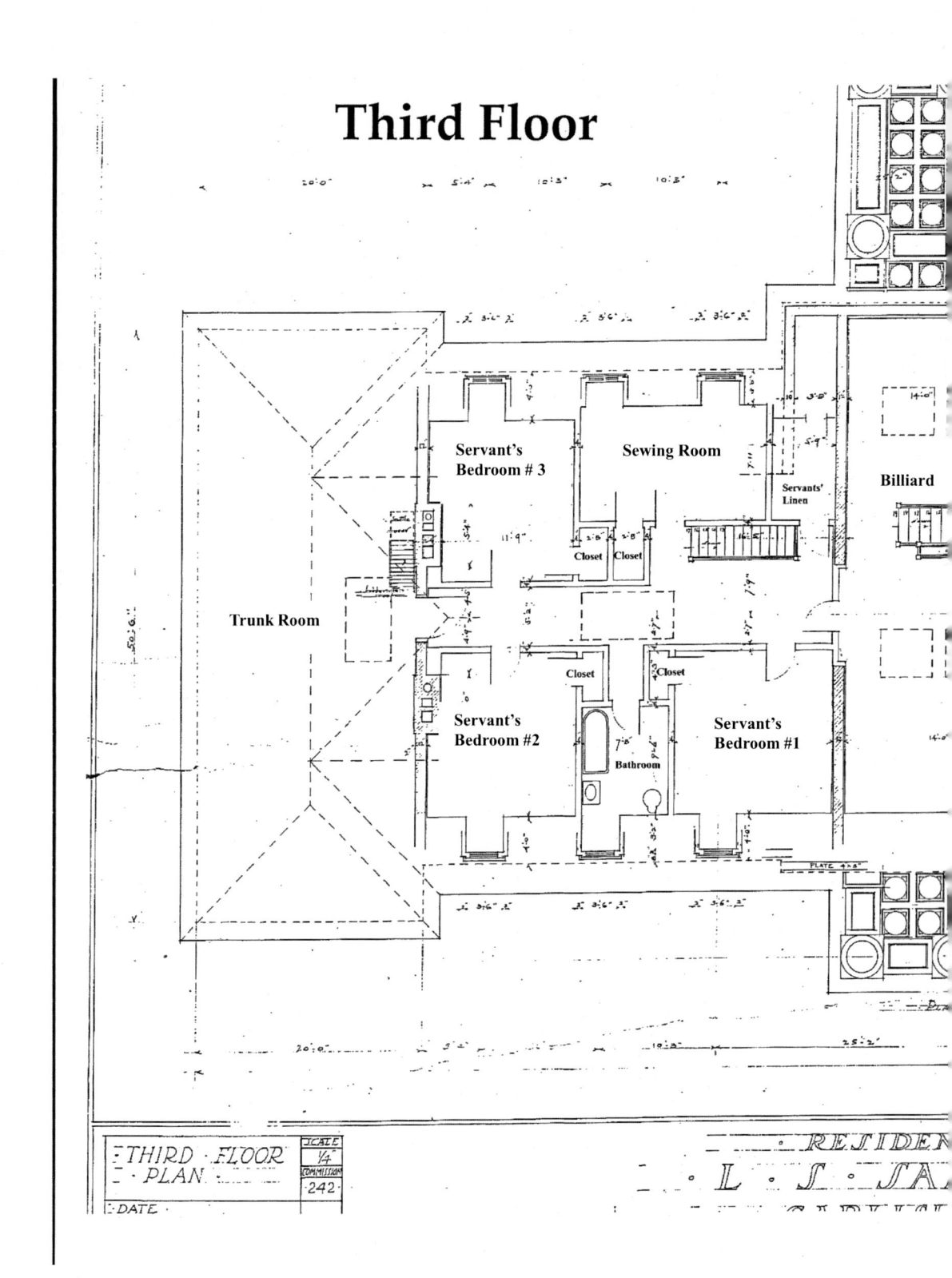

Third Floor

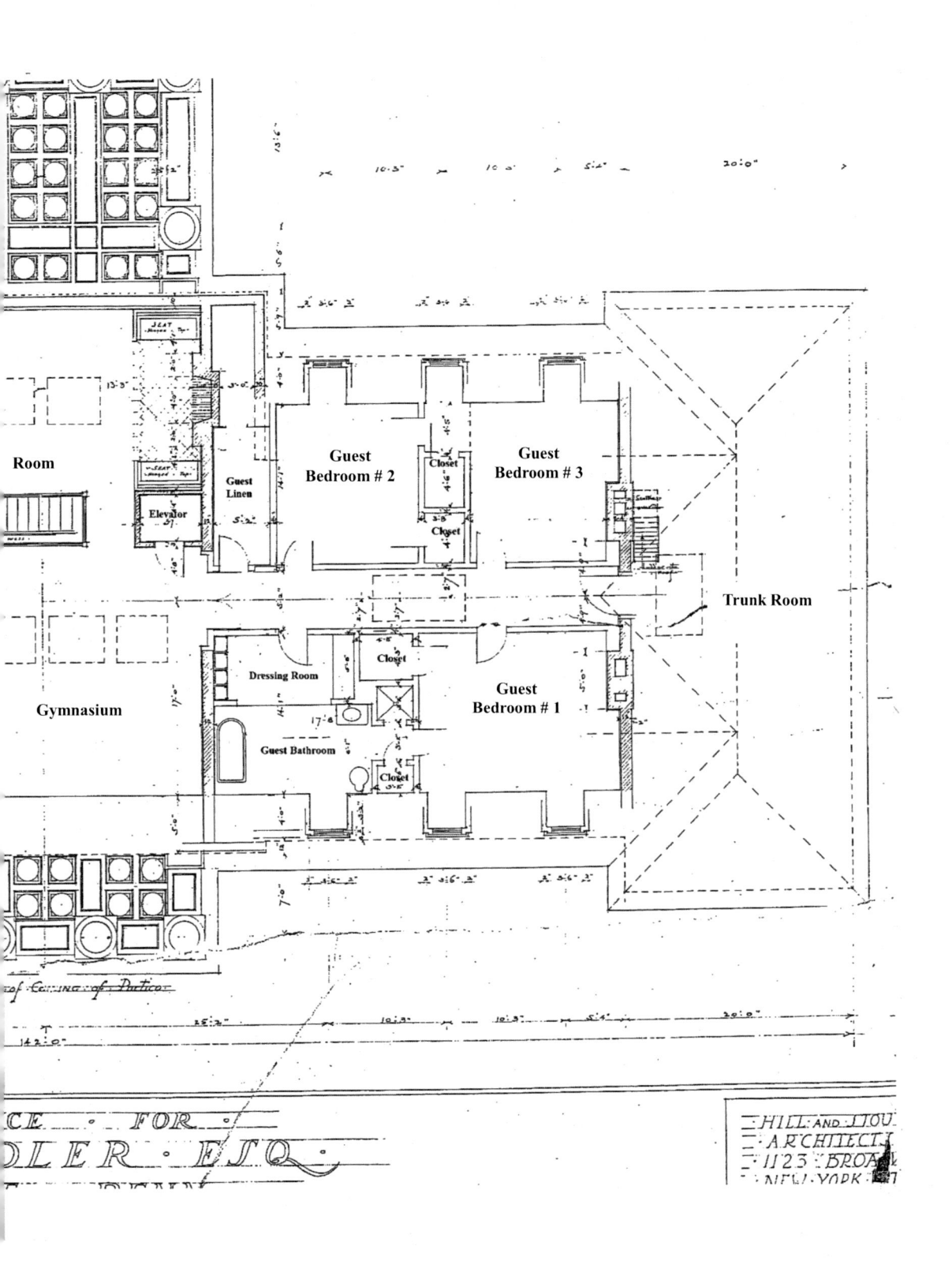

Third floor blueprint drawn by Hill & Stout in 1909. Rooms labeled for informative purposes. The small squares, shown in the above blueprint, denote skylights.

Cumberland County Historical Society, Carlisle, Pa

Gymnasium and Billiard Room

      Similar to Albion Point was the location of the gymnasium and billiard room, which were located on the third floor. The gymnasium was the larger of the two and was divided from the billiard room by the staircase that allowed access to the second floor. Unlike the gymnasium, the billiard room contained a fireplace along with a pair of wooden deacon benches that were located on either side.

      According to a furniture label found underneath one of the benches in 2011, they were custom made for the billiard room by the William Baumgarten and Company of New York, and contained a seat that had a "hinged top", which allowed for extra storage space.[24] Located directly in front of the fireplace and in between the two benches was a floor made of tile that resembled cobblestones.

      Each of the rooms was illuminated with an abundance of sunlight that came from the large skylights. Besides the skylights located in the gymnasium and billiard rooms, there was also a skylight located at either end of the third floor and inside the trunk rooms.

The fireplace inside the billiard room.

Courtesy of Thornwald Home

The built-in cabinet that was located to the left of the fireplace.

Courtesy of Thornwald Home

Guest Bedrooms and Servants' Quarters

Located in the west wing were three guest bedrooms that shared a single dressing room and bathroom. Similar to Mrs. Sadler's bathroom was the guest bathroom, which also contained a shower. Across from the dressing room was the guest linen closet, and located next to bedrooms one and three was a large trunk room.

While the west wing contained the guest bedrooms, the east wing contained the servants' quarters. The servants' quarters was blocked off from the rest of the third floor by a single door. Similar to the guest bedrooms, the servants' bedrooms also shared a single bathroom. Across from the bathroom was the servants' sewing room and linen closet.

Due to the layout of the servants' quarters, and the single stairway that allowed access from the basement to the third floor, the servants' were able to go completely unnoticed when the couple entertained their many friends and family members at their residence.

Despite the many rooms that were designated for the servants' of Thornwald, there are few records that indicate the couple had additional hired help, other than those named in the local papers or those mentioned in their wills. Even those who did work at Thornwald, such as William J. McCulley, Mr. and Mrs. Lewis Sadler's private chauffeur, did not live there and instead lived at his residence along South West Street in Carlisle.[25] The only servant known to reside at Thornwald was Lewis Sadler's negro butler, David G. Graham, who resided at Thornwald between 1920 and 1922.[26]

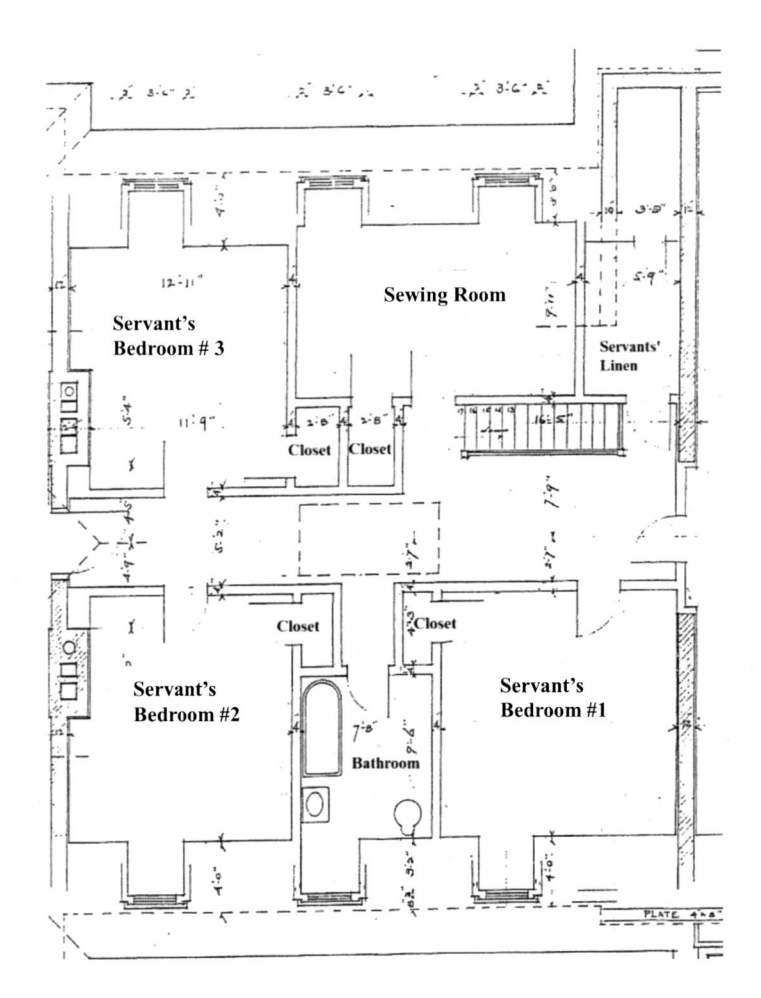

A section of the third floor blueprint drawn by Hill & Stout in 1909, showing the servants' quarters.

Cumberland County Historical Society, Carlisle, Pa.

Basement

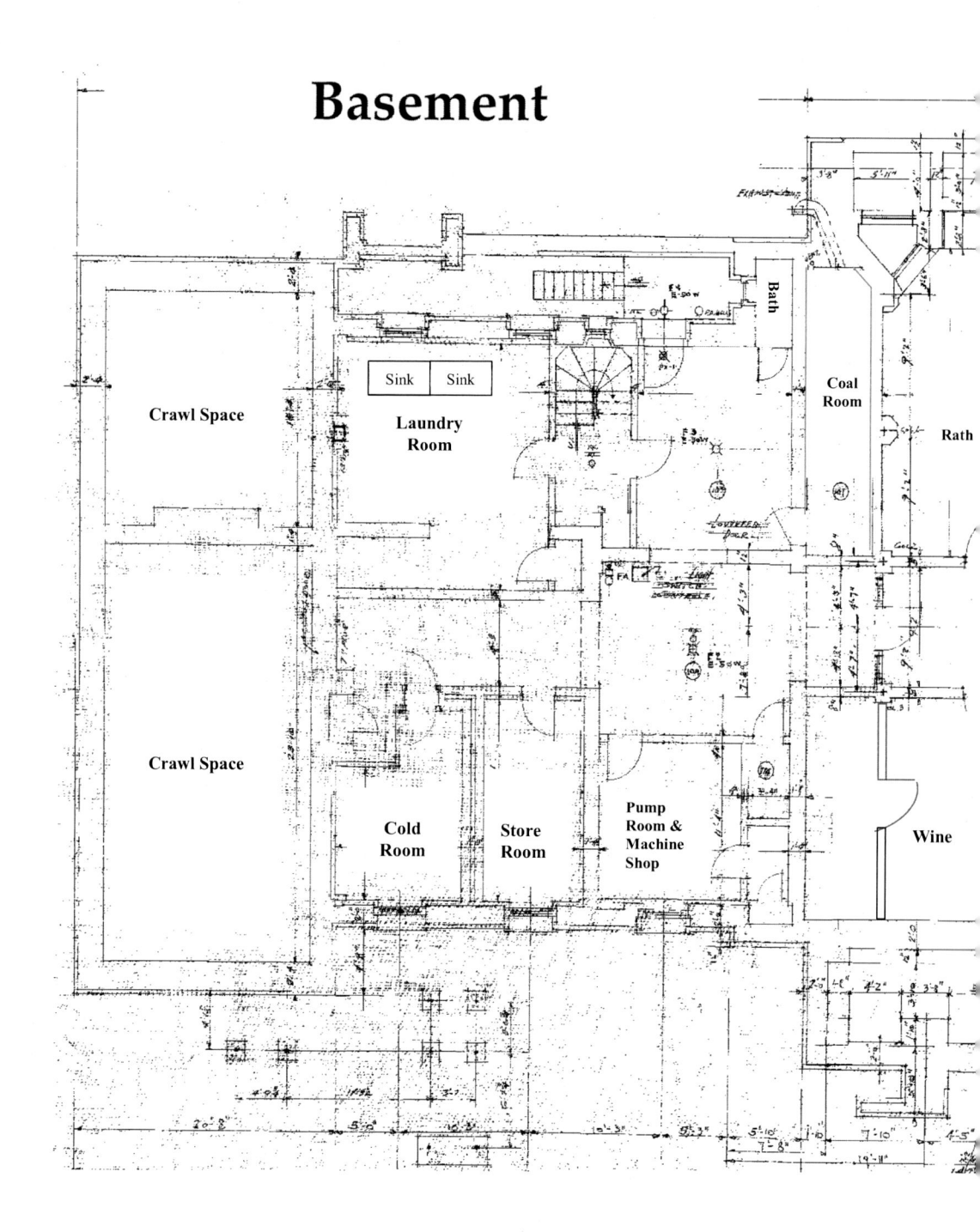

- Bath
- Coal Room
- Bath
- Crawl Space
- Sink | Sink
- Laundry Room
- Crawl Space
- Cold Room
- Store Room
- Pump Room & Machine Shop
- Wine

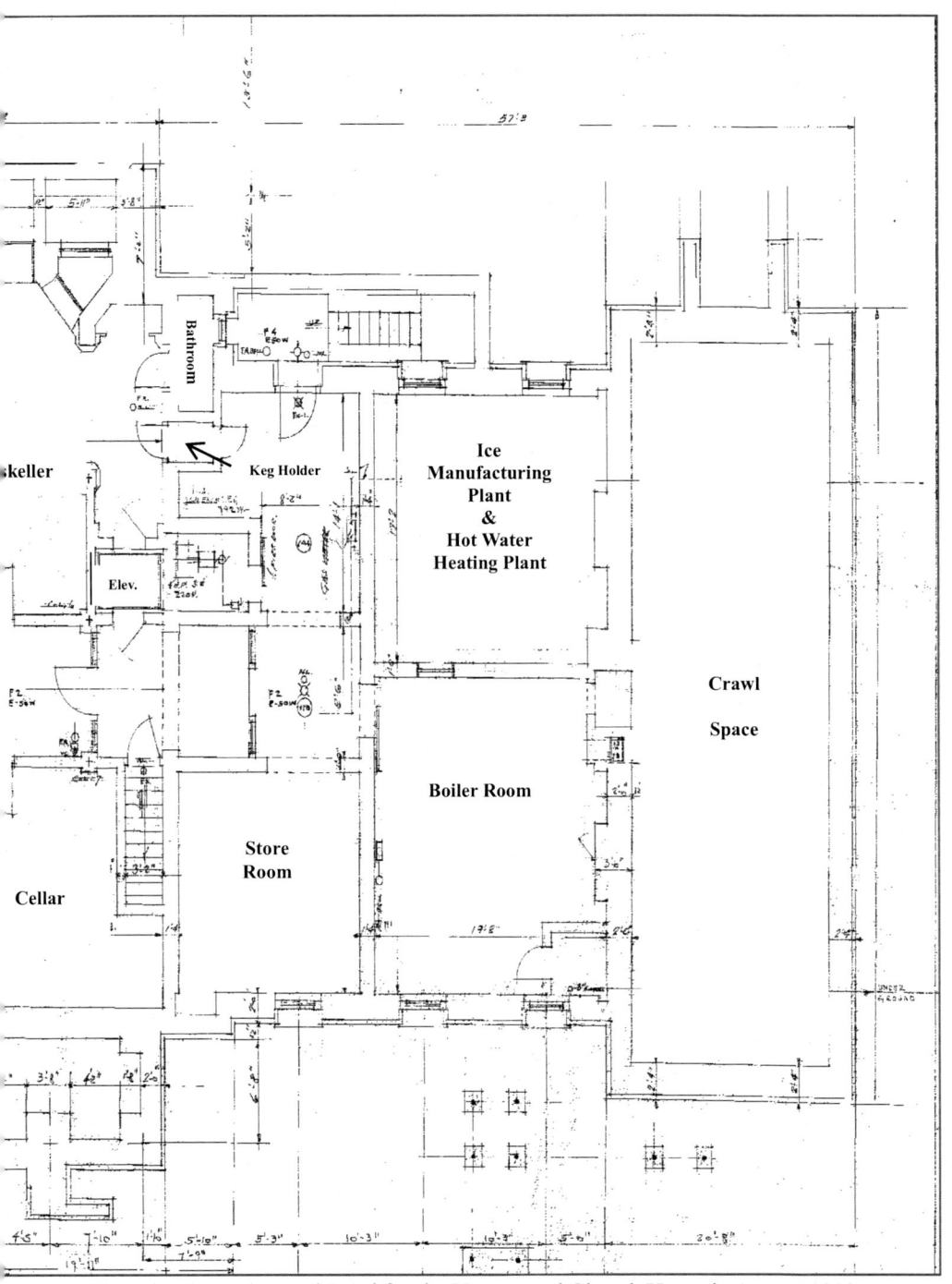

Blueprint drawn by Paul Reed for the Homewood Church Home in August 1959. Rooms relabeled to show how the basement might have functioned in 1911. Rooms labeled from observations made on May 1, 2011 by the author, along with observations made of Hill and Stout's blueprint of the second floor, drawn in 1909, that showed the location of the cold room, store room and the pump room and machine shop.

Note the bathroom located next to the entrance to the basement, on the opposite page. This bathroom was located directly below the servants' dining room, and was used by the servants', since they were not allowed access to the bathrooms on the first floor.

Cumberland County Historical Society, Carlisle, Pa.

The powerhouse to the mansion was in the basement, where there were a number of rooms designated for a certain purpose. Among the rooms included a boiler room, laundry room, store room, the servants' bathroom, an "ice manufacturing plant", "hot water heating plant", "cold room", "pump room and machine shop", along with the Sadlers wine cellar and rathskeller, or "beer hall".[27]

Overall, the basement was a far cry from that found in the average home at the turn of the century. Unlike the laundry room, coal room, and boiler room that were typical of the time was the ice manufacturing plant, pump room and machine shop, rathskeller, and wine cellar.

It is unknown, exactly the location of ice manufacturing plant and hot water heating plant in the basement. However, the two may have been located in the large room that was adjacent to the boiler room, which was also the location of the Carlisle water main. While the ice manufacturing plant produced ice for refrigeration purposes, the plant also may have been used to produce ice for central air to cool the first floor during the hot summer months.

The basement looking east these rooms were located directly under the breakfast and dining rooms, servants' dining room and kitchen.

Courtesy of Hurley Auctions

The basement looking west these rooms were located directly under the office, reception room and library.

Courtesy of Hurley Auctions

The wooden partitions that sectioned off the wine cellar and rathskeller. Upon completion of Thornwald, in 1911, each partition contained a door along with glass inside the windowpanes. In the photograph above, the entrance to the rathskeller is to the left and the wine cellar is to the right.

Photo by author

The storeroom, which was located beside the boiler room.

Photo by author

The sinks inside the laundry room. Also, in this room, was a small closet that was used for storage.

Photo by author

A close-up view of one of the sinks that was located inside the laundry room. The sinks were installed on October 4, 1910.

Courtesy of Rkia Hall

A section of the storeroom, which was located beside the pump room and machine shop in the basement.

Photo by author

The large compressed air tank, which was located inside the pump room and machine shop, forced water up to the third floor.

Photo by author

Wine Cellar

A large room located outside the wine cellar, and across the hall from the rathskeller, was used to store additional kegs. *Courtesy of Hurley Auctions*

The door that lead into the wine cellar. *Photo by author*

The many shelves inside the wine cellar that could hold nearly 1,000 bottles of wine. Also located in this room, was a sink.

Photos courtesy of Hurley Auctions

Rathskeller

The rathskeller was reminiscent of a German rathskeller having an arched concrete ceiling, a floor made of tile that gave the appearance of cobblestones, along with the doors in the room that were German in design and contained "blown orange [bottle] glass". Hanging from the ceiling were "two German marionbuds" and located on the far wall was an oak bench.[28] Located on either side of the bench was a built-in cupboard where kegs could be stored away. Each cupboard contained walls covered in white Old Bridge tile bearing resemblance to the English tile found in the rest of the mansion while the cupboard doors were inset with orange bottle glass. In addition, the cupboards also contained a basement window that was protected by a bronze grate along with a light fixture. Also in the rathskeller, was a built-in wet bar, a bathroom, a keg holder, and the entrance to the elevator all of which were each concealed by an oak door containing orange bottle glass.[29]

While it is unknown, the Charles P. Biggin Company of Philadelphia, who specialized in making ornamental cast and wrought iron, may have made the ornate wrought iron hinges that were on the doors of the rathskseller. The company made a number of pieces for the mansion, including the lampposts that lined the driveway, along with the cast-iron grates that covered the exterior basement windows, along with the cast-iron gates that were located in front of the exterior basement doors.[30]

The main door inside the rathskeller that led out into the hallway. Note the cobblestone tile in the picture above, which was similar to that found in front of the fireplace in the upstairs billiard room.

Photos courtesy of Thornwald Home

Above: A section of the arched ceiling, which was just one of the many features that were reminiscent of the German rathskeller.

Courtesy of Thornwald Home

Left: One of two symbols that were imbedded in the floor of the rathskeller. Both symbols were identical, and portrayed two birds facing a fleur de lis. According to a historian, who specialized in European history, the symbol stood for good luck for the home.

Courtesy of Rkia Hall

Above: One of two cupboards that were used to store large kegs. The inside of the cupboard was lined with Old Bridge tile.

Above right: The focal point of the rathskeller.

Right: The additional rooms inside the rathskeller. The door to the left was the built-in wet bar while the door to the right was the bathroom.

Photos courtesy of Thornwald Home

Left: The built-in wet bar.

Courtesy of A. Keating

Below: The keg holder. The photo to the right depicts what the back of the keg holder looked like from the hall. The keg holder was conveniently located near the outside door where the kegs were delivered to the basement.

Not shown in the photograph, is a set of cast-iron refrigeration coils that were located next to the keg holder, which allowed the keg to stay cold when the rathskeller was used for entertaining.

Photos by author

Since both the large room inside the wine cellar, along with the rathskeller, were used to store large kegs, the basement was designed for easy rolling of the kegs when they were delivered to Thornwald.

Located in the rear of the mansion were two flights of stairs, located on opposite sides of the rear entrance that led to the basement. Each stairway bore smooth sides that allowed the kegs to roll down into the basement.[31] In addition, the concrete floor in the basement was specially sloped at either end to allow the kegs to be rolled down into either the wine cellar or rathskeller.[32]

One of two sets of steps that were located on either side of the rear entrance that led to the basement. Note the smooth sides, which allowed for easy rolling of the kegs when they were delievered to Thornwald. The cast-iron gate, pictured right, was made by the Charles P. Biggin Co. of Philadelphia and was another added security feature for the baement, in addition to the iron grates that covered the basement windows.

Photo by author

Furnishings

Despite the magnificent interior of Thornwald, the couple further embellished their stately mansion with period furnishings that were reminiscent of the eighteenth century including early mahogany Hepplewhite and Sheraton furniture along with a number of pieces made of early English mahogany.[33]

A number of the pieces came from New York, such as the benches located inside the billiard room, which were made by the William Baumgarten & Company. Other pieces came from England, such as the painting of the 17th century gentleman in the library, while some came as far away as Russia; such was the furniture from the Sadlers master bedrooms.[34] In order to protect their valuables, the Sadlers put their monogram on their silverware (see page 148), along with branding a few of their pieces of furniture with a branding iron that contained the name "Thornwold".

Despite the wealth of mahogany furniture that adorned the rooms of the mansion, fine oriental rugs covered the floors while large oil paintings by notable artists hung on the walls. Even the dressers inside the butler's pantry contained a number of fine china, glass, and sterling silver wares that the couple had purchased from around the world. Altogether, the interior of Thornwald was reminiscent of the early English home.

A William Baumgarten & Company tag found in September 2011 underneath one of the benches in the upstairs billiard room.

Courtesy of Rkia Hall

The "Thornwold" branding iron.   *Courtesy of Bob Rowe*

Chapter 9

Additions to the Thornwald Estate

The "commodious garage" built in May 1912.   *Photo by author*

    Although Thornwald was completed in May 1911, by the following year the couple began to add a number of noteworthy additions that were of mention in the Carlisle area papers.
    Prior to this time, Thornwald did not contain any outbuildings, a gate at the entrance to the long road that led to the mansion, nor a brick wall along the Walnut Bottom Road. Passersby along the Walnut Bottom Road could catch a glimpse of the mansion whenever they crossed over "Sadler's Hill".[1] However, by the spring of 1912, work had begun on adding a number of noteworthy additions to their Thornwald Estate.
    Towards the end of April 1912, Lewis Sadler put a number of masons to work at constructing a "brick and concrete automobile garage" which would later become the Sadlers "eight-car garage" upon its completion.[2] By the following month, *The Evening Sentinel* announced that Sadler was having yet another garage constructed on the grounds just off of Walnut Bottom Road. Upon completion the "commodious garage" was unlike any other in all of Carlisle containing walls lined with white tile.[3] Certainly, Sadler had enough room to store away his prized Pierce-Arrows touring car, which his brother Wilbur Jr. often enjoyed parading his friends from New Jersey around in when they were in Carlisle.[4]

Months later, plans were already underway for the "entrance gateway", which was to be constructed at the main entrance to the mansion along with a brick wall that would run parallel with Walnut Bottom Road. In charge of drawing up the plans, were Hill and Stout of New York, who in 1909 had drawn up the blueprints for the mansion.[5]

Mrs. Sadler had her own vision in mind when it came to the entrance gateway. She envisioned an entrance similar to that of an English home, which she had seen in Charles Latham's *In English Homes.* The entrance consisted of a pair of iron gates between two pillars that were connected by a wall on either side.

In addition to the gate, she wished to have a set of steps constructed on either side of the wall that would allow one to walk over the wall instead of passing through the gate. However, instead of the steps, Hill and Stout recommended that gates be placed "along the front wall". Therefore, upon completion, the main entrance contained two cast iron gates that were placed on either side of the main entrance instead of the set of steps that Mrs. Sadler had earlier suggested.[6]

Circa 1915 view of the entrance gateway, pedestrian gateway, and wall taken from the Walnut Bottom Road. The wall was built in 1914 by the Sheafer brothers of Carlisle.

Cumberland County Historical Society, Carlisle, Pa.

HILL AND STOUT
ARCHITECTS
TOWNSEND BUILDING, BROADWAY & TWENTY-FIFTH STREET
NEW YORK

FREDERICK PARSELL HILL
EDMUND COFFIN STOUT, C.E.
VINCENT ROBERTS, C.E.

TELEPHONE 780 MADISON SQUARE

August 14, 1912

L. S. Sadler, Esq.
Carlisle, Pa.

Dear Mr. Sadler:-

Under separate cover we are sending Mrs. Sadler the perspective of the gates, showing the curved ramps of the wall omitted, but leaving the curves by the side of the gates which our Mr. Hill said could not by omitted from our design. In place of the curved ramps we are showing the wall in accordance with the picture in the English Book which Mrs. Sadler showed Mr. Hill yesterday and which was similar to one which we showed you here at one time. This is all right from our point of view.

In compliance with your order of yesterday we are preparing the working details for the Entrance Gateway and the masonry wall that extends along the Highway boundry of your property, but before we can complete these working drawings, we shall have to have a little further information; namely; the specified grades of the Highway which you said you have, and the confirmation of your expressed preference for making the walls of tapestry brick. Mrs. Sadler preferred steps up and over the wall and down on the other side, instead of Gateways as we suggested at 3 or 4 different points along the front wall. This will cost more, but it is satisfactory to us from the point of view of design, and unless you disapprove, we shall proceed this way.

As regards the height of the walls, we are going ahead on the assurance that it is to be 7 to 7 1/2 feet high. Any higher than this would be excessive and look badly. In some places as you know the ground changes slightly; here another 6 in. or thereabouts might help.

Will you please let us have an answer to these points by Monday of next week if possible, so that we will loose no time.

Yours very truly,

Hill and Stout

FPH

Letter addressed to Lewis Sadler from Hill and Stout of New York dated August 14, 1912.
Copy of the letter found in the "Thornwald" drop file at the Cumberland County Historical Society, Carlisle, Pa.

Gateway entrance to Thornwald looking towards Walnut Bottom Road. Photo by A. A. Line
While it is unknown, it is likely that the cast-iron gates may have been made by the Charles P. Biggin & Company of Philadelphia.

Cumberland County Historical Society, Carlisle, Pa

The entrance gateway and pedestrian gateway, to the right, as seen from the Walnut Bottom Road. Photo by A. A. Line.

Cumberland County Historical Society, Carlisle, Pa.

Left: A section of the entrance gateway as it appeared in 1973.

Below: The entrance gateway looking out towards the Walnut Bottom Road.

Photos courtesy of Thornwald Home

{ 112 }

Two years later, Sadler had constructed a seven-foot tall brick wall, which would run parallel with Walnut Bottom Road. For nearly three years, Thornwald was open to the outside, and therefore anyone wishing to walk across the Walnut Bottom Road onto the estate could do so. Hill and Stout drew up the plans for the wall along with the entrance gateway in 1912 although the couple held off on constructing the wall until two years later.[7]

The construction of the wall was such big news in Carlisle that an article pertaining to the construction appeared in *The Evening Sentinel* on October 3, 1914 entitled "$50,000 for a fence at Sadler Home: Magnificent Property To Be Enhanced In Beauty". The paper reported that the wall would run a length of a half a mile long along the Walnut Bottom Road and cost a staggering "$50,000" or a whopping one million dollars today.[8] A.J. Spotts was in charge of laying the concrete foundation, and Sheafer Brothers was to do the brickwork.[9] Four years ago, the Sheafer Brothers were involved in laying brick and tile at the mansion.[10]

Although it was big news in Carlisle, the news also traveled as far as Gettysburg where an article, which appeared in the *Adams County News* on October 10, 1914, read "$50,000 for fence-that much for one at Sadler Home near Carlisle". The wall was the last phase of construction for the estate with the exception of the nine hole golf course, which was later created behind the brick wall.

By the following year in November 1915, Sadler further enlarged Thornwald by purchasing seven acres of ground from George H. Stewart who owned the Toll Gate Farm in South Middleton Township. Sadler had previously known Stewart from the Farmers Trust Company where he served on the board of directors along with serving on the board of directors for the Valley Traction Company. On November 23, 1915, Sadler purchased the seven acres of land for 755.63.[11] At the close of 1915, Thornwald now contained a total of fifty-three acres of natural woodlands and meadows and was the most lavish estate in all of Carlisle.

A section of the brick wall that ran parallel with Walnut Bottom Road.

Courtesy of Homewood Retirement Centers

Chapter 10

Living in High Society

Prior to the completion of Thornwald, Sadler became well acquainted with living among the upper class. During his years at Cottage Hill, he enjoyed extensive vacations to Europe with his wife along with witnessing the daily chores being performed by hired servants', such as the Boslers cook and chambermaid.[1] Therefore, upon the completion of Thornwald in 1911, the couple wasted no time in hiring William J. McCulley as their private chauffer and electrician.[2]

McCulley was nearly twenty-five years of age when he went to work for the couple. However, despite the servants' quarters at Thornwald, he did not reside there and instead lived nearby at 314 South West Street across from the Franklin School.[3] McCulley had purchased the home just a week after the mansion was officially completed. Years later in 1917, he sold his residence along South West Street and moved into an apartment, which was located above the Farmers Trust Company where Lewis Sadler served as the bank's president.[4]

During their first year at Thornwald, the couple did not fill it with a family of their own since Mrs. Sadler would never bear any children and the same went for her sister, Helen. It is unknown whether or not the sisters had any complications with pregnancy, although it is believed that they may have chosen not to have children due to having lost both their parents at an early age. Mary was eighteen years of age and Helen was just fourteen when they lost both their parents. Therefore, it is no wonder that when it came to the construction of Thornwald, their residence was designed for entertainment purposes and not to accommodate a family of their own. However, on a few occasions the couple had the opportunity to entertain a few children from New York City.

Nearly three months after Thornwald was completed the couple invited two "fresh air children" from New York City to stay with them for a short period of time. Even Sylvester took in a child.[5] However, this was not the only time that the couple entertained the children from New York. A year later, Mr. and Mrs. Lewis Sadler along with Dr. and Mrs. Horace Sadler each took in two children. The children stayed two weeks at Thornwald and must have felt as if they were living a fairy tale.[6]

Although the mansion was designed for entertaining, there were few social gatherings at Thornwald that were of mention in the Carlisle area papers. However, on June 26, 1912, the couple entertained sixteen of their close friends in honor of their tenth wedding anniversary. According to the *Carlisle Evening Herald* the mansion was "beautifully decorated" for the occasion. Among the guests present that day, included "Representative and Mrs. Marlin E. Olmstead, Henderson Gilbert and Mr. Ericson" all of whom were from Harrisburg. That evening the guests enjoyed wining and dining with the couple while sweet strains of music could be heard coming from a "Neopolitan mandolin player".[7]

When they were not in the company of friends or enjoying their new piece of paradise, they were often seen golfing at the Harrisburg Country Club or dancing the night away at the Carlisle Armory.

> **OLMSTED GUEST HERE**
>
> Mr. and Mrs. L. S. Sadler Observe Tenth Wedding Anniversary
>
> Mr. and Mrs. L. S. Sadler last evening celebrated the tenth anniversary of their marriage at their mansion home, "Thornwold," and sixteen guests were present. Among the persons from out of town were Representative and Mrs. Marlin E. Olmsted, Henderson Gilbert and Mr. Ericson, all of Harrisburg.
>
> Musical selections were rendered by a Neapolitan mandolin player from New York city. The house was beautifully decorated.

Carlisle Evening Herald, 27 June 1912

The Carlisle Cotillion Club hosted a number of dances at the Armory each year. Both Mr. and Mrs. Lewis Sadler and Dr. and Mrs. Horace Sadler were members of the club with Mary Sadler having served as president of the club during 1911 and 1912.[8] Each December the couple along with Dr. and Mrs. Horace Sadler danced the night away at the annual "Charity Ball" that was held inside the Carlisle Armory. On one occasion in December 1914, the couple did the honors of leading the "grand march" inside the Armory, which was considered by *The Evening Sentinel* as a "brilliant spectacle".[9]

Despite the dances at the Carlisle Armory, the most extravagant galas took place in Harrisburg at the Chestnut Street Hall. In May 1913, the couple was present at Harrisburg's May Fete, which took place inside the Chestnut Street Hall. There they danced the night away along with Mrs. Edward Biddle and Miss Parker both from Carlisle. Also, in attendance were Governor and Mrs. Tener of Pennsylvania.[10]

Although their life had changed little from their years at Cottage Hill, they no longer took extensive vacations like those they had taken prior to the completion of Thornwald. Prior to this time, they were known to travel to New York and Europe and at one time they spent two months touring the Mediterranean.[11] However, two years after the completion of Thornwald in February 1913, the couple took a much-needed trip to Europe. *The Evening Sentinel* reported that the couple had sailed from "Brooklyn on the 'Amerika' to Europe" where they spent "six weeks in Paris and other continental cities". For nearly two months, the couple toured through Europe and Northern Africa before arriving home in Carlisle on April 15, 1913.[12] This may have been their last trip across the Atlantic for in later years they were only known to travel to the Pacific Coast and stay nearby at the Bedford Springs Hotel.[13]

Outside of Thornwald, Sadler continued to be among the leading citizens in Carlisle although he no longer worked out of his father's law firm. Instead, he followed in the footsteps of his brother-in-law, Frank C. Bosler who despite his bachelor of law degree had majored in banking. Currently Bosler was president of the Carlisle Trust Bank, along with a director of the Farmers Trust Company, which was located across from the law office of Sadler and Sadler.[14] In May 1910, Sadler became president of the Farmers Trust Company upon the death of Peter Wertz.[15]

View of the grillwork on the Farmers Trust Company building, copied from a postcard. Lewis S. Sadler was president of the bank from 1910 – 1921.

Cumberland County Historical Society, Carlisle, Pa.

Prior to his death, Wertz had been president of the Farmers Trust Company and manager of the Standard Chain Company along with a member of Carlisle's Board of Trade where Sadler had been a member along with his brother, Horace and Frank Bosler.[16] Upon his death, both positions were in need of being filled.

On May 5, 1910, just some months after the death of Wertz, the *Carlisle Evening Herald* announced that the man who had been selected to fill the vacancy as president of the Farmers Trust Company was none other than, Lewis Sadler. It may have come as no surprise to some, since according to the paper he had held the largest stock at the bank and ranked high in both "business and financial circles".[17] However, he was not the only one to benefit from Wertz's death. Two weeks later, the *Carlisle Evening Herald* announced that his youngest brother, Dr. Horace Sadler, was selected as manager of the Carlisle Standard Chain Company, a position that he continued to hold for several years until the factory closed in 1919.[18]

An advertisement for the Farmers Trust Company

Residence and Business Directory of Carlisle, Cumberland County, Pa., 1911- 1912

Outside of his duties at the bank, Lewis Sadler took an interest in both Republican politics and the healthcare of the citizens of Pennsylvania. In November 1911, he and his brother, Sylvester were considered by *The Evening Sentinel* as "financial backers" to the Republican Party and by the following year, he ran for Republican National delegate.[19] However despite the "nice sum" of "$666" that he had spent during his campaign, he was not elected.[20]

In July 1913, he along with his brother, Horace, and their father were among the men to endorse the new Carlisle Hospital project. The new hospital was designed to replace the old and outdated Todd hospital which had been in operation for nearly seventeen years.[21] In addition, even Mrs. Mary Sadler and her sister, Helen played a role in the healthcare of Carlisle's citizens by becoming "honorary members" of the Visiting Nurses Association.[22] Later, Helen, also served on the hospital's auxiliary in 1919.[23] By the following year in 1914, the construction of the new Carlisle Hospital had begun and in the summer of 1916, it was officially open to the public.[24]

Prior to the creation of the new Carlisle Hospital, Lewis Sadler currently sat on the board of trustees of the Pennsylvania Lunatic Hospital along with the Hahnemann Medical Hospital in Philadelphia.[25] Under Governor Tener's administration, he was selected as chairman of a commission that was in charge of selecting a site for the construction of a hospital for "inebriates" and individuals that were addicted to drugs.[26]

The Evening Sentinel
29 April 1912

View of the Carlisle Hospital from Parker Street, c. 1920.

Cumberland County Historical Society, Carlisle, Pa.

The Inn at Ragged Edge, the former home of Moorhead C. Kennedy, Vice President of the Cumberland Valley Railroad.

Courtesy of Lew Martin

CARLISLERS INVITED

Among Carlislers invited to M. C. Kennedy's social stunt at "Ragged Edge," Saturday, were C. S. Brinton, A. R. Rupley, John Hays, L. S. Sadler, S. B. Sadler, Esqs., and Judge Sadler.

H. H. Mercer and J. L. Shelley, Esqs., of Mechanicsburg, received invitations as did George H. Stewart, of Shippensburg.

The Evening Sentinel, 25 September 1911

Outside of his busy lifestyle, he still found time to wine and dine amongst the notable dignitaries of Pennsylvania. Every fall, he accompanied his siblings, Wilbur and Sylvester, and their father to Chambersburg where they enjoyed the fine festivities at Ragged Edge along with other directors of the Cumberland Valley Railroad. The galas at Ragged Edge often brought a number of notable men from across Pennsylvania and surrounding states together for an afternoon of wining and dining.[27]

In October 1914, Horace accompanied his siblings to Ragged Edge where they participated in a baseball game against Governor Slaton of Georgia and Governor Tener of Pennsylvania along with a number of other men. Tener had previously known Sadler from his visit to Thornwald in May 1911.[28]

However, this was not the last time that Sadler would wine and dine with the governor of Pennsylvania. During his time serving on the commission, which was in charge of selecting a site for the inebriate hospital, he established close ties with Governor Brumbaugh and his staff.

On April 17, 1915, Sadler attended a dinner at the Executive Mansion that was given in honor of former president, William Taft.[29] The following month, he returned once again to the executive mansion this time to attend a dinner in honor of the members of the Supreme Court.[30]

ENTERTAINED JUSTICES

L. S. Sadler Among Notables at Governor's Dinner

Governor Brumbaugh entertained at dinner last evening at the Executive Mansion in honor of the members of the Supreme court. The favors were American Beauty roses with American Beauty ribbons and covers were laid for Chief Justice J. Hay Brown, Justice S. Leslie Mestrezat, William P. Potter, John P. Elkin, John Stewart, Robert Von Moschzisker and Robert S. Frazer, Jasper Y. Brinton, Attorney General Francis Shunk Brown, Highway Commissioner Robert J. Cunningham, Judge Thomas D. Finletter, Robert W. Gawthrop, Second Deputy Attorney General William M. Hargest, J. Levering Jones, Deputy Attorney General William H. Keller, M. C. Kennedy, Judge George Kunkel, J. Banks Kutrz, Judge S. J. M. McCarrell, Lewis S. Sadler, Judge William H. Shoemaker, John C. Swartley, Secretary of the Commonwealth Cyrus E. Woods, and Acting Private Secretary Paul N. Furman.

The Evening Sentinel,
25 May 1915

L. S. Sadler, of this place, was a guest at the dinner given by Governor Brumbaugh to former President William Howard Taft at Harrisburg.

The Evening Sentinel,
17 April 1915

Chapter 11

A Black Cloud Looms Over Thornwald

By 1916, Mr. and Mrs. Lewis Sadler had lived at Thornwald for nearly five years and were married for almost fourteen years although it would be their final year together as husband and wife.

In the beginning of January of that year, Sadler attended yet another dinner at Ragged Edge in Chambersburg. This time the dinner was in honor of his brother, Sylvester, who was the newly elected judge of Cumberland County.[1] Their father, Wilbur Fisk Sadler, had previously served his second term as judge of Cumberland County serving from 1905-1915.[2]

In the fall of 1915, Sylvester ran against Democrat Edward Biddle, Jr. and won by a "great majority" therefore continuing his father's legacy. Furthermore, it came as no surprise to *The Carlisle Evening Herald* who claimed his election as county judge was "expected".[3] For the next four years, Sylvester governed the county courthouse until 1920. In that year, he was appointed justice of the Supreme Court under Governor William C. Sproul.[4]

Months later, in June 1916, Lewis Sadler joined his father, Wilbur, at becoming a member of a committee, which was in charge of looking into the construction of a new law school that would replace the present Emory Hall. Among the other members of the committee were William Trickett, Caleb S. Brinton, and J.L. Shelley. His father, Wilbur Fisk Sadler, served as president of the board, which perhaps was due in part to his close ties with the law school for the past twenty-seven years. Later, the new law school was built along South College Street and upon its completion in 1918, it was given the name Trickett Hall in honor of the law schools dean, William Trickett.[5]

Circa 1933 photograph of Trickett Hall. Upon completion in 1918, the main entrance of the law school coincidentally mirrored the architecture of the rear entrance of Thornwald.

Cumberland County Historical Society, Carlisle, Pa.

Mrs. Mary Bosler Sadler enlarged from the Sadler-Bosler wedding photograph taken on June 26, 1902 at Cottage Hill.

Cumberland County Historical Society, Carlisle, Pa.

During this time, Sadler continued to spend time with his wife. Together they attended a dance in January at the residence of Mr. and Mrs. Frank Payne in Harrisburg. The dance was in honor of Mr. and Mrs. Jacob Fronheires of Johnstown, Pa. Also in attendance at the dance were Dr. and Mrs. Horace Sadler along with their close friends Mr. and Mrs. Raphael Hays of Carlisle.[6]

Several months later, on July 1, 1916, the couple hosted a dinner at Thornwald in honor of Mr. and Mrs. Frank Bosler. The dinner even made the "personal mention" column in *The Evening Sentinel* where the paper remarked how the mansion was "beautifully decorated" for the occasion. However, this would be the last noteworthy event to take place inside the mansion for some time.[7]

Months later, in September of that year, the couple was staying at their summer home, Rose Balcony, when Mary came down with food poisoning. Immediately, they returned to Carlisle and sought medical treatment at the nearby Carlisle Hospital where she was admitted on September 18, 1916. Although she had sought immediate medical attention, her condition never improved. The following day, she passed away at just forty-four years of age.[8] That day *The Evening Sentinel* announced the passing of Mrs. Mary Eliza Bosler Sadler and remembered her as "[the] most charitable woman of the town", and having "[a] bright and cheerful disposition".[9]

The funeral took place three days later at Thornwald, and was the first to occur inside the mansion. The services were conducted by Rev. E.H. Kellogg of the Second Presbyterian Church where the couple had been long time members. The pallbearers included Dr. Leon T. Ashcraft of Philadelphia and notable gentlemen from Carlisle including Dr. Harry A Spangler, Raphael S. Hays, M. Parker Moore, J. Montgomery Mahon, and Guy H. Davies. Interment was private and took place inside the Ashland Cemetery.[10]

Despite the Sadler plot that currently existed inside Ashland Cemetery, Lewis Sadler purchased a separate burial plot on October 18, 1916, for $1,000.[11] The plot that he had purchased was in the center of the cemetery, and across from the Bosler burial plot. On the ground, he had constructed Ashland Cemetery's first and only mausoleum, the Sadler Mausoleum. The mausoleum was constructed in memory of his late wife, Mary Eliza Bosler Sadler.

Although it is unknown who constructed the mausoleum, upon its completion in 1917, the mausoleum closely mirrored the front portico of Thornwald. In addition, the mausoleum contained a pair of bronze gates and a stained glass window in the rear along with containing two pairs of bronze vents that were located on either side that were identical to those that covered the basement windows of the rathskeller.

Shortly after Sadler had purchased the lot of ground for the future mausoleum, his brother, Wilbur Sadler Jr., arrived home in Carlisle. Prior to his arrival, Wilbur too had been sick with food poisoning, which he had acquired back in July.[12] However, due to the demands of his position as Adjutant General, he was unable to rest and therefore his condition continued to grow worse. Nearly two months later, in August, he was stricken with heart disease while preparing the New Jersey National Guard for their services along the Mexican border.[13]

His declining condition sent him away to New York to seek medical attention although he was unable to recover. Therefore, in October, just a month after Mrs. Sadler's death, he returned home to Carlisle. Upon arriving in Carlisle, he did not seek the nearby Carlisle Hospital for prompt medical treatment or the family home along North College Street. Instead, he set out for Thornwald where he believed with a little rest amongst the peaceful scenery he could recover and return shortly to his duties as Adjutant General of New Jersey.[14]

Circa 1900 photograph of Wilbur Fisk Sadler, Jr. taken from the Sadler family photograph by Choate.

Cumberland County Historical Society, Carlisle, Pa.

However, days turned into weeks and although at times it appeared as if he was getting better his condition soon became worse. Three days prior to his death, he lay in bed unconscious. On November 10, 1916, he passed away at forty-five years of age.[15] His death marked the first death at Thornwald and the second funeral to take place at the Sadler residence within just one year.

Wilbur Fisk Sadler, Jr. was to Trenton, New Jersey as his father was to Carlisle, Pennsylvania. He was both a bachelor and a high-class citizen within the great city of Trenton. He had owned several high rises including the State Gazette Building and the United Cigar Stores along with "bachelor apartments" at No. 9 West State Street, which was his private residence.[16] He was the Adjutant General of New Jersey for nearly seven years prior to his death and was an influential part of the New Jersey National Guard.

According to the *Evening Times* in 1916, he was "responsible for re-organization of the National Guard and the adoption of the more advanced school of training". He also initiated for the passage of a Retirement Act, which allowed for the same retirement age of the regular army be applied to the National Guard, which was passed by the state in 1911. In the years to come, he also was involved in the restoration of the Trenton Barracks along with creating a park system for the city of Trenton.[17]

Outside of his duties as Adjutant General, he was an active member of St. Michael's Episcopal Church serving as a vestryman. He was also a member of several organizations in both New Jersey and Pennsylvania including; member of the Sons of the Revolution, Society of Colonial Wars, the Trenton Club, Trenton Country Club, Markham Club of Philadelphia, Duquesne Club of Pittsburgh, secretary of the Mercer County Automobile Club, and a member of a Masonic fraternity in Trenton.[18] Although quite a busy body, in his spare time he did extensive research both on the Sadler and Sterrett families, which today is on record at the Cumberland County Historical Society in Carlisle, Pa.[19]

His funeral took place at Thornwald on November 13, 1916. The funeral drew hundreds of people from across New Jersey and Pennsylvania. That day special trains, from New Jersey arrived in Carlisle carrying a boxcar full of floral tributes along with a number of public officials such as U.S. Senator elect Joseph S Frelinghuysen, former Governor John Fort of New Jersey. However, Sadler's good friend, President Wilson, could not be present for the funeral and instead sent a telegram expressing his deepest condolences to the Sadler family.[20]

Rev. William Eldy Rector, from Trenton, New Jersey conducted the funeral services that day while the pallbearers consisted of Governor James Fielder and staff of New Jersey.[21] Afterwards, interment took place inside the Ashland Cemetery.

With the passing of Wilbur Jr. also came a great inheritance for the siblings Lewis, Sylvester, and Horace. According to the Gettysburg *Star and Sentinel,* Wilbur Jr. had left $250,000 or a staggering $4.8 million today to his brothers in his will. As for his residence in New Jersey, his valet David B. Graham inherited the property upon his death.[22]

Although he was gone, he was not forgotten by the city of Trenton, New Jersey. A few weeks after his death, the Masonic Historical Association placed a bronze tablet on the main floor of the Old Masonic Temple in Trenton in his honor. According to the *Carlisle Evening Herald,* Sadler was an "organizer of the association and one of the prime promoters for the preservation of Masonic treasures in New Jersey".[23]

Later, The Board of Freeholders of Mercer County, New Jersey, too, would honor Sadler by placing a memorial lamp on the Willow Street Bridge in Trenton while Mayor Fredrick Donnelly of Trenton issued that a memorial booklet be published which upon its completion in 1916 was entitled "A Memorial Tribute to Wilbur F. Sadler, Jr.".[24]

Above left: The Sadler Mausoleum located inside the Ashland Cemetery in Carlisle.
Above right: The pair of bronze gates
Bottom: The inside of the mausoleum. To the left, are the tombs of Mr. and Mrs. Lewis Sadler & Dr. and Mrs. Horace Sadler. To the right, are Sylvester and Wilbur Jr. Followed by Mr. and Mrs. Wilbur Fisk Sadler.
Photos by author

Chapter 12

A Man of Distinction

Following the sudden death of his wife and his eldest brother, Sadler's life now took a turn in a different direction. Currently, he still maintained his position as president of the Farmers Trust Company and continued to attend the galas at Ragged Edge in Chambersburg every fall although now his life began to mirror that of his late brother, Wilbur Sadler Jr.

Early on, Sadler had close ties with the Governor of Pennsylvania, Martin G. Brumbaugh, and on occasion, he even wined and dined with him at his Executive Mansion in Harrisburg. Therefore, when the Governor created the Committee of Public Safety, during World War I in March 1917, he did not hesitate in naming Sadler as a member of the committee.[1]

According to *Philadelphia in the World War 1914-1919,* the Committee of Public Safety was considered the "war emergency body" and was created "to mobilize and conserve the civil resources of the state for the benefit of the Federal war program". Furthermore, the committee served as the "functioning arm" of the Pennsylvania Commission of Public Safety and Defense. At the beginning there were only 300 members, but grew to nearly 15,000 and later became known as "the largest public organization ever created in Pennsylvania". Those who served on the committee did so without compensation. Appointed to serve as executive manager of what was later known as the Pennsylvania Council of National Defense, was Lewis Sadler.[2]

Throughout the next two years, Sadler busied himself with the duties bestowed upon him, often attending numerous executive meetings at the Girard Trust Company in Philadelphia. There he was involved in discussing various transactions of money and issues relating to the Council of National Defense with other members of the committee.[3] During his time in Philadelphia, he became a member of both the Racquet and Rittenhouse clubs and continued to frequent at the Union League.

Among the members of the Union League, was William C. Sproul, who had known Sadler from being a member of the Pennsylvania Commission of Public Safety and Defense.[4] Prior to the establishment of the committee, both Sproul and Sadler were members of the Union League and served on the board of directors of the Valley Traction Railway in 1914. Four years later, in 1918, Sproul was elected as governor of Pennsylvania and in January of 1919, he appointed Lewis Sadler as his commissioner of highways.[5]

Early on, the *North American* considered Sadler an "ideal man for the position" due to his rank in business and politics although there was a group of men from Alleghany who felt otherwise. According to the *North American,* the "Penrose-Babcock Leslie machine" was upset at hearing the news since they were hoping for the "appointment" of Pittsburgh mayor, Joseph G. Armstrong. However, Armstrong lacked both "business and executive ability" that were among Sproul's prerequisites for the position.[6] Therefore, Armstrong was not elected. Furthermore, Sadler was one step ahead of Armstrong, since early on he had expressed an interest in Pennsylvania's highways.

In June 1915, Sadler, along with Camp Hill mayor, J.W. Milhouse, spoke with State Highway Commissioner Cunningham regarding the possibility of constructing a road through Camp Hill. However, *The Harrisburg Telegraph* reported that building such a road through Camp Hill was uncertain at the time.[7] However, this was only the beginning of his many attempts at giving the Cumberland Valley a number of "excellent roads". During this time, he even was influential in the construction of the Lincoln Highway that was constructed "from Chambersburg through the central part of the state".[8]

Formal portrait of Lewis S. Sadler by Marcecau, Philadelphia

Cumberland County Historical Society, Carlisle, Pa.

Assistant State Highway Commissioner George H. Biles
Photograph taken from Gov. Sproul's Cabinet, c. 1920

*Pennsylvania Historical and Museum Commission,
Pennsylvania Archives, MG_218*

State Highway Commissioner Lewis S. Sadler.
Photo by Marceau, Philadelphia

*Cumberland County Historical Society,
Carlisle, Pa.*

Prior to beginning his duties as Pennsylvania's new commissioner of highways, Sadler had the honor of having the Sproul family at Thornwald in January 1919. William Sproul was to arrive within a few days in Harrisburg to be sworn in as governor of Pennsylvania, although the family would spend a few days at Thornwald before settling into the Executive Mansion.[9] On January 21, 1919, William C. Sproul was sworn in as governor of Pennsylvania.[10]

The following day, *The Evening Sentinel* announced those that were selected to serve on Sproul's cabinet included, Lewis Sadler, who was appointed state highway commissioner, and George H. Biles, who was appointed as assistant state highway commissioner.

On January 22, 1919, Sadler once again entertained at Thornwald but this time he hosted a dance "in honor of the members of the inaugural party". However, Governor Sproul could not attend the dance since he had to look after his mother who had fallen ill. Those that were in attendance included Mrs. Sproul, Mrs. Henry Klaer, Mr. and Mrs. Francis Hall, Dr. and Mrs. William E. Wright, Mr. and Mrs. Henderson Gilbert along with Lt. John Sproul.[11]

However, despite his new position in society, his career as the new commissioner of highways was not off to a good start. Already, he had declined two invitations that he had received regarding the "good roads convention". According to *The Evening Sentinel*, he was to give an address at the convention regarding his plans for the roads of Pennsylvania although at the time he was not ready to "announce any plans or policies".[12]

By the following month, Sadler's plan for the highways of Pennsylvania was revealed in the *Carlisle Evening Herald* which announced that the state would have a "lateral road construction" also known as a "primary road system".[13] Prior to his administration, the roads in Pennsylvania were laid out in a "haphazard manner" and therefore there was no "connected system of highways" at the time.[14]

LEWIS S. SADLER'S DISTINGUISHED GUESTS

Governor-elect William C. Sproul and family are guests of Lewis S. Sadler, at the latter's home, "Thornwald," College Street and Walnut Bottom Road. The party included Mr. and Mrs. Sproul, the Governor-elect's mother, his daughter, Mrs. Henry Klarr and daughter and Lieutenant Jack Sproul, U.S.A. They arrived from their home, in Chester, about six o'clock Saturday evening. Mr. and Mrs. Sproul will leave for the Executive Mansion at five o'clock this evening and after the inauguration the family will remain here until Thursday.

The Evening Sentinel, 20 January 1919

Governor William Cameron Sproul
Photo by Harris & Ewig

*Courtesy of the Library of Congress
LC-DIG-hec-19345*

MR. SADLER TO GIVE DANCE

Lewis S. Sadler, of Carlisle, will give a small dance on Wednesday evening at his home, Thornwold, in honor of the members of the inaugural party.

The Evening Sentinel, 21 January 1919

FORM NO. 712
COUNTY Montgomery
TOWNSHIP
BOROUGH Bridgeport
APPL. NO.
ROUTE NO. 143-E

Pennsylvania

STATE HIGHWAY DEPARTMENT
HARRISBURG, PA.

LEWIS S. SADLER
COMMISSIONER
GEORGE H. BILES
ASSISTANT COMMISSIONER
WILLIAM D. UHLER
CHIEF ENGINEER
JOSEPH W. HUNTER
TOWNSHIP COMMISSIONER

October 27, 1919.

Secretary of Borough Council,
Bridgeport, Penna.

Gentlemen:

    I am enclosing herewith duplicate copies of agreement covering the construction of State Highway Route No. 143, lying within your borough, with the request that you execute these agreements in the spaces provided and return to this Department as soon as possible, accompanied with an itemized statement of your indebtedness, showing your authority for the increase over 2 percent, if the same has been increased.

    This work is advertised, bids to be received October 31, and as no contract will be awarded until these agreements, properly executed, are in our possession, I would ask that you give this matter your immediate attention.

Yours very truly,

Lewis S. Sadler.

JLS/EMB

Lewis S. Sadler,
State Highway Commissioner.

Letter addressed to the Secretary of Borough Council of Bridgeport, Montgomery County from State Highway Commissioner Lewis Sadler. The letter concerns the construction of State Highway Route No. 143. The letter is from Lewis Sadler's student drop file at the Dickinson College Archives and Special Collections, Carlisle, Pa.

$10,000 PAID OVER FOR PIKE

Party Chops Down Toll Gates

The $10,000 purchase money for the Carlisle-Hanover turnpike was paid over to the sequestrator in Carlisle Tuesday by subscribers to the fund, and the deed turned over to the State Highway Department. Nine of the contributors to the $10,000 fund left Hanover at 8:30 Tuesday morning. The party came in two automobiles, and consisted of Chief Burgess, H.G. Newcomer, G. Stanley Shirk, Charles Brough, G. H. Shirk, C. J. Delone, Melvin Sheffer, H. S. Ehrhart, Guy W. Bange and Philip N. Forney.

On arriving in Gettysburg, they were met by Senator Beales, who accompanied the party on the journey. The party reached Carlisle about 10:30 a. m., and paid over the money to the sequestrator of the turnpike company and received the deed. They then left Carlisle and arrived in Harrisburg, where luncheon was partaken of at the Penn-Harris Hotel. There was no speechmaking. At the end of the meal the deed was presented to State Highway Commissioner Lewis Sadler. Guests at the luncheon were: Commissioner Sadler, Robert S. Spangler, speaker of the house of representatives, S. S. Lewis, of the attorney general's staff. The party left Harrisburg at 4:30 p. m., arriving at the Altland House, Abbottstown, where supper was served.

On the homeward trip the four toll gates along the pike were chopped down by members of the party and left lying, scrap heaps along the road. The party arrived home about 9 p. m.

The Evening Sentinel, 23 July 1919

Therefore, when Governor Sproul and Sadler devised the plan they wanted to construct roads that would benefit the state as a whole and furthermore give Pennsylvania "the greatest highway system in America", which Sadler had envisioned.[15]

For the project, the state allotted a "huge sum" of money in the form of bonds, which totaled "$50,000,000". Upon hearing of the large sum, the county delegates were outraged and asked for a "slice for their home counties" and immediately confronted Sadler regarding the proposed road project. However, in reply he said, "'I will not comprise with a poor thing'". A statement that he was said to have made "hundreds of times". For he believed, "'When we begin our work it will be well done. It shall never be said of me that I built a makeshift road--- or that in an effort temporarily to satisfy the demands of a community I put down a pavement which would not last'".[16]

The highways that were about to be constructed across Pennsylvania were to be made of steel reinforced concrete, which was the same material used in the construction of Thornwald. Just as Thornwald seemed like it could withstand time so Pennsylvania's highways were to be built with the same concept in mind, or as *The Carlisle Evening Herald* put it Sadler would construct the roads so that they "will last and not peel off".[17]

Furthermore, since a number of the roads were to be built from "the proceeds of bond issues", Sadler conceived the idea that the roads should still be in good order when the bonds reached their full maturity once saying, "We will build no short-time roads with long-time bonds". By the close of 1919, there was nearly 200 miles of "durable highway", and by the following year the number would double to approximately 400 miles.[18]

During this time, Cumberland County was already seeing many changes during Sadler's control of the Highway Department. In the summer of 1919, the State Highway Department was already in the process of macadamizing West High and South College Streets. Later, the Highway Department macadamized the main street that led through Mount Holly beginning at the railroad bridge and ending at the Holly Inn.[19] Also at this time, Sadler had the State Highway Department concrete the road that led to Rose Balcony along with the Walnut Bottom Road that led to the Stone House, a tavern that he was known to frequent at on occasion.[20]

COMMISSIONER FORT ILL HERE.

Federal Trade Commissioner J. Franklin Fort, former Governor of New Jersey, who came here last night to address the Carlisle Chamber of Commerce, is quite ill at the home of State Highway Commissioner Lewis S. Sadler, Walnut Bottom Road. He was unable to make his scheduled address and it is said suffers a slight stroke.

The Evening Sentinel, 17 April 1919

John Franklin Fort

Courtesy of the Library of Congress
LC-DIG-ggbain-00713

    Besides creating a number of macadamized roads within the county, he was also involved in the abolishment of the Carlisle-Hanover Turnpike. In July 1919, Governor Sproul issued that the Carlisle-Hanover turnpike be abolished and therefore on July 23, 1919, the gates on the turnpike were officially torn down. That evening, Sadler attended a dinner at the Penn-Harris Hotel in Harrisburg where he received the deed for the turnpike therefore allowing the State Highway Department in complete control of the road.[21]

    When Sadler was not occupied behind his desk or traveling with his chief engineer, Col. William D. Uhler, inspecting the state highways, he did find time to hold a few social galas at Thornwald. In May 1919, just months after his election as commissioner of highways, he held a dinner for a few distinguished gentlemen. Those whom attended the dinner included Senator Boies Penrose, Representative State Chairman and Senator, William Evans Crow along with his good friend Governor William C. Sproul.[22] Days prior to the gentlemen arriving at Thornwald for the dinner, former New Jersey Governor John Franklin Fort had left Thornwald after spending the past few weeks there.

    Prior to this time, Fort was a member of the Federal Trade Commission and was scheduled to give a speech at the Carlisle Chamber of Commerce on April 16, 1919. However, upon arriving in Carlisle, he suffered a stroke. Instead of seeking medical treatment at the local Carlisle Hospital, he went to Thornwald. Fort was no stranger to Sadler, since he had known his brother Wilbur, and had attended his funeral at Thornwald in 1916.

    For the next few weeks, Fort recovered at Thornwald staying away from the local newspaper reporters that were often inquiring as to his condition. Days after arriving at Thornwald, *The Evening Sentinel* reported that Fort was "unable to talk" and had suffered paralysis of his left side.[23] Nearly a week later, Fort left Thornwald after spending Easter with Commissioner Sadler although his condition never improved. He died nearly two years later, in November 1920, at age sixty-eight.[24]

Wilbur Fisk Sadler at age seventy-two, taken April 1912. Photo by Mathilde Weil, Philadelphia.

Cumberland County Historical Society, Carlisle, Pa.

    A few weeks later, Sadler hosted yet another dinner at Thornwald this time for members of the Supreme Court on the evening of May 21, 1919. Among those in attendance that evening was Judge McPherson along with six judges from the Supreme Court and Governor Sproul.[25] Although, this was not the last time that Sproul would make an appearance at Thornwald. The following month, Sadler hosted two more dinners at Thornwald. This time the members of the "Legislative Correspondents' Association" along with Governor Sproul were among the guests at the mansion.[26] However, this would be the last noteworthy dinner at Thornwald until the following year.

    There was little time for Commissioner Sadler to entertain at Thornwald, since he was often on the road from Thursday to Saturday inspecting the highways with his Chief Engineer, William Uhler. At times, he was known to be so busy that he even skipped lunch.[27] Although a majority of his time was spent inspecting the state highways, he did find time to make a view public appearances.

    In February 1920, Sadler made an appearance at a banquet at the Hotel Washington in Chambersburg. By the following month, he was present with Chief Engineer, Uhler in Easton where they gave a speech at the Easton highway meeting.[28] However, if his job was not enough wearing on him at the time, in July of that year; he faced the sudden death of his father and two-time Judge of Cumberland County, Wilbur Fisk Sadler.

    On June 29, 1920, his father suffered a massive heart attack on his way home from his law office along West High Street. However, he did not recover and died shortly afterwards on July 3, 1920, at his residence along North College Street at eighty years of age. Three days later, Rev. A Houck of the Methodist church conducted a private funeral at the Sadler residence along North College Street. The pallbearers were members of the Cumberland County Bar. Among the notable men in attendance at the funeral included Governor William C. Sproul and Supreme Court Judge John Stewart along with other notable lawyers from the surrounding area. Afterwards, entombment took place inside the Ashland Cemetery at the Sadler Mausoluem.[29]

    Afterwards, Sylvester continued to live out of the Sadler home along North College Street. By the following year, he purchased the home from Lewis for $7,000. The house had been in the hands of his older brother ever since the home had gone up for sheriff sale in February 1899.[30]

> GOVERNORS THIS EVENING
> General John J. Pershing, General W. W. Atterbury, and the half hundred Governors and Governors-elect will arrive at the Sadler home this evening. It is expected between seven and eight o'clock.

The announcement appeared in *The Evening Sentinel* on December 2, 1920, announcing the arrival of General John J. Pershing, William Wallace Atterbury and Governors' from across the United States at Thornwald.

Five months later, Lewis Sadler hosted by far the largest gathering ever witnessed in Carlisle for some time at Thornwald. On December 2, 1920, *The Evening Sentinel* announced that "General John J. Pershing, General W.W. Atterbury and half [a] hundred Governors and Governs-elect" would arrive at Thornwald that evening "between seven and eight o'clock".[31]

Their arrival was such big news in Carlisle that a number of Carlisle citizens turned out to watch the parade of automobiles make their way towards Thornwald. Generals' Pershing and Atterbury along with Moorhead C. Kennedy of the Cumberland Valley Railroad arrived by a "special train" that had come from Harrisburg. Upon arrival in Carlisle, the train came to a stop at College Street and from there the men were driven by automobile to Thornwald as motorcyclists from the State Police followed behind.[32]

Thornwald was beautifully decorated for the occasion. Upon entering the mansion, sweet sounds of stringed instruments and singing filled the mansion that was furnished by Italian gentlemen from New York. That evening the guests enjoyed a delectable dinner that was furnished by a caterer from Germantown, Pennsylvania. Concluding the festivities for the evening was a dance that was given in honor of the "ninety" guests who had come to Thornwald.[33]

The following day, a number of people lined the streets to wish "General Perishing and party" goodbye as they left for New York that day.[34] Afterwards, news ceased regarding the gatherings at Thornwald, although Sadler continued to entertain a number of statesmen at his home during his time as highway commissioner.

By the following year, Sadler was once again out on the roads inspecting the state highways. During this time, he even made a few public appearances one which included a visit to the Hotel Casey in Scranton where he spoke before several members of the Lackawanna Motor Club. Unlike his brother, Sylvester, who had excelled at public speaking, Commissioner Sadler "disliked public speaking" and therefore was known to have "made less than a half a dozen speeches" during his time as highway commissioner of Pennsylvania.[35]

DISTINIGUISHED GUESTS AT SADLER DINNER

General Pershing and Governors Entertained

State Highway Commissioner Lewis S. Sadler entertained at his home, "Thornewold," Thursday night, Governors and Governors-elect of more than half the states in the Union, General John J. Pershing and party, Gen. W. W. Atterbury and party and other men in state official circles. General Pershing and his marshalls and General Atterbury, M. C. Kennedy and others arrived on a special train over the P. R. R. from Harrisburg which stopped at College street and from there they were taken in automobiles to the Sadler mansion.

Italians from New York played stringed instruments and sang and the caterer was from Germantown, Philadelphia.

The Governors came in automobiles from Harrisburg. General Pershing and party went to New York today.

Motorcycle patrolmen of the State Police Force escorted the Governors here. Following the dinner at the Sadler home a dance was held in honor of the guests, about ninety in number.

A large number of Dickinson students and townspeople greeted General Pershing at High and College streets. The students gave him a yell and the great soldier responded with a salute.

The Evening Sentinel,
3 December 1920

General John J. Pershing
Photo by Harris & Ewig

Courtesy of the Library of Congress
LC-DIG-hec-07393

Brigadier General William W. Atterbury
Photo by Bain News Service

Courtesy of the Library of Congress
LC-DIG-ggbain-12498

The above photographs and the photograph on the following page depict concrete road construction during the fall of 1921 in an unidentified location in Pennsylvania. In the photograph, at the top of the page, note the sheets of steel that were used to reinforce the concrete. The steel reinforced concrete was the same material used in the floors of Thornwald, and therefore it is no wonder that Sadler constructed the highways of Pennsylvania using the same material.

Photos from author

Photo from author

After Commissioner Sadler had delivered his speech at the Hotel Casey that day, the crowd cheered for him and declared that he was their "next choice as governor of Pennsylvania".[36] However, this was not the first time that he had heard those words. At the start of his career as highway commissioner in 1919, he made an appearance in Scranton where a number of people suggested he run for governor. However, at the time he had "no intentions" to fill a "political position" and furthermore, believed that the Highway Department should have no connections with politics.[37]

In the fall of that year, he made his last public appearance in Erie along with Governor Sproul and Governor Davis of Ohio at the opening of the stretch of highway that connected Pennsylvania with Ohio.[38] By the close of 1921, 670 miles of concrete roads were constructed making Pennsylvania number one in the nation in concrete road construction.[39]

In January 1922, *The New York Times* ranked Pennsylvania among the states who were constructing highways for the future. Up until this time, Sadler already had taken the steps in ensuring that the roads were built with durability in mind. Now, the issue that was at hand was constructing roads that could handle the traffic fifteen to twenty years from now. He insisted that everyone who currently used the highways do their part in maintaining the roads.

Furthermore, he believed a number of the roads were currently being damaged due to overloaded trucks. In order to prove that his theory was correct, he wasted no time in launching an investigation to show that "one thousand passenger cars will not do the damage to a roadway that is caused by one three-ton truck with an unsprung overload two tons beyond the trucks capacity".[40] In the end, the results were conclusive and thereafter the state legislature put a weight limit on trucks.

By this time, Sadler had served as highway commissioner for three years although by now he was starting to feel the effects of being "overworked".[41] According to the *Highway Engineer & Contractor*, the position of highway commissioner was a "killing one", and certainly, it was. Former Highway Commissioner Edward M. Bigelow died a year after leaving office while Robert J. Cunningham died during his term as highway commissioner. Even J. Denny O'Neil, whom Sadler had succeeded in January 1919, was at this time considered an "invalid".[42] Despite the strain that his position as commissioner was currently having on his health, he continued his work as usual and therefore ignored Sylvester's advice of taking a rest.[43] In January 1922, Sadler was once again on the road although this time he was on his way to Philadelphia to attend the funeral of Senator Boies Penrose.

The death of Senator Penrose opened up a vacancy that he believed he could most likely fill. However, much to his surprise, Governor Sproul chose former chairman of the Pennsylvania Council of National Defense, George Wharton Pepper as Penrose's replacement. Upon hearing the news, he was overcome by both disappointment and grief since he felt that he had a good chance at replacing Penrose due to his close friendship with Governor Sproul.[44]

On January 16, 1922, he returned home to Thornwald after being away at Penrose's funeral in Philadelphia. Upon arriving home, he came down with pneumonia and shortly afterwards was confined to his bed. Sadler now lay in bed awaiting his final hours, similar to his brother Wilbur who had succumbed to pneumonia and later passed away in November 1916.

On Thursday, January 19, 1922, Sadler took a turn for the worse. Dr. H.A Spangler from the Carlisle Hospital was called at once to Thornwald to aid him from his ailing condition. Throughout the night, the doctor stayed with him until early the next morning. Afterwards, he was left in the company of his secretary and chauffer, William J. McCulley and butler, David Graham. At 9:40 a.m. on Friday, January 20, 1922 he passed away at forty-seven years of age.[45] Coincidently, he had passed away almost three years to the day when Governor Sproul appointed him highway commissioner of Pennsylvania.

Upon hearing the news of his death, Dr. and Mrs. Horace Sadler immediately returned from their trip in Florida while Sylvester and Governor Sproul made their trip home from the Supreme Court in Philadelphia. Both Sylvester and Governor Sproul were awestruck upon hearing of his death since Sproul had not spoken to him in "ten days" while Sylvester's nightmare from the night before now had become a reality.[46] According to *The Evening Sentinel,* Sylvester awoke at four o'clock in the morning after having a nightmare that his brother had died. Upon hearing that his nightmare had indeed become a reality, he left "at once" for Carlisle.[47]

On the day of his death, *The Evening Sentinel* published the obituary of Commissioner Sadler in the newspaper and reported that his death was the result of a "hemorrhage" caused by pneumonia. He was remembered as a "most distinguished citizen" and the paper furthermore told of the dinner, which he had hosted for the governors a few years prior in December 1920.[48]

The Evening Sentinel was not the only one to tell of his passing. Even the *Dickinsonian* told how his death had shocked the community and threw the Republican party into "confusion", since he was a "leading candidate in the approaching Gubernatorial Contest".[49] Besides his obituary being announced in the local papers, even *The New York Times* announced his passing along with the *Highway Engineer & Contractor*, which released an exhaustive obituary the following month summarizing his past three years as highway commissioner and further remembering him for his durable road construction.

According to *Highway Engineer & Contractor*, upon his death, 1,400 miles of his "dream roads" had become a "reality" and the work continued even after his death. Besides retelling his history as highway commissioner, the magazine also told how he was responsible for increasing the salary of his state highway officials with the "exception of his own".

A few months prior to his death, he gave his Assistant Commissioner, George H. Biles, an increase of $4,000 making his annual salary $12,000, which exceeded the annual salary of the governor of Pennsylvania. It was the biggest increase next to his chief engineer who received a $2,500 raise to $10,000 per year. The magazine also recalled how Sadler drove "his own car" to Harrisburg and asked for no compensation of bills that he had accumulated while inspecting the state highways.[50]

The following day, another short article relevant to his passing appeared in *The Evening Sentinel* this time entitled "Governor Sproul's Tribute", which read as follows:

> The sudden death of Commissioner Sadler has shocked me almost beyond expression. I had not known that he was seriously ill, although he had not yet been in his office for the past ten days.
>
> Lewis Sadler and I had been closely associated for many years and I have had no friendship which I valued more highly than his. He was earnest, loyal, and notably sincere in all his friendships, and his taking at such an early age is certainly a calamity.
>
> Lewis Sadler was one of the finest public servants whom I ever knew. He was energy and efficiency personified. The great system of public highways in Pennsylvania is his monument. Absolutely unselfish and untiring in his desire to serve, he devoted himself incessantly to the duties of his great post. He had the confidence of people to a marked degree and every one admired his wonderful conception of the great undertaking he had planned to carry out.
>
> I mourn the loss of a true friend, a splendid official and a noble and patriotic citizen of the Commonwealth.[51]

The funeral took place on the afternoon of Monday, January 23, 1922. The county courthouse closed at noon that day, while the Dickinson Law School remained closed for the entire day. Across the commonwealth, state offices were closed, and the American flag remained at half-mast, which was still in its present position since the death of Senator Penrose.[52]

The scene at Thornwald was similar to the funeral of Wilbur Sadler Jr., which had taken place some years prior in November 1916. No cars were permitted on the grounds of Thornwald, and therefore they could only park along South College Street and Walnut Bottom Road. A special train escorted members of the Supreme Court along with a few Pennsylvania state officials including Governor Sproul to Thornwald. Inside the library at Thornwald, numerous floral tributes surrounded the mahogany casket.[53]

Rev. Glenn M. Shaffer of the Second Presbyterian Church in Carlisle presided over the services, which according to *The Evening Sentinel* were "brief and simple".[54] The pallbearers were from the Farmers Trust Company in Carlisle, whom afterwards placed the casket inside the Sadler Mausoleum located in Ashland Cemetery. A few months later, both Horace and Sylvester donated $10,000 to the Carlisle Hospital in memory of their brother.[55]

Chapter 13

The Inheritance

Following the death of Commissioner Sadler, Assistant Commissioner George H. Biles was appointed by Governor Sproul to "direct the affairs of the Pennsylvania State Highway Department" therefore, continuing the work that Sadler had begun just three years ago by creating the "greatest highway system in America".[1]

However, his death was not the last within the Highway Department that year. Several months later in October of that year, Sadler's former Chief Engineer, William Uhler, passed away from a cerebral stroke.[2]

During this time, Sylvester became the sole heir to his brother's Thornwald Estate along with its contents. Besides inheriting the mansion, he also inherited $100,000 worth of bonds at the Farmers Trust Company.[3]

Upon acquiring Thornwald, it did not take long until he sold the Sadler home along North College Street. In September of that year, he sold the home to the Pennsylvania Sigma Phi Alumni Association for $18,500 and moved into Thornwald taking with him the many volumes of books that he had stored at the Sadler residence for many years.[4] Thereafter, the home was occupied by the Sigma Phi Fraternity until in 1963, the house was torn down to make way for the present day Holland Union building.[5]

Although Sylvester had inherited Thornwald, he did not spend much time there due to his duties at the Supreme Court in Philadelphia. Prior to his brother's death, he had served both as judge of Cumberland County (1915-1920) and as justice of the Supreme Court, a position that he held since January 3, 1921.[6]

Formal portrait of Sylvester B. Sadler taken in 1921. Photo by Chandler.

Cumberland County Historical Society, Carlisle, Pa.

The great city of brotherly love had become his second home. His office was located on the third floor of City Hall, which overlooked the hustle and bustle of suburban Philadelphia. During his time in the city, he became a member of the Philadelphia Art Club, the Pennsylvania Historical Society, and the Union League where he was later known to keep a "suite of rooms".[7] Due to his extended time in Philadelphia, Sadler soon transferred the deed to his youngest brother and sister-in-law, Dr. and Mrs. Horace Sadler, the following year on January 8, 1923.[8]

Albion Point, the home of Dr. and Mrs. Horace Sadler, was sold in October 1923 to Mr. and Mrs. George Hays of Carlisle. Photo by A.A, Line.

Cumberland County Historical Society, Carlisle, Pa

Prior to the transfer of sale, the couple currently lived at Albion Point where they had spent the last fourteen years of their married life together. Upon acquiring Thornwald, they sold Albion Point some months later in October 1923 to Mr. and Mrs. George Hays of Carlisle.[9] Later, the mansion was torn down in the 1960's to make way for a shopping plaza.[10]

Currently, Thornwald still appeared much the same way as when Mr. and Mrs. Lewis Sadler had owned it although upon acquiring the mansion, Dr. and Mrs. Horace Sadler brought with them the many antiques that had adorned Albion Point for many years therefore adding to the beautification of the residence. However, they were not alone and like Mr. and Mrs. Lewis Sadler, they too had a private chauffeur named, Frank Gleim. Like McCulley, Gleim too did not live at Thornwald and instead lived at his residence along F Street in Carlisle.[11]

During their first year at Thornwald, the couple adjusted to their new home, which was unlike living at Albion Point. In comparison, Thornwald was located on the outskirts of town away from the hustle and bustle of everyday life while Albion Point was in close proximity to The Frog & Switch Manufacturing Company, the Carlisle Gas & Water Company along with the Cumberland Valley and Gettysburg & Harrisburg Railroads.[12] While both homes were large in size, Thornwald was fit for a king containing a number of rooms such as those found in the basement along with the servants' quarters which were not often seen in homes of the time nor that of Albion Point. While the grounds of Thornwald could not compare to the prestigious landscape of Albion Point, the estate did contain a golf course, which the couple often enjoyed although only for a short time.

Above: Circa 1930 photograph of Mrs. Helen Sadler with a glass right eye. Photograph by E.F. Foley of New York.

Cumberland County Historical Society, Carlisle, Pa.

Right: News article that appeared in *The Evening Sentinel* on October 20, 1924.

MRS. SADLER LOSES EYE

Struck by Golf Club While Playing at Thornewold

Unaware that her husband was about to swing a heavy golf club in demonstrating a golf stroke, Mrs. Horace T. Sadler, Carlisle, stooped to pick up a golf ball and was struck in the right eye by the club, a mid-iron, on Saturday afternoon on the golf links of the Sadler home, Thornewold, near Carlisle.

The blow made necessary an operation in which Mrs. Sadler's eye was removed. Her condition was reported to be good last night.

The accident occurred early in the afternoon after Mr. and Mrs. Sadler had been on the links for some time. Mrs. Sadler was taken into her home where the operation was performed. Dr. George de Schweinitz, of Philadelphia, and Dr. Helen M. Stewart, of Chambersburg, eye specialists, were called and after a consultation decided to remove the eye.

The Sadlers had just returned the day before from their country home at Allenberry.

    By the following year in October 1924, Mrs. Helen Sadler would fall victim to a horrific golfing accident . Prior to her accident, the couple was away at their summer home, "Allenberry", and upon returning home a few days later they decided to enjoy a round of golf .

    While on the links that day, Horace wanted to demonstrate a new "golf stroke" to Helen. However, as he proceeded with his demonstration she was unaware of him raising the "mid-iron" high into the air as she picked up her golf ball. The iron came down hard, and Horace hit his beloved wife right in the eye. Immediately, she was escorted off the green into Thornwald where an operation was performed to remove her right eye.[13]

    That day, Dr. George de Schwemitz of Philadelphia and Dr. Helen M. Stewart of Chambersburg preformed the first surgery to occur inside the mansion. Together, they successfully removed her right eye, and afterwards replaced it with a glass one, which Helen would continue to wear throughout the remainder of her life.[14]

    However, the couple would no longer enjoy the golf course at Thornwald, and therefore it soon grew over although throughout the next several years they did find time to enjoy their summer home, known as Allenberry, which was located just outside of Boiling Springs.[15]

    Prior to Allenberry, there was Rose Balcony, which was the summer home of Mr. and Mrs. Lewis Sadler. There they entertained a number of their friends over the years. Upon Mrs. Sadler's sudden death in 1916, Lewis became the sole heir of the two tracts of ground that contained their summer home. By the following year, Sadler sold the two tracts of ground consisting of nearly 250 acres to his brother Dr. Horace

Sadler.[16] Over the next few years, Horace bought and sold surrounding ground, which included the sale of Rose Balcony in 1925.[17]

During this time, he began to develop the grounds of, Allenberry, which included the construction of a caretakers house known as "White House" and remodeling the old bank barn into a place where they could entertain.[18] Overall, he had done a considerable amount of work to make it a place they could enjoy when they were away from Thornwald.

Above: The Mansion House at Allenberry, circa 1900, during the time it was owned by the Boslers. The Mansion House was just one of the many buildings that made up Dr. and Mrs. Horace Sadler's summer estate.

Bottom Right: A modern day photograph of the Mansion House

Photos courtesy of Charles Heinze

Chapter 14

The Final Years of Justice Sylvester Sadler

During the first few years that Dr. and Mrs. Horace Sadler lived at Thornwald, they continued to share the mansion with Sylvester although he was often away in Philadelphia. However, just as his oldest brother, Wilbur Jr. had done when he lived in New Jersey so Sylvester, too, returned home on various occasions to be with his family. However, in August 1928, Sylvester did not return home to visit his brother, but this time to attend the funeral of his beloved mentor and friend, William Trickett.

For over fifty years, Trickett practiced out of the Sadler and Sadler law firm along West High Street and even roomed there during his final years on the first floor.[1] Trickett was a part of the Sadler family due to his close relationship with Wilbur Sadler and his son, Sylvester, whom he served as a mentor for during his years at the law school. Therefore, it came as no surprise that upon his death Trickett was buried beside the Sadler Mausoleum in Ashland Cemetery. Furthermore, Sylvester became the sole heir to his estate, which was valued at 126,399.04.[2]

Afterwards, Sylvester was chosen to fill the vacancy left by Dean Trickett as dean of the Dickinson Law School until 1930.[3] Presently, he served as president of the law school's Board of Incorporators, a position that he filled upon the death of his father in July 1920.[4] Prior to this time, he was deeply involved with the law school ever since he graduated in 1898 when he served as a professor of law at the school. In 1929, the law school dedicated the *Commentator* in his honor and further remembered the life of their former dean, William Trickett.[5]

During this time, he maintained a busy schedule since he now served as both dean of the Dickinson Law School along with serving as justice of the Supreme Court in Philadelphia. His life was filled with both meetings and court cases and now he had little time to spend at Thornwald, although he did not serve as dean of the law school for long.

By 1930, Walter Harrison Hitchler was elected the new dean of the law school, and therefore, the weight that he had carried for the past two years was now lifted from his shoulders.[6] However, he continued to carry a "heavy case load" at the Supreme Court and therefore, his life now mirrored that of his siblings who too succumbed to being overworked.[7]

In December 1930, Sylvester came down with a cold, although he was unable to take a rest due to his duties at the Supreme Court. Instead of resting, he continued working as usual inside the courtroom and therefore, never fully recovered from his illness. By the following year, and with little improvement from his cold, he looked towards Thornwald in hopes of being able to recover.[8]

Thornwald indeed may have been the Sadlers last hope for recovery, since the mansion was secluded from the outside world along with being well ventilated. Both Wilbur and Lewis, Sylvester's two oldest siblings, had both sought Thornwald in their final days along with former Governor Fort of New Jersey who looked to Thornwald after suffering a stroke upon his arrival in Carlisle in April 1919. Each had his reasons for coming to the mansion in the woods, although, they did not recover. While Wilbur and Lewis died some days after their arrival, Fort went on to live nearly two more years before he passed away on November 17, 1920.[9] Now Sylvester, too, looked to Thornwald as his last resort.

On February 3, 1931, Sylvester's private chauffer, John Dysert, drove him home to Thornwald. Sylvester was hoping that with a little rest he would be able to return to his duties at the Supreme Court within a few days. However, instead of taking a rest he continued working out of his law office along West High Street. His brother, Horace urged him to rest, but Sylvester would not heed his advice. Shortly afterwards, his cold reemerged, and therefore no more would he be seen outside the walls of Thornwald. This time he had to rest, and he knew it.[10]

Judge Sylvester Sadler in judicial robe. Photo by Ralph W. Johnston.

Cumberland County Historical Society, Carlisle, Pa.

He had come down with pneumonia, and for days, he lay in bed. Dr. H. A. Spangler, who had come to the aid of his brother Lewis during his final hours, now was also at Thornwald. However, little could be done, since the pneumonia had ravaged his ailing body. At 10:45 a.m. on March 1, 1931, Sylvester Sadler passed away at fifty-four years of age.[11]

Throughout the next two days, leading up to his funeral, which was to occur on March 4, 1931, *The Evening Sentinel* remembered the life of former county judge and Justice of the Supreme Court, Sylvester Baker Sadler. The paper regarded him as a member of "one of Carlisle's most distinguished families" along with a "most eminent member of the supreme bench" and how he "served on the local bench with much distinction" throughout his term as county judge.[12] Furthermore, his secretary J. Earl Quigley shared with the paper how he remembered Sylvester as being a generous man, and often gave "anonymous" gifts to charity.[13]

While *The Evening Sentinel* recounted his final hours at Thornwald for those who were unaware of his ailing condition, Horace grieved over the loss of his brother. He received several condolences in the mail, one that included a letter from Governor Pinchot.[14]

On the day of the funeral, the courthouse closed for the day, so county officials could attend the funeral of Justice Sylvester Sadler. More than two hundred people, including justices of the Supreme Court, attended the funeral that day. Inside the library, "profuse" floral tributes surrounded the mahogany casket along with the many volumes of books Sylvester had in his collection for the last fifty years.[15]

Rev. Dr. Glenn M. Shafer of the Second Presbyterian Church conducted the services that day. The pallbearers were justices of the bar, with the exception of Col. Thomas B. Kennedy Jr., who was president of the Pennsylvania Railroad. Afterwards, entombment took place inside the Ashland Cemetery where Sylvester joined his former loved ones inside the Sadler Mausoleum.[16]

Within a few days after the services, news carried as far as Gettysburg as to the value of Sylvester's estate. The *Gettysburg Times* declared that his estate was worth a mere "$750,000" which today would be equivalent to 10.6 million dollars.[17] Within his will, he included his chauffer, John Dysert, his secretary, J. Earl Quigley, and the servants' at Thornwald, Frank Gleim and Richard Grant. According to his will, Dysert was to be cleared of all debt, which included his house on Louther Street and receive $10,000. Quigley was to receive $50,000 worth of bonds at 5% interest, and both servants' at Thornwald were to receive $2,000 each.[18]

As for Dr. and Mrs. Horace Sadler, upon the death of Sylvester they received two plots of ground in Monroe Township from J. Earl Quigley, which further enlarged their Allenberry Estate.[19] Due to the death of Sylvester, and the inheritance left by his siblings who had passed away some years ago, Horace had inherited every penny.

At the time of his brother's death, Horace was unemployed. Unlike his siblings who worked all their lives to earn a living, Horace rarely worked. For nine years, Sadler was the manager of the Carlisle Standard Chain Company until it closed in March 1919.[20] Afterwards, for the next several years he went unemployed and therefore fell back on the Sadler-Bosler inheritance. Then in 1933, during the midst of the Great Depression, he went back to work. This time he got a job working as vice president of the Farmers Trust Company where his brother, Lewis Sadler, had served as the banks president for nearly ten years.[21]

Following the death of Sylvester in March 1931, Horace donated a number of books from his brother's voluminous book collection to the nearby Cumberland County Historical Society. The books consisted of local histories along with books written on the state of Pennsylvania and New Jersey.[22]

Three months later, in June of that year, Horace became president of the Dickinson Law School's Board of Incorporators, therefore filling the vacancy left by his brother. During this time, he had an artist from Virginia by the name of Miss. Fletcher, draw four self-portraits. Each of the three self-portraits was of Wilbur Fisk, Sylvester, and Lewis Sadler with the fourth being of the law school's former dean, William Trickett. Each of the men had played an intricate part in the law school over the years with William Trickett and Wilbur Sadler being at the forefront in the reestablishment of the law school. On November 6, 1931, Horace Sadler presented the portraits to the Dickinson Law School, which were then hung inside the lobby of Trickett Hall.[23]

Pictured above left is Wilbur Fisk Sadler, followed by his son, Sylvester Sadler, above right, and William Trickett, bottom left. Not pictured, is the painting of Lewis Sadler, which is no longer owned by the law school, location unknown. Photographs from slides

Courtesy of the Penn State University Dickinson School of Law

Chapter 15

The Final Years at Thornwald

A view of Thornwald, from the front lawn, as it appeared in 1935.

Cumberland County Historical Society, Carlisle, Pa.

    Throughout their final years together, Dr. and Mrs. Horace Sadler enjoyed the tranquility of Thornwald although it was no longer spelled as, "Thornwold". There is little known as to the change in the spelling, although one individual whose father had known of the Sadlers claimed the spelling had come about after Mrs. [Helen] Sadler had sent invitations out to a number of guests who were to come to "Thornwold" for dinner. Upon receiving the invitations, back from the company who had printed the invitations she was awestruck at seeing that "Thornwold" was spelled as "Thornwald", and from then on, the mansion was presumed have been spelled as "Thornwald".[1]

    During this time, they no longer lived at Thornwald year round like Mr. and Mrs. Lewis Sadler had done in years prior. Instead, the couple now spent their winter months in Florida. There they lived out their time at the Breakers Resort Hotel located in Palm Beach wining and dining amongst the wealthy.[2] In February 1935, the *Palm Beach Daily News* reported that the couple was among the guests who attended

The rear entrance of Thornwald as it appeared in 1935. The gentleman posing in the photograph is Frank Gleim, Dr. and Mrs. Horace Sadler's chauffeur.

Cumberland County Historical Society, Carlisle, Pa.

Side view of Thornwald taken in 1935.
Frank Gleim, standing next to the main entrance, poses for the photograph.

Cumberland County Historical Society, Carlisle, Pa.

DEALER ACCUSED WITH NEGRO BUTLER

Charged by Police with Receiving Stolen Goods

C. P. Parsons, proprietor of a second-hand store at 46 West Louther Street, was charged with receiving stolen goods in an information made this afternoon by Chief of Police Harvey Kuhns before Justice of the Peace Frank M. Fasin.

Parsons bought hundreds of pieces of china, glass and silverware stolen by Richard Grant, a butler, from the home of his employer, Dr. Horace T. Sadler, of Thornwald and Allenberry. Grant was arrested last week and later most of the stolen articles were recovered at Parsons' store.

The merchant, giving police every assistance, frankly admitted buying countless articles of tableware from Grant in the past year but denied knowing they had been stolen.

The Evening Sentinel,
14 January 1935

Enlarged photo of Sylvester Sadler's monogram "SBS", that appeared on his sterling silver hand mirror with floral design.

Cumberland County Historical Society,
Museum Collection, Carlisle, Pa.

a luncheon at the Beach Club that was hosted by Mr. and Mrs. Howard Garmany of the "Breakers".[3] That year, the couple was happy to get away from Thornwald. Just a month prior to them leaving for Florida, they had discovered that their butler had stolen a number of precious valuables, including silverware and glassware, from the mansion.

Prior to 1930, Frank Gleim was the only individual who worked for the Sadlers often driving them around town and escorting them to and from, Allenberry. However, by 1930, the couple hired a "negro butler" named, Richard Grant.[4]

Grant was in his early thirties at the time of hire and previously worked many years for the Pennsylvania Railroad.[5] Upon his employment at Thornwald, he did not move into the mansion despite the servants' quarters on the third floor. Instead, just like a number of the men who came to work at Thornwald, he resided at his residence located at 211 North Pitt Street in Carlisle.[6] During his first year working for the distinguished couple, he often worked at both Thornwald and Allenberry and by the following year in March 1931, he inherited a considerable amount of money upon the death of Sylvester Sadler.[7]

Upon his death, both Frank Gleim and Richard Grant received a large sum of $2,000 each, which today would be equivalent to nearly $27,000.[8] The inheritance was large, and therefore it was not long until Grant found a way to make even more money. Both Dr. and Mrs. Horace Sadler were among the wealthiest couple in all of Carlisle, and the interior of Thornwald boasted with an array of fine china, silver and glass wares, which just a few years later began to disappear from the mansion.

During this time, the couple was too busy to notice that their butler, Richard Grant was taking their precious valuables from the mansion and trading them in for cash. Throughout 1934, Grant made off with a number of silver and glass wares and took them down to Parson's furniture store along Louther Street. However, Parson had no idea that the wares had come from Thornwald nor did he recognize the monogram on the silver that bore witness that it belonged to Dr. and Mrs. Horace Sadler.

For nearly a year, the theft went unnoticed. Then in January 1935, a woman who was shopping at Parson's store recognized the monogram on a piece of silverware, which she believed to belong to Dr. and Mrs. Horace Sadler. Immediately, she made a trip to Thornwald to confront the couple about the possible theft. Upon discovering that a piece of silverware had made its way outside the walls of Thornwald, Horace immediately contacted the Carlisle police.

Soon afterwards, on January 10, 1935, Richard Grant was arrested. According to the *Gettysburg Times,* the total amount of items stolen from Thornwald was valued at "$7,000" or $108,000 today.[9] After apprehending Grant, police took action on Mr. Parson's, who had dealt the valuable goods along Louther Street. Although Grant no longer worked at Thornwald, Frank Gleim continued to work for the Sadlers for the next fifteen years.[10]

By 1935, Dr. and Mrs. Horace Sadler were married for over twenty-five years. Horace was now fifty-eight years of age and Helen was sixty. Outside of Thornwald, Horace remained working as vice-president of the Farmers Trust Company, while Helen stayed at home in the company of their English Springer Spaniel.

During this time, they rarely held large dinners, such as Lewis Sadler had done in previous years. However, on May 2, 1935, the couple took the opportunity to entertain a "number of prominent persons" at Thornwald who were in town for the inauguration of Dickinson College's twentieth president, Dr. Fred P. Corson.

Among the guests who attended that evening, included U.S. Senator Lester J. Dickinson of Iowa and Harry P. Fletcher of Greencastle. Fletcher was chairman of the Republican National Committee and was slated to give a speech at the student celebration for Dr. and Mrs. Fred Corson, the following day. At this time, Thornwald was also home to their "house guests", Justice John W. Kenhart and his wife, who were also in town for the inauguration.[11]

Although the galas at Thornwald were few in between, the couple often enjoyed entertaining their close friends, which included but not limited to, Mr. and Mrs. Ephraim Adams, William Fetter, Dr. E. J. Plank and Mr. and Mrs. Henry Line.[12] While at Thornwald, the men often spent their time playing poker inside the library. In the summer of 1935, Ivan Carter, a Carlisle photographer, even took pictures of Dr. Sadler and his friends playing poker at Thornwald.

Although poker was a big hit at Thornwald, what the couple may have enjoyed most of all was giving their guests a grand tour of the mansion, which often included retelling stories of how Lewis Sadler had entertained a number of distinguished men at Thornwald during his time as state highway commissioner.

Dr. Sadler's dog

Pennsylvania Historical and Museum Commission, Pennsylvania State Archives

MG-329 Ivan Carter Collection, neg._1470

The following photographs were taken by Ivan Carter on May 22, 1935 at Thornwald, and are the only pictures that exist of the interior during the time it was owned by the Sadlers.

Seated left to right are Dr. Horace Sadler, Dr. Edward Roberts Plank and William J. Fetter. Note the revolver on the table.

Cumberland County Historical Society, Carlisle, Pa.

Seated left to right are Dr. Edward Roberts Plank, Dr. Horace Sadler and William J. Fetter.

Pennsylvania Historical and Museum Commission, Pennsylvania Archives, MG_329 Ivan Carter Collection, neg._1391

Seated left to right are Ephraim L. Adams, Dr. Horace Sadler, and E. Sheaffer.

Cumberland County Historical Society, Carlisle, Pa.

Seated left to right are Dr. Horace Sadler, E. Sheaffer, and Ephraim L. Adams.

*Pennsylvania Historical and Museum Commission, Pennsylvania Archives,
MG_329 Ivan Carter Collection, neg._1395*

In the winter of 1940, Mr. and Mrs. Henry Line got an opportunity to have their tour of the mansion. Line had fixed a number of clocks for Dr. and Mrs. Horace Sadler, which included a grandfather clock at Allenberry. Just a few weeks prior to their arrival, Line had sent the couple a bouquet of flowers. Upon them receiving the flowers, they called him at once and asked if he would come to Thornwald for a visit and bring his wife.[13]

That evening Mr. and Mrs. Henry Line were given "a nearly complete tour" of the mansion, which at the time was elegantly decorated for Christmas. During their tour he had the opportunity to ride a machine which simulated horseback riding in the upstairs "exercise room" and hear stories of how Lewis Sadler had entertained the governors from across the United States in 1920 at the mansion. Although there were a number of stories that were told that evening, the most amusing story was hearing how the intoxicated guests would ride the elevator "almost to death", which was quite understandable considering how the elevator serviced all four floors.[14]

During their tour that evening, Mr. and Mrs. Henry Line were shown the rathskeller. According to Henry Line, the rathskeller was "the most impressive thing at Thornwald". Upon concluding their tour for the evening, the couple was given a bottle of "pre-World War I Highspire Whiskey" which was considered by Line to have been "the best rye whisky that had ever been produced in Pennsylvania" during that time.[15]

Mr. and Mrs. Henry Line were not the last to be entertained at Thornwald. Throughout the next ten years, the couple would continue to entertain their many friends at the mansion.

During this time, on April 1, 1944, they sold their fifty-seven acre Allenberry Estate, to Charles Heinze.[16] The couple had enjoyed entertaining a number of their friends at Allenberry over the years although they were now in their mid-sixties and no longer held large gatherings at their summer home as they had in previous years. Nearly four years later, the couple would sell yet another piece of prime real estate, and this time it was Thornwald.

Both Dr. and Mrs. Horace Sadler had neither children nor heirs except for Helen's nephew, Frank C. Bosler Jr., who was the only surviving son of Frank and Elizabeth Swank Bosler.[17] Frank had moved to Wyoming some years prior to them selling Thornwald and currently owned the Old King Ranch, which consisted of nearly 40,000 acres.[18]

Since they could no longer keep Thornwald within the family, they sold the fifty-three acre estate in 1948 to the Old Folk's Home of the Potomac Synod-Reformed Church for $100,000.[19] Despite the sale, the couple continued to live out of the mansion for the next two years.

During this time, they spent their final years together as husband and wife. In May 1950, Helen became critically ill and shortly afterwards was admitted to the Carlisle Hospital. However, despite the medical treatment that she had received, she passed away on May 18, 1950, at age seventy-three.[20] Coincidently, she had spent her final hours at the Carlisle Hospital where her sister, Mary, also passed away in September 1916.

That day her obituary appeared on the second page of *The Evening Sentinel*. She was regarded by the paper as the youngest of the Bosler family along with having been a member of both the Second Presbyterian Church and the Carlisle Garden Club. That day a private funeral service took place at Thornwald and afterwards entombment occurred inside the Ashland Cemetery at the Sadler Mausoleum.[20]

Thornwold Sold For Church Home

Three synods of the Evangelical and Reformed Church have made arrangements to acquire "Thornewold," the 51-acre estate of Dr. and Mrs. Horace T. Sadler, for use as a home for the aged.

Charles R. Todd, Carlisle manufacturer and prominent layman of the church, who with John C. Wentzel, also of town, acted for the Potomac, Mercersburg and Southern Pennsylvania Synods in the local negotiations, said that no date for transfer of the estate has been fixed.

"Thornewold will remain the property of Dr. and Mrs. Sadler just as long as they wish to continue to reside there," Todd emphasized. "In the meantime the estate will be strictly private private property, just as it is now."

30 Rooms in House

The residence on the estate has 30 rooms. As a home for the aged it could easily accommodate 40 guests just as it is and an additional 20 guests with some inside changes, Todd said.

The estate, which is located on the southwest edge of town along the Walnut Bottom highway, and is shut off from the view of passersby by a high tapestry brick wall one-quarter mile long, was built 36 years ago by the late Lewis Sadler, highway commissioner of Pennsylvania under Gov. Sproul and a brother of the present owner. During Mr. Sadler's life many men prominent in state and national government, the late Boise Penrose and William Vare among them, were entertained there.

It has numerous lawns, gardens and woodland areas. In addition to the residence there is a caretaker's cottage and a five-car brick garage and maintenance shop.

The house, built of specially made tapestry brick 18 inches long and six wide, has four large porches. There is an elevator from basement to third floor. Some of the rooms are paneled throughout.

A visiting churchman who is in the construction business estimated that the residence would cost $760,000 to construct under present-day prices. He said the quality of many of the materials is unavailable today.

Three Synods Involved

Official name of the purchasing organization is the Old Folks Home of the Potomac Synod of the Reformed Church, which maintains a home for the aged at Hagerstown. The Hagerstown home also serves the Mercersburg and Southern Pennsylvania Synods.

Todd said that the three synods will continue to operate the Hagerstown institution. Plans to make a major addition to that home have been changed following decision to acquire Thornewold. The addition will be smaller than first planned.

It was reported that Dr. Sadler's decision to dispose of Thornewold was speeded by the assurance from the churchmen that the property will be substantially maintained in its present form and constantly kept in good order.

Several years ago Dr. and Mrs. Sadler disposed of their other large estate, Allenberry, near Boiling Springs.

The Evening Sentinel, 9 July 1948

Chapter 16

The End of an Era

Following his wife's death, Horace left Thornwald for the Breakers Resort Hotel in Palm Beach, Florida where he stayed for "several weeks".[1] Upon returning home to Carlisle, he packed his bags and moved out of Thornwald and thereafter the estate was overseen by his caretaker, "Stence Miller".[2]

Thereafter, he rented an apartment at 28 South Pitt Street, which was not far from his former home. Coincidently, Joseph Noble, the same man who had sold Lewis Sadler the forty-six acre lot of ground inside Noble's woods in 1909, once owned the home.[3] However, no longer was the home owned by Noble and instead was now home to the Farm Bureau Insurance Company along with Fashion House Women's Clothing. Dr. Sadler along with George Ritter, were tenants inside the home and lived on the second floor overlooking the hustle and bustle of South Pitt Street.[4]

Noble House at 28 South Pitt Street in Carlisle, c. 1910. Photo by A. A. Line.

Cumberland County Historical Society, Carlisle, Pa.

Photograph of Dr. Horace Sadler at age fifty-nine taken on May 21, 1935 by Ivan Carter.

Pennsylvania Historical and Museum Commission, Pennsylvania Archives, MG-329- Ivan Carter Collection, neg_1378

James "Stence" Miller, observing a birdhouse on the grounds of Thornwald in May 1953. Photo by James Steinmetz.

Cumberland County Historical Society, Carlisle, Pa.

The Sadler Curtilage   *Postcard from author*

For the next three years, Horace lived out of his apartment along South Pitt Street. During this time, he witnessed the construction of the Sadler Curtilage, which was built next to the Dickinson Law School in 1952 as the student dormitory. The dormitory was built in honor of his father, Wilbur Fisk Sadler, who played an influential role in the reestablishment of the law school in 1890.[5]

That year, in December 1952, Horace also got the opportunity to be interviewed by John Vernon Hertzler, Jr., who was currently in the process of writing a booklet about Thornwald for the First Reformed Church of Carlisle.

The purpose of the booklet was to give members of the church an inside look at the history of Thornwald including the layout of the "thirty-nine rooms".[6] Furthermore, it would be the first glimpse inside the mansion since *The Evening Sentinel* gave its readers an inside look during construction on August 16, 1910.

Left: The cover of "Thornwald" by John Vernon Hertzler, Jr. Copy of the booklet is located inside the "Thornwald" drop file at the Cumberland County Historical Society, Carlisle, Pa.

The rear entrance of Thornwald, as it appeared on May 27, 1953. Photo by James Steinmetz.

Cumberland County Historical Society, Carlisle, Pa.

    On December 29, 1952, Hertzler walked the grounds of Thornwald and furthermore was given a grand tour of the mansion by Mrs. James Dewalt. On the outside, Thornwald had changed little although it was now overgrown by a number of trees along with climbing ivy. However, despite its present appearance, the grounds were still enhanced with beauty.
    A number of walking paths still wound through the endless woods leading up to the main entrance which was "surrounded by beds of ivy, holly and rhododendron". Where once was located the nine-hole golf course along the Walnut Bottom Road now was a large open lawn that was bordered by "numerous beds of forsythia, peonies, and sweet peas". Dotting the landscape were also "statues of little elves and gnomes" along with a bronze statue that was transformed into a fountain.[7] The statue, known as "The Offering", was sculpted by Grace Neal in 1921 and sat directly in front of the main entrance overlooking the mansion.

Side view of the rear entrance of Thornwald, as it appeared on May 27, 1953. Photo by James Steinmetz.

Cumberland County Historical Society, Carlisle, Pa.

Main entrance of Thornwald as it appeared on May 27, 1953. Photo by James Steinmetz.

Cumberland County Historical Society, Carlisle, Pa.

Side view of the main entrance showing the vine clad walls. Photo taken on May 27, 1953 by James Steinmetz.

Cumberland County Historical Society, Carlisle, Pa.

Grounds of Thornwald as seen from the loggia on May 27, 1953. Photo by James Steinmetz.

Cumberland County Historical Society, Carlisle, Pa.

The main entrance gateway as it appeared on May 27, 1953, looking from the Walnut Bottom Road.
Photo by James Steinmetz.

Cumberland County Historical Society, Carlisle, Pa.

Left: The gnomes that were located along the outside loggia.

Below: "The Offering" statue that overlooked the main entrance of Thornwald.

Photos taken on May 27, 1953 by James Steinmetz.

Cumberland County Historical Society, Carlisle, Pa.

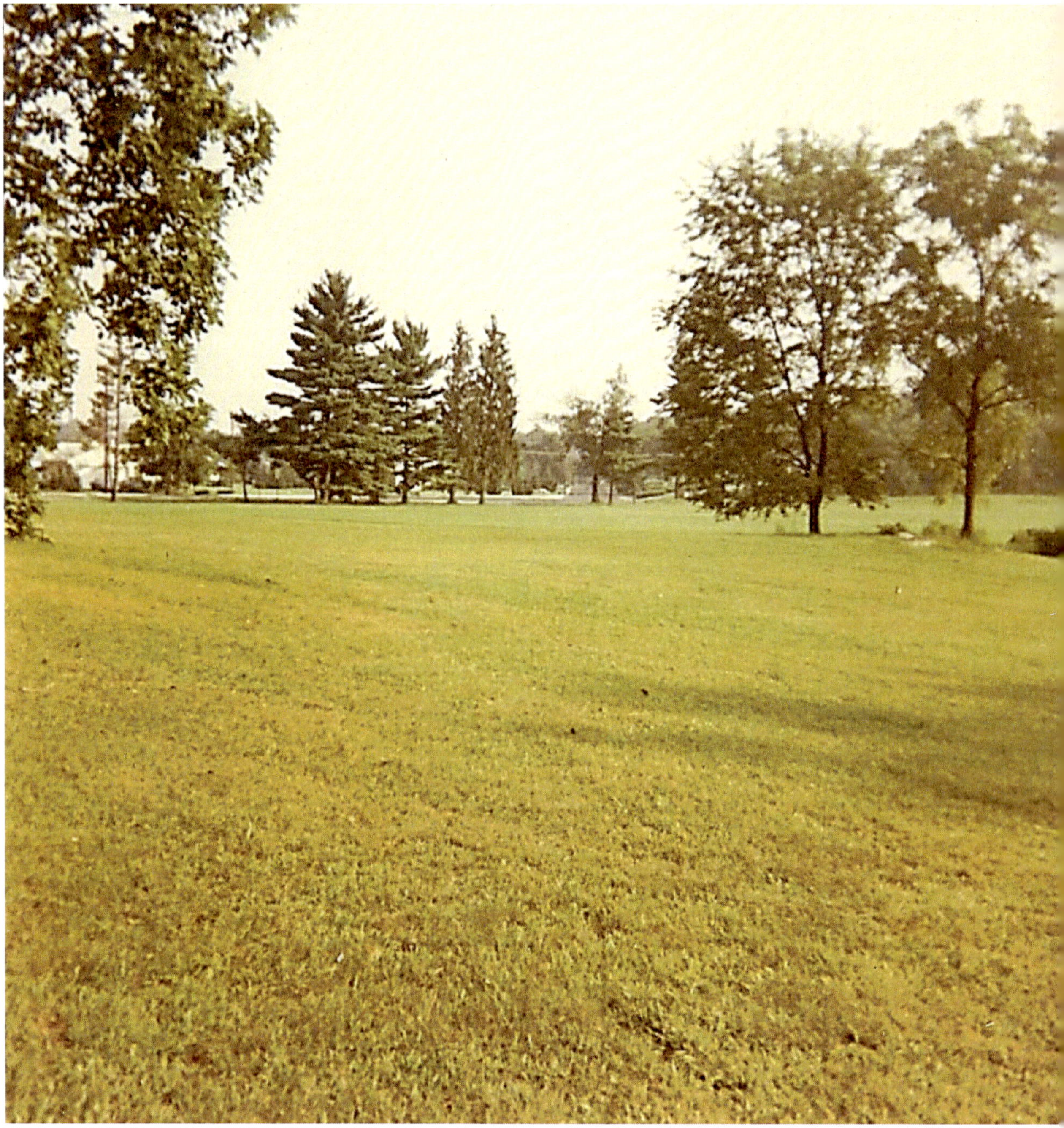

The large open lawn, which at one time boasted the nine hole golf course.
On the opposite page, behind the grove of pine trees, is the Walnut Bottom Road.

Courtesy of Thornwald Home

Above: The peony bushes in full bloom.

Right: One of the many flowerbeds at Thornwald.

Photos courtesy of Thornwald Home

One of the many walking paths that encompassed Thornwald.

Courtesy of Thornwald Home

View of the library as it appeared in 1954 facing the front lawn.

Courtesy of Homewood Retirement Centers

    While the grounds resembled "the estate of an English noble", the interior still boasted with a wealth of antique furnishings that gave Thornwald the appearance of a king's castle.[8] Upon entering the mansion, Hertlzer noticed the wealth of oil paintings that hung on the oak paneled walls in the main hall. Two of the oil paintings that were located in the main hall were done by the "renowned artist, Jonas Lie". At the top of the grand staircase, there were also two more oil paintings, one known as "The Valley of the Durdent" by Julien Depré and the other by Bernard De Hoog, known as "A Humble Interior".[9]

    As Hertlzer walked into the library, he could not help but notice the "richly carved fireplace with hugh black andirons" along with the oil painting "of a seventeenth century gentleman" which was "inset within a highly carved oak panel". Covering the floor was a "red oriental rug" that sat directly in front of the fireplace. According to Hertzler, the rug was valued at "$3,000".[10]

    Inside the reception room or what was now known as the "music room" were a number of "french-styled chairs" that were placed around the room.[11] At one time, a Steinway player piano graced the room, which Mrs. Helen Sadler enjoyed showing their guests how it could play all on its own.[12]

    Down the hall, inside the dining room, was a large "mahogany table to which belong twenty Chippendale chairs" and located on one side of the room were "two mahogany buffets" each bearing "three stirling silver candlesticks".[13] The candlesticks in the room were just one of several pieces of sterling silverware in the mansion. At the time, pieces included everything from "silver carving sets and serving pieces" to "silver ramekins" and "Sheffield candlesticks". Besides the silverware, there was also an abundance of fine china stacked away in the "dressers" of the butler's pantry pieces such as "Minton",

View of the library as it appeared in 1954 facing the rear lawn.

Cumberland County Historical Society, Carlisle, Pa.

"Rose Canton", "Villeroy", "Bach", "Copeland", and "Meissen" along with numerous pieces of fine glass and silverwares. Certainly, there was enough dishware to entertain hundreds of guests at Thornwald.[14]

Even the second floor contained several pieces of furniture, everything from the "mahogany luggage carrier" to the "walnut and mahogany night tables" and the several "Sheraton Carved High Poster Beds".[15] While a number of pieces had come from Europe, those in the master bedrooms had come from Russia.[16]

The master bedrooms had changed very little from the time when Mr. and Mrs. Lewis Sadler had lived at the mansion, and even Mrs. Sadler's former bedroom still contained the feminine charm. Her bedroom was the only evidence of a woman living in the mansion, except for the downstairs music room. Everywhere you looked, there was no evidence that a woman had lived in the mansion since the interior of Thornwald was completely masculine in design. According to Hertzler, Mrs. Sadler's bedroom was known as the "Queen Anne Room" due to "the lampshades bearing a Queen Anne's lace design".[17]

Up on the third floor, the guest rooms and servants' quarters also contained a variety of antique furniture. It is likely, that since the rooms were rarely occupied that Dr. and Mrs. Horace Sadler may have used the rooms for storage. Despite the rooms on the third floor, the gymnasium contained numerous pieces of exercise equipment including "rowing machines, power driven bicycles, two horses, punching bags, archery set [and an] exerciser". Adjacent to the gymnasium was the billiard room, where a "Brunswick-Balke collender Combination Pool and Billiard table" still sat directly in the middle of the room.[18]

Besides the numerous pieces of furniture that adorned the mansion, even the rathskeller was not overlooked. According to Hertzler, the rathskeller was "the most unusual of all the rooms at 'Thornwald'". Located in the center of the room was a "long table" that was surrounded with a number of chairs and adorning the table and the ledges around the wall were a number of "German steins". Overall, Hertzler believed the rathskeller was "a comfortable, informal room highly reminiscent of the famous German rathskellars" and certainly, it was.[19]

Although Hertzler had received the grand tour that day in December 1952, he was still not finished writing his booklet on Thornwald. Therefore, it would be several months until the citizens of Carlisle could finally read for themselves what was hidden behind the walls of Thornwald all these years. However, Horace would never get the chance to read Hertzler's "Thornwald" although he already knew for himself all about the mansion both inside and out.

On February 27, 1953, Dr. Horace Sadler passed away inside his apartment along South Pitt Street in Carlisle at seventy-three years of age. The following day his obituary appeared on the fourth page of *The Evening Sentinel*. In comparison to his brothers' obituaries, his was short and to the point and did not include a great deal of detail in regards to his final hours nor did it include where the funeral services would take place. However, the paper did herald him as one of Carlisle's "most wealthiest men" and remembered him as being "generous" and one whom did not "seek credit" for his financial contributions to the community.[20] Furthermore, the paper told how he enjoyed following the construction of old buildings and was responsible for the election of Fred S. Reese as judge of Cumberland County a few years ago.

Days later, a private funeral took place, although it did not occur at Thornwald. Instead, the funeral services took place at the J.R. Shulenberger Funeral Home in Carlisle.[21] Afterwards, entombment took place inside the Ashland Cemetery at the Sadler Mausoleum. All four members of the Sadler family, Wilbur Jr., Lewis, Sylvester, and Horace died in the order in which they were born with Wilbur Jr., the first-born, who died in 1916, followed by Lewis in 1922, Sylvester in 1931, and now Horace in 1953.

Upon his death, he left $10,000 to Miss Ruth Hemminger of the Farmers Trust Company and "the proceeds of an insurance policy" to his neighbor, Mrs. Gladys Ritter. Within his will, he also included his caretaker, John X. "Stence" Miller, and his former chauffeur, Frank Gleim, both of whom received $10,000, which they would each receive at $100 a month. While these individuals received a considerable amount of money upon his death, neither one was named the sole beneficiary.[22]

When Dr. Sadler first drew up his will on July 1, 1951, he carried out the wishes of his brother, Sylvester Sadler, who had passed away in 1931.[23] According to Sylvester's will, if Horace was deceased prior to 1931, he wished for the Farmers Trust Company to pay income to the Carlisle Hospital.[24] Therefore, when Dr. Sadler drew up his will in 1951, he kept his brother's wishes in mind by creating what he called the "Sadler Foundation".[25]

For many years prior to his death, Dr. Sadler had served on the Carlisle Hospital's Board of Trustees and prior to his wife's death in 1950; the couple had made financial contributions to the hospital. Once in September 1934, Dr. and Mrs. Horace Sadler contributed $5,000 towards an addition to the hospital's annex.[26] In addition, they were also known to contribute money towards the purchase of an x-ray machine.[27]

Now, in 1953, the hospital had received its largest contribution. This time, the money was in the form of a trust, which was under the management of, Fredrick J. Templeton.[28] At the time of Dr. Sadler's death, the amount of the trust was estimated between four and five million dollars and today helps fund the Carlisle Area Health & Wellness Foundation.[29]

A few months passed after the death of Dr. Horace Sadler, and now Thornwald stood as a lasting monument to the citizens of Carlisle of the Sadlers contributions to the community and their impact on the states of Pennsylvania and New Jersey. Although the Reformed Church had purchased the fifty-three acre Thornwald Estate some years ago, upon Sadler's death in February of that year, all debt was to be cleared and therefore the church ended up paying less than $40,000 for the estate.[30] Included with the sale were the numerous furnishings that still adorned the mansion. One individual who walked through the mansion during this time remembers seeing everything in its place from the dishes in the butler's pantry to the pool table still on the third floor.[31] However, just three months later the Reformed Church scheduled an auction to sell several items from the mansion.

Sadler Will Creates Foundation To Pay Income To Hospital

Visiting Nurses Association To Share in Bequest; Estate Estimated at $4,000,000

The Carlisle Hospital was named chief beneficiary in the $4,000,000 estate of Dr. Horace T. Sadler, under terms of his will which was probated this morning in the office of Register of Wills Luther M. Bectem.

Dr. Sadler, who died unexpectedly Feb. 27 at his home, 23 South Pitt Street, created the Sadler Foundation from which Carlisle Hospital will annually receive 90 per cent of the income from the trust fund which will be administered by the Farmers Trust Company as trustee. The remaining 10 per cent of the income from the trust fund will go to the Visiting Nurse Association.

The income that the hospital will receive annually will amount to approximately $100,000, while the Visiting Nurses Association is expected to receive around $10,000 annually under the terms of the will to which five codicils were written. The will was drawn up July 1, 1951.

Miss Ruth Hemminger, of the Farmers Trust Company, was bequeathed $10,000 outright. Gifts of $10.00 each were made to John X. Miller, North Bedford Street, and Frank Gleim, 133 F Street, former employes of Sadler. Their bequests will be made on a $100 a month basis, the will directs.

Mrs. Gladys Ritter, 23 South Pitt Street, was bequeathed the proceeds of an insurance policy.

Dr. Sadler's will directs:

Includes All Property

"ITEM 1. All of my estate, real, come from the said Sadler Foundation shall be distributed by my trustees from time to time as deemed necessary, in the following manner:

Divides Income

"Ninety per cent thereof for the upkeep and maintenance of the Carlisle Hospital; 10 per cent for the employment of visiting nurses under the direction of the Carlisle Hospital, who shall furnish assistance to those residing in Carlisle and vicinity who may be deemed worthy and to be in need; the said assistance to be furnished in the homes of the patients and to include the necessary medical and other supplies for those who are ill or disabled and dependent and whose care has been delegated to the nurse or nurses so selected. It is not my purpose to provide pen-

---

Left: *The Evening Sentinel*, 6 March 1953

Bottom: Carlisle Hospital Board of Trustees, c. 1948. Dr. Horace Sadler is seated on the far left. Photo appeared in the July 1949 *Shuttle*.

Cumberland County Historical Society, Carlisle, Pa.

Chapter 17

The Sale of the Sadler Heirlooms

The largest auction to ever take place at Thornwald occurred on May 27, 1953. Prior to the auction, Dr. Sadler had stated in his will that he wished for the furnishings to be sold in "New York or Philadelphia" if "satisfactory prices cannot be obtained in Carlisle".[1] However, the church would have no trouble drawing antique lovers and treasure seekers to the auction.

The auction bill gave a detailed description of each item that was to be sold that day. The items ranged from several pieces of "antique and fine modern furniture", "antique imported china and cut glass" and early silverwares to "unusual bronzes", "brass and pewter wares", and "antique oriental rugs". Also listed in the sale bill, were a few paintings and engravings along with other "miscellaneous items" such as the exercise equipment from the gymnasium and the curtains that once adorned the mansion. Every item was to be sold that day, with the exception of those items that could be used "to the best advantage" by the nursing home.[2]

A day prior to the big sale, *The Patriot News* released an article giving the details of the sale from noting Paul Gilbert from Lebanon as the auctioneer along with the location of the auction which was to be held on the "south portico".[3] For those who did not get a glimpse of the auction bill, the paper also included a brief listing of some of the noteworthy antiques, which included:

> early inlaid Hepplewhite sideboard and chairs, a pair of Adams serving tables, early mahogany twin tables, a mahogany Sheraton sofa, a rare early inlaid mahogany Hepplewhite bow front chest of drawers, an old mahogany English sea captain's desk, early American Chippendale and Sheraton bureaus, a rare Hepplewhite corner cabinet and antique oriental rugs.[4]

Two metal ewers from Thornwald sold at auction on May 27, 1953. Photo by James Steinmetz.

Cumberland County Historical Society, Carlisle, Pa.

Announcing The Public Auction of

The Rare Antique Furniture, Fine Oriental Rugs, Quality China and Glassware and Modern Furnishings

of The Horace Sadler Mansion and now the property of "The Homewood Church Home" — Sadler Unit of The Evangelical Reformed Church

Sale to be held at the Residence at the edge of town in Carlisle, Penna., along Route No. 33 or better known as the Walnut Bottom Road.

SALE TO BE HELD

Wednesday, May 27, 1953

beginning at 10 A. M. DST. and continuing until all is sold.

NOTE: The furnishings to be sold are the original furnishings of the large thirty room Sadler Home and they are being sold, as they cannot be used to best advantage in the home. This goods is of the finest quality and you will not be disappointed as there will be plenty of fine merchandise and we would like to sell it all.

Cut shows the entrance to the Sadler's Unit Home at Carlisle, Pa., now the property of the Homewood Church Home, Inc., of the Evangelical and Reformed Church.

ANTIQUE AND FINE MODERN FURNITURE

ANTIQUES—Early English Walnut Server or Hunt Board with solid walnut top over three long drawers and small cupboard doors with neat vase and ring turned legs and stretcher base, 6' long. Rare Early Adams Carved Mirror with urn and floral design at top and repeated floral design on the frame. Old English Mahogany Chippendale Credenza with two small and one long drawer in top part and with carved marlborough legs on the base. Gilt Oval Wall Mirror with raised leaf scrolls and blossom design. Pretty Ivory and Gold Decorated Living Room Suite, consisting of a Sofa, Two Arm Chairs and Three Side Chairs with cane panels and needle point seats.

Early Inlaid Hepplewhite Sideboard and Hepplewhite Chairs, Pair Adams Serving Tables

Antique Hepplewhite Inlaid Buffet with brass rail gallery around the solid top, with front having drawers and doors, all with pretty satin wood line and oval inlay on the tall square tapered legs, 71½" long. Old Mahogany English Large Tilt-Top Table with wide inlayed band on top and bulbous turned pedestal with four scroll legs that have line inlay and brass castored end. Five Matching Inlaid Mahogany Sheraton Dining Chairs, Two Arm and Three Side Chairs, lattice type open slat backs with satin wood inlays and square tapered legs with spade feet, slip seats covered in figured gold damask. Inlayed Mahogany Empire Sideboard with solid top, short backboard and full open center front, each side has one small drawer over two paneled doors, carved bracket type feet. Pair of Fine Adams Type Carved Mahogany Serpentine Front Serving Tables with carved aprons and square tapered legs. Antique English or Italian Carved Cassone or Chest on frame of walnut wood with nice stretchered base. Rare Long Early English Oak Carved Chest with pretty carved urns and scrolls on the front, sides and the hinged lid.

Early Mahogany Twin Tables, Chests of Drawers, Tables, Chairs, Sofas, Etc.

Pair of Antique Sheraton Mahogany Dining Tables with full swell fronts and with reeded turned legs, about 45" x 75", open and in the rough. Early Antique English Mahogany Bow Front Chest with four long drawers that have lion head brasses and short shaped seat with early solid ends. Early Mahogany Shaving Mirror with arched top holding a mirror and ogee type base having six small drawers with neat scroll feet.

Antique Mahogany Hepplewhite Fold Top Card Table with square tapered legs. Several Early English Yewwood Windsor Armchairs with bowed backs, and broad shaped saddle seats with cabriole type legs. Pair of Inlayed Adams Type Cane Seat Side Chairs with urn splat in back. Early English Walnut Poudre of Dressing Table with double hinged lid enclosing a dressing cabinet with one drawer below and neat shaped legs with stretchers. Early English Swell Front Dresser with mirror and inlayed posts, two small over three long swelled drawers with solid ends over cutout feet. Fine Mahogany Sheraton Sofa with nicely arched back, fluted bulbous turned arm supports and eight turned reeded legs, upholstered in rose damask. Two Early English Oak Bannister Back Chairs with cutout tops, paneled backs with carving, valouted arms and neat turned legs with stretcher bases, early 1700 period. Rare Early Inlayed Mahogany Hepplewhite Bow Front Chest of Drawers, two small swell front drawers over three long with holly line inlay and oval brasses, inlayed shell on the cutout skirting. Oval Gilt on Wood Wall Mirror with raised floral festoons.

First page of the four-page auction bill, which gave a detailed description of the items that were to be sold that day. Sale bill found in the "Thornwald" drop file at the Cumberland County Historical Society, Carlisle, Pa.

{ 173 }

An 1886 bronze bust of Bismarck that was sold at auction on May 27, 1953.
Photo by James Steinmetz.

Cumberland County Historical Society, Carlisle, Pa.

Two bronze figures, sold at auction on May 27, 1953.
Photo by James Steinmetz.

Cumberland County Historical Society, Carlisle, Pa.

A signed, Charles Cumberworth bronze statue that was sold at auction on May 27, 1953. Photo by James Steinmetz.

Cumberland County Historical Society, Carlisle, Pa.

A circa 1880 bronze fountain entitled "Fontana delle Tartarughe". The fountain was modeled after the one built by Giamco della Porta, and sculpted by Taddeo Landini, in Rome, Italy in 1580. In 1999, a similar fountain sold for a whopping $9,944 at Christie's auction in London. Photo by James Steinmetz.

Cumberland County Historical Society, Carlisle, Pa.

On the day of the sale in May 1953, the first floor of the mansion was turned into a showroom. Every item was put on display for the auction, and therefore a number of the rooms were emptied, including the library, which was the location of the Sadlers exhaustive book collection. Since the book collection was to remain inside the library, the bookcases were emptied on the day of the auction to make way for the many pieces of silverware and glassware that were to be sold that day. After the sale, the several items that remained, such as the Sadlers book collection, were put back in place by the nursing home.

In the above photograph, Urie Lutz, standing left, and Glenn Todd, right, of the Homewood board of trustees, observe one of the many bronze sculptures that were up for auction on May 27, 1953. Located on either side of the mantle, are two silhouette portraits, which according to the auction bill; one was signed "T.R. Knox, Carlisle", and the other "Rev. V. E. Thom, Carlisle".

Photo taken on May 27, 1953, by James Steinmetz
Cumberland County Historical Society, Carlisel, Pa

Sadler Family Possessions Go Under Hammer at Thornwald Auction

An estimated 1,500 to 2,000 persons, some purchasers and many just curious about the palatial home of the well-known Carlisle family gathered on the tree-shaded lawn of the estate yesterday for a day-long auction of rare furnishings, china, silver and rugs. Here Auctioneer Paul K. Gilbert cries the wares from the mansion's west portico. The sale will resume this morning at 10 a.m. and continue until the last of the treasured possessions are gone.

Photograph and caption taken from the May 28, 1953 Harrisburg *Evening News*

On the morning of Wednesday, May 27, 1953, cars drove into Carlisle from nearly five different states to get a front row parking spot at Thornwald. A number of parking attendants directed the cars that day to their designated parking spot on the front lawn of Thornwald. Those who were anxiously waiting for the auction to begin that morning could also enjoy a bite to eat from the Reformed Church's refreshment stand.

By the start of the auction that morning, approximately two thousand people were roaming the grounds of Thornwald.[5] Some were there to buy while some were there to get a sneak peak at the inside of the mansion. Among the people that day, was James Steinmetz, who was inside the library taking pictures of some of the bronze sculptures that were to go up for sale that day. Also at the auction, was a reporter from *The Evening Sentinel*, who was gathering the full details for the following day's paper.

The auction began promptly at ten o'clock that morning on the outside porch, located to the left of the rear entrance. From that location, Lebanon auctioneer, Paul K. Gilbert, auctioned off the items. The items that day may have went cheap for some, but other items such as the fine oriental rugs fetched between $200 and $500 dollars (2010: $1,611.47-$4,028.67). A Borglum bronze bust went for $195 (2010: 1,571.18) while eight Chippendale chairs fetched $372 (2010: $2,997.33). However, the highest priced item of the day was a "Sarouk rug with rose field and large blue medallions and colored floral and banded borders" measuring 13' by 20' which sold for $920 (2010: $7,412.76).[6]

During the auction, there were several people taking their precious items out to their car to be taken home with them. Certainly, there was plenty of hustle and bustle by noon that day. So much so, that a reporter from *The Evening Sentinel* recalls having seen a woman carrying a glass, fish aquarium out to her car when one of the glass panels slipped out and crashed to the ground. By days end, the Homewood Church Home made "$13,000" (2010: $104,745.55) from the sale that day.[7]

Despite the sale in June 1974, a few of the heirlooms still remained inside the new Homewood Church Home. Pictured left is one of two paintings by Jonas Lie, which at one time hung inside the main hall of Thornwald and were later owned by the nursing home. However, today only this one still belongs to the present day, Thornwald Home, and hangs inside a residential lounge.

Photo by author

    However, after the sale had ended that day there were still several items left inside the mansion. Therefore, the following day, a second auction was held at Thornwald. *The Evening Sentinel* ventured to guess that the total amount raised that day would be between "$3,000 or $4,000 more" than the total of $13,000 brought on the previous day.[8]

    Although a majority of the items were sold over the course of the two day auction, there were still several items left inside the mansion. Such items included oriental rugs, oil paintings, along with numerous pieces of furniture, glass and silverwares, and the Sadlers book collection, all that became property of the Homewood Church Home.

    Despite the large sale in 1953, it certainly was not the last sale of the Sadler heirlooms. Nearly twenty years later in 1974, Homewood vacated Thornwald and moved into their newly built nursing facility, which today is known as Thornwald Home. Thereafter, a number of the heirlooms along with various pieces of furniture that had come out of the mansion were auctioned off on June 8, 1974 at the new nursing home.[9]

    However, despite the sale, the Sadlers book collection remained inside the library of Thornwald along with other heirlooms that were left behind, therefore becoming the property of the Carlisle Area School District, who had purchased the estate in April 1972. Sometime after 1973, the "1,300 or so books" were taken out of the library and stored in the Carlisle junior high school.[10]

    The books were in perfect condition at the time and almost appeared as if they were not read.[11] The books included numerous works by both English and British novelists and poets along with books on American and European history. Some of the books were even inscribed, such as *Poems of Jean Ingelow*, which was inscribed with the message "Minnie Bosler from Uncle Herman, Christmas 1888".[12]

    In the fall of 1977, the books were sold by bid at a silent auction that was run by the Carlisle Area School District. This was the last auction of Sadler heirlooms, although over the next few years a few pieces would show up at local auctions, such as those that were sold at auction in 1983.[13] However, today it is a rarity, such as the pair of bronze andirons that were sold at Cordier's Auction in May 2010.

    For several years, the andirons adorned the fireplace inside the library and remained there even during the time that it was run as a nursing home. However, sometime after the nursing home moved out of the mansion, the andirons were sold at auction in 1983, before being sold at Cordier's Catalog Auction in Camp Hill on May 23, 2010. That day, the pair of andirons fetched $2,100, which was more than what the Sadler heirlooms brought at the sale in 1953. Furthermore, the pair of andirons served as a sample of the fine furnishings that once adorned Thornwald.

On the preceding pages, are a few items that came from the Thornwald Mansion. Today the items are owned by Thornwald Home, unless otherwise noted.

Photos by author

The grandfather clock that was sold at auction in 1974. Today the clock sits inside the main lobby of Thornwald Home.

The statue that at one time overlooked the Thornwald Mansion, was previously owned by Thornwald Home.

A signed portrait of Abraham Lincoln by William Bicknell, which was printed for members of the Bibliophile Society. Mary Bosler Sadler was a member of the Boston, Massachusetts, Bibliophile Society.

One of two Wilcox candelabras

Circa 1940, Old English Melon tea set

A Melford cup, made by Wallace

An unmarked serving tray

The andirons and the fireplace set at one time were located inside the library at Thornwald.

Courtesy of Thornwald Home

The fireplace set that was once located inside the library at Thornwald. The fireplace set was made by the William H. Jackson Company of New York, the same company who made the mantle for the second floor bedrooms.

The pair of bronze andirons that once sat inside the fireplace at Thornwald were sold at auction on May 23, 2010, for $2,100.

Courtesy of Cordier Auctions

Chapter 18

Homewood

View of Thornwald on March 6, 1954 with fire escapes. Photo by James Steinmetz.

Cumberland County Historical Society, Carlisle, Pa.

Upon Homewood acquiring the property in the spring of 1953, Thornwald was overgrown with a number of vines that clung to the sides of the mansion along with a number of overgrown shrubs and trees. During the final three years that Dr. Sadler owned the property, there was little done as far as maintaining the grounds. However, upon Homewood acquiring the property, a number of the shrubs and trees were cut away and once again, Thornwald boasted with life although the grounds were not the only area to receive special attention. During this time, the mansion underwent a $25,000 renovation to make it fit for the approximately "25 guests" and staff.[1]

Prior to Dr. Sadler's death, plans were already drawn up for a pair of fire escapes along with three pairs of "smoke screens" and two stairwells that were installed on the second floor, further bringing the building up to code.[2] Over the next few months, a number of men worked at making the necessary renovations to the mansion, and by the end of September 1953, the mansion was fit for occupancy although now it took on a different appearance.

Above: Postcard of the Homewood Church Home
Below: Homewood Church Home sign located along Walnut Bottom Road

Courtesy of Thornwald Home

First Floor

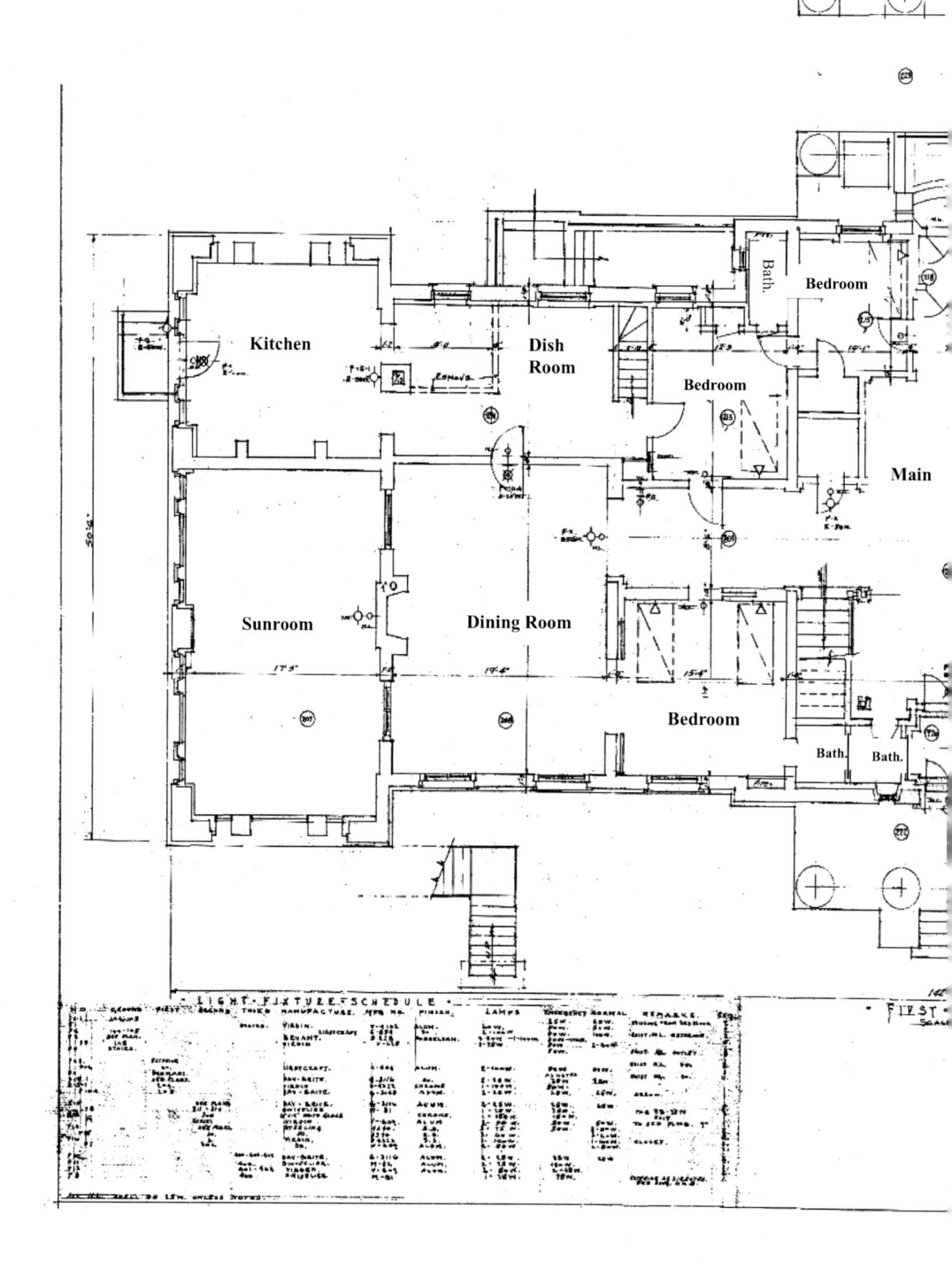

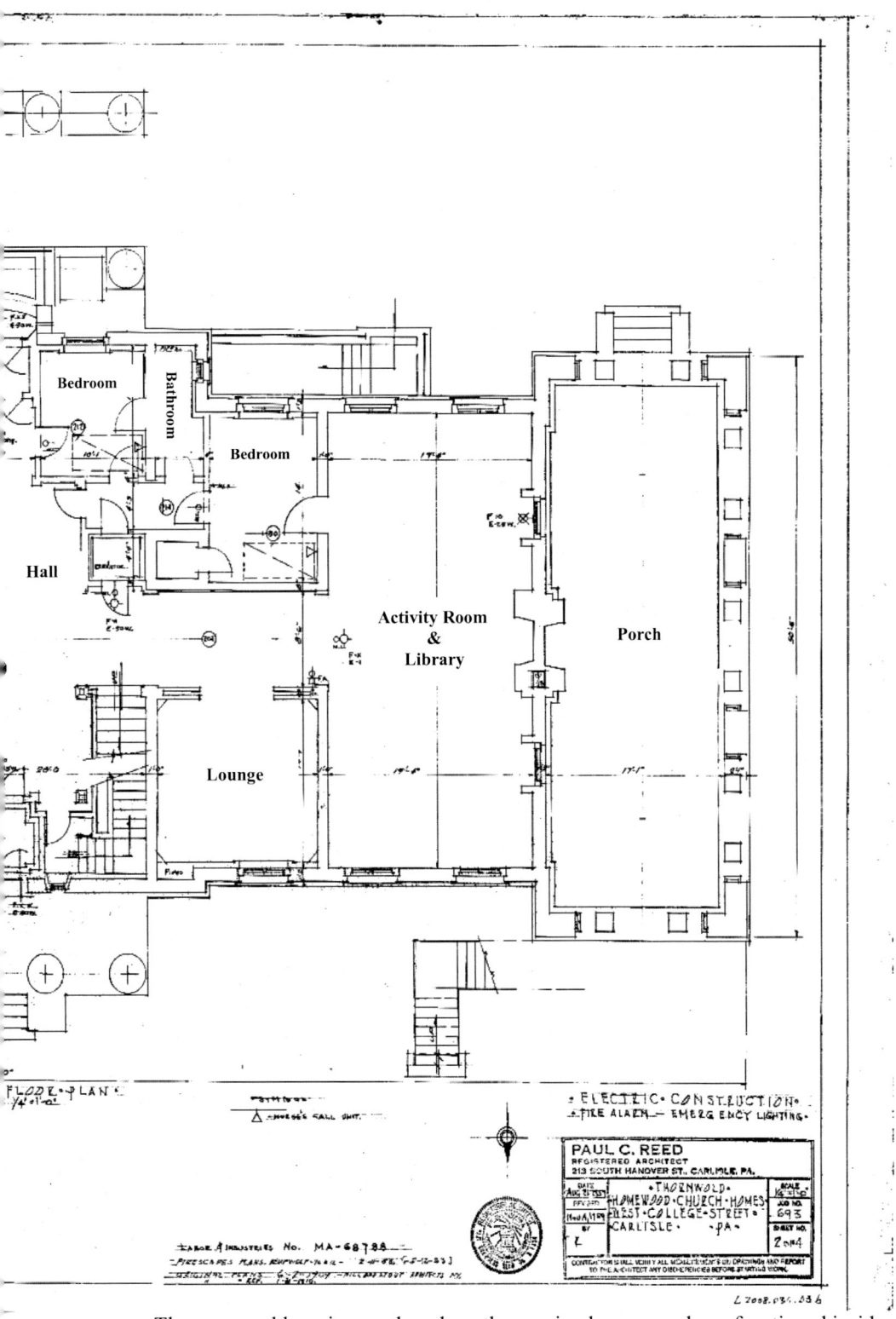

There are no blueprints to show how the nursing home may have functioned inside Thornwald, during its first few years, other than those drawn by Paul Reed in August 1959, when the mansion underwent a second renovation. Rooms labeled to show how the first floor functioned at the time of the nursing home. (For 1909 blueprint, see pages 66-67).

Cumberland County Historical Society, Carlisle, Pa.

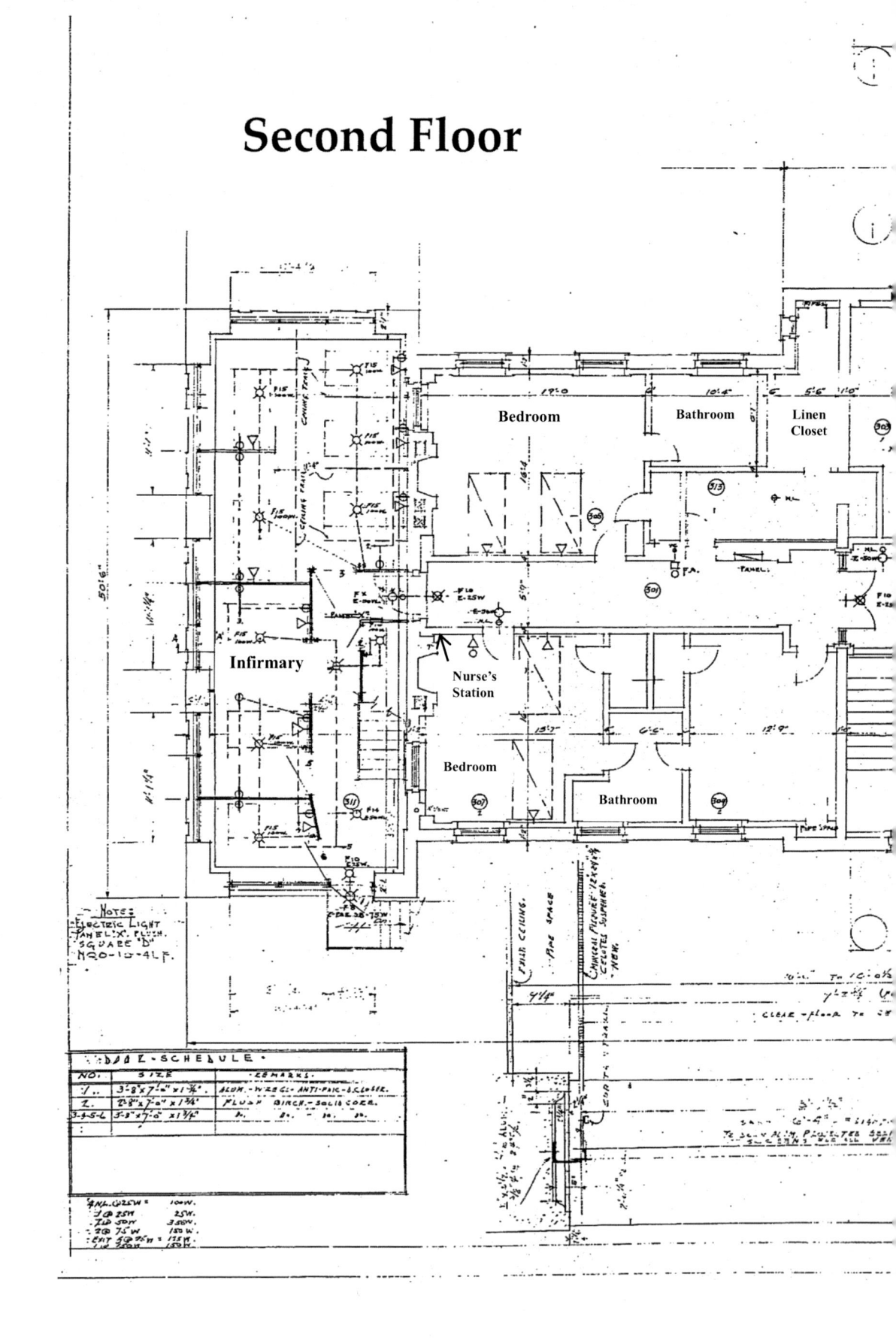

Second Floor

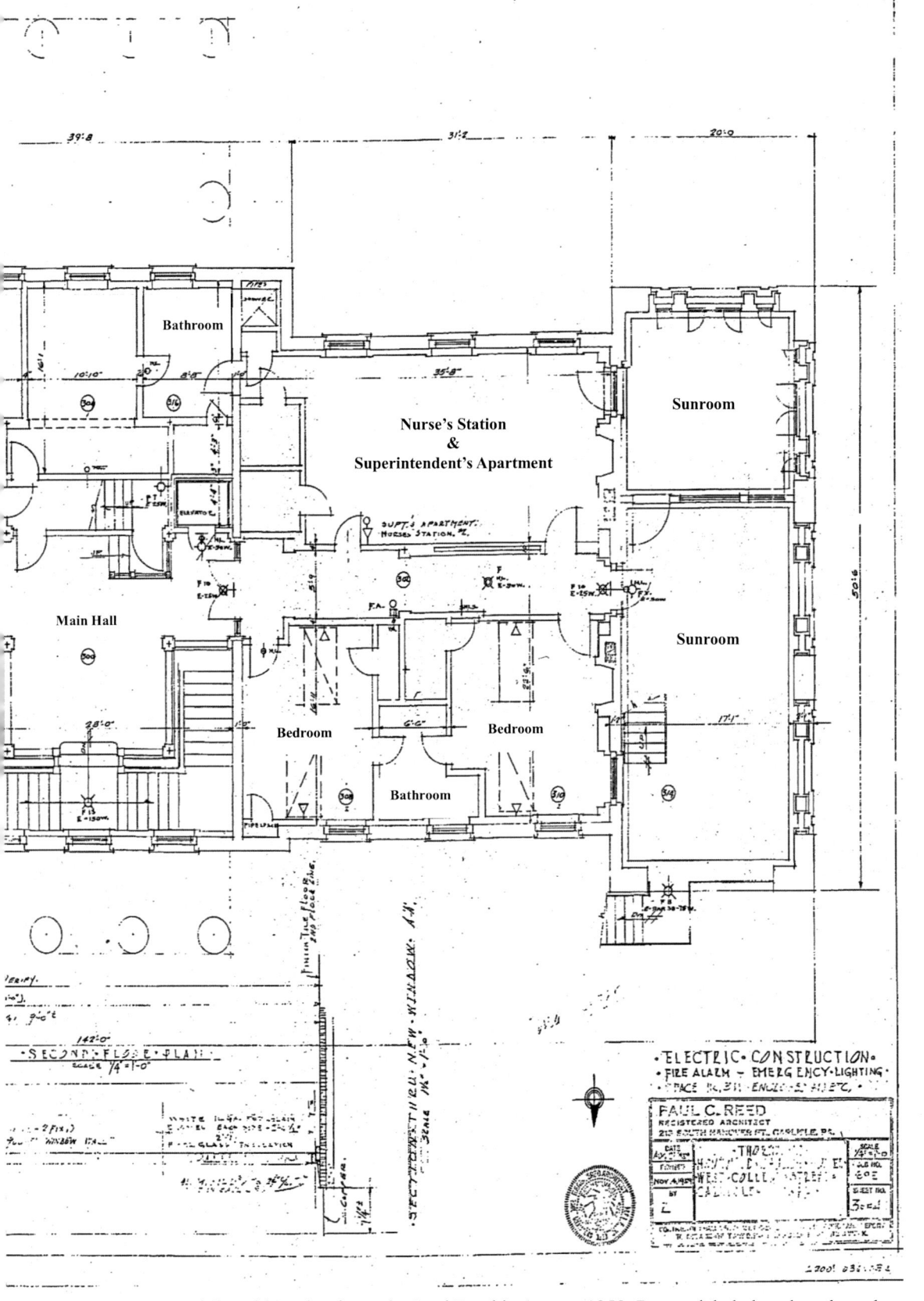

Second floor blueprint drawn by Paul Reed in August 1959. Rooms labeled to show how the second floor functioned at the time of the nursing home. (For 1909 blueprint, see pages 84-85).

Cumberland County Historical Society, Carlisle, Pa.

Third Floor

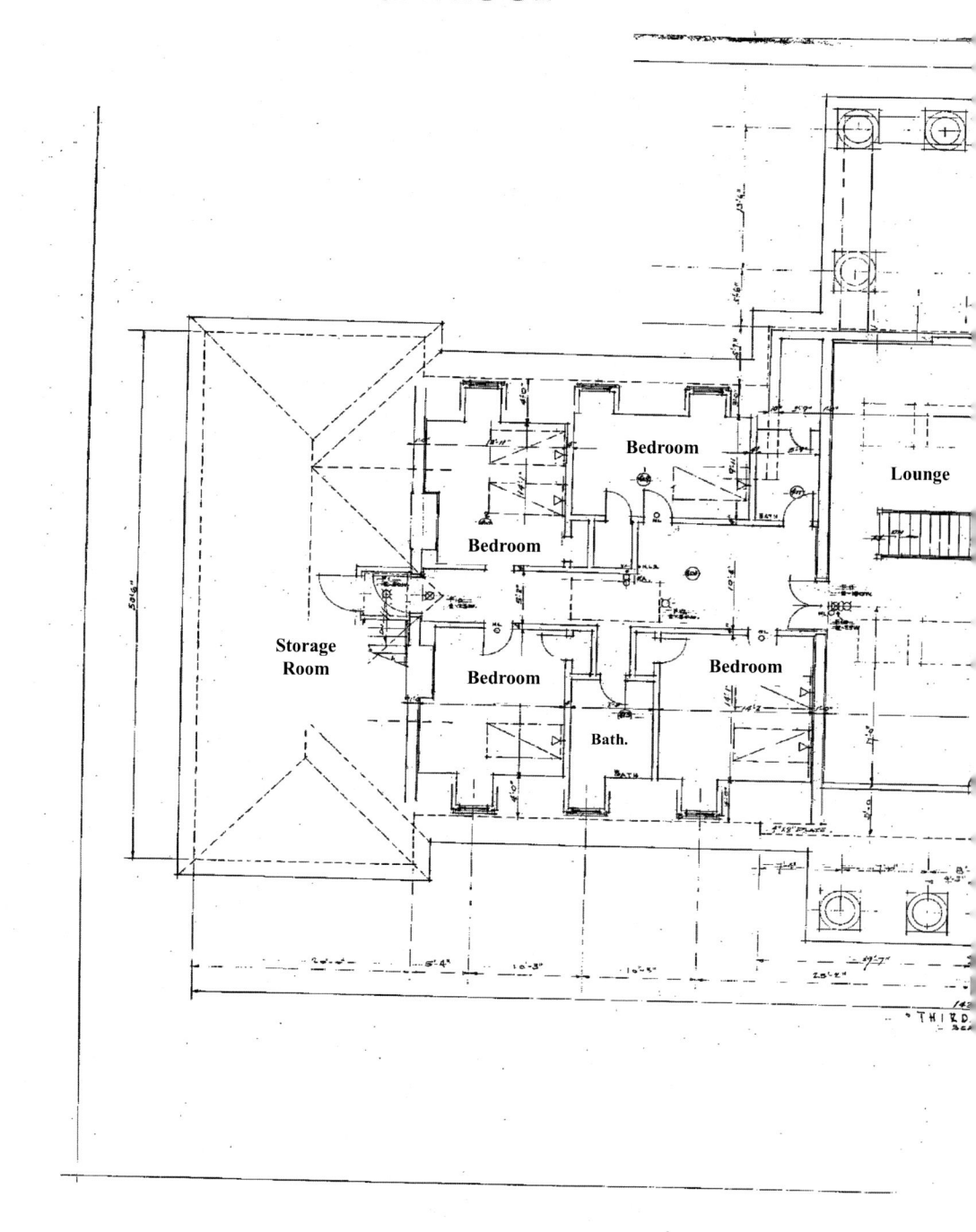

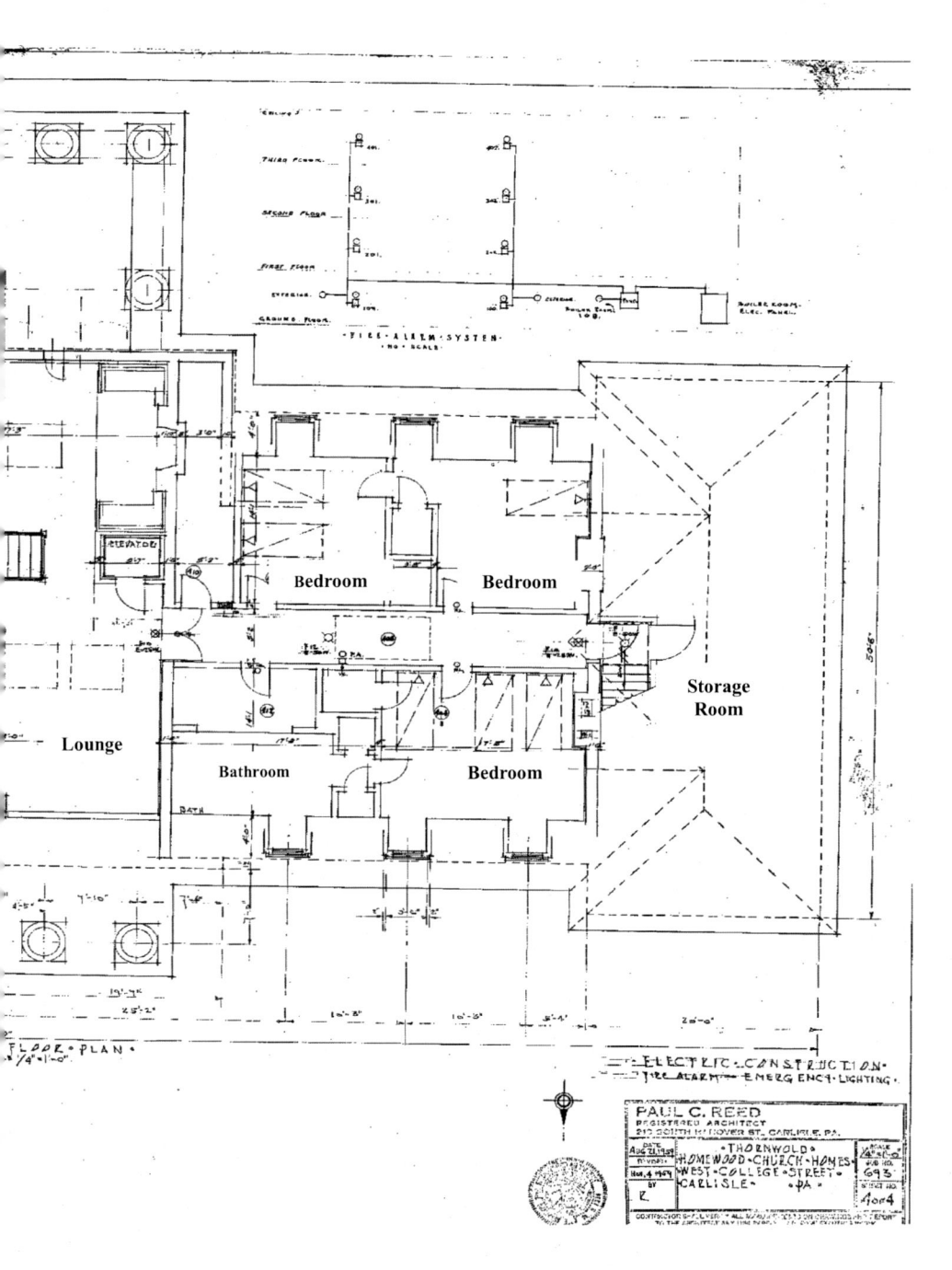

Third floor blueprint drawn by Paul Reed in August 1959. Rooms labeled to show how the third floor functioned at the time of the nursing home. (For 1909 blueprint, see pages 90-91).

Cumberland County Historical Society, Carlisle, Pa.

On the first floor, the main hall still contained a floor of parquetry although in later years it was covered in gray carpet. While some of the rooms on the first floor were left untouched, the ladies and men's dressing rooms, Mr. Sadler's office, the servants' dining room, and breakfast room were later turned into bedrooms. While the first floor had undergone few changes, the second floor, which was once the location of Mr. and Mrs. Lewis Sadler's master bedrooms and additional bedrooms, underwent extensive renovations.

A view of the library from the main hall as it appeared in 1973. To see how it appeared in 1954, see pages 168-169 in this book. Note the items, in the above photograph, which were once owned by the Sadlers, and were just a sample of the fine furnishings that still adorned the mansion.

Courtesy of Thornwald Home.

Where once was the long hallway, which ran the entire length of the house, now were a pair of double doors known as "smoke screens" that divided the hallway into two corridors. Besides the pair of double doors there was also another set of doors located at the bottom of the stairwell leading up to the third floor directly in front of what once was Mrs. Sadler's den.

Although a number of the rooms retained their original appearance, both of the master bedrooms along with the loggias at either end underwent extensive renovations. Mrs. Sadler's former bedroom now was home to a nurse's station and a supervisor's apartment, while Mr. Sadler's former bedroom was turned into a double room.

At either end of the second floor, each of the screened in loggias now contained a staircase that led up to the third floor. In later years, they were enclosed with each serving a specific purpose. The loggia, located in the west wing, functioned as a sunroom while the loggia adjacent to the bedrooms in the east wing, was turned into an "infirmary".[3]

A view from the hallway looking towards the west wing. The set of steps to the left in the photograph led to the third floor.

Courtesy of A. Keating.

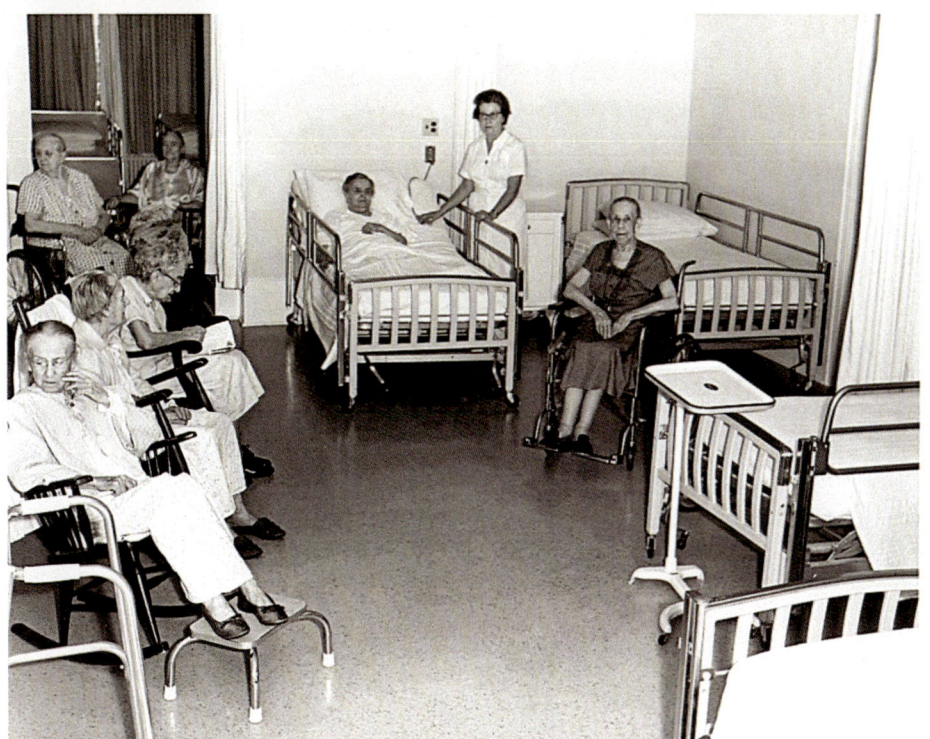

A section of the infirmary

Courtesy of Homewood Retirement Centers

While the second floor had undergone extensive renovations, the third floor underwent few changes. The former billiard room and gymnasium were left untouched and now were used as a lounge. Located on either side of the lounge were a total of seven bedrooms, three double and three single and one room that contained three beds. Despite the location of the bedrooms in the mansion, the residents' of the home preferred sleeping on the third floor rather than the second floor.[4]

Bible study

Courtesy of Homewood Retirement Centers

The residents of Homewood spending their leisure in the former billiard room. Photo taken by James Steinmetz on February 12, 1957.

Courtesy of Homewood Retirement Centers

On September 30, 1953, the first "guests" arrived at Thornwald or what was now known as the "Sadler Unit" of the Homewood Church Home. In later years, Homewood simply referred to it as the "Sadler Home". That day, they enjoyed their first meal inside the dining room and later got their picture taken inside the library with Superintendent Rev. Mark Wagner and his wife, along with Mrs. James DeWalt. DeWalt served as both the caretaker and housekeeper of the nursing home.[5]

The following day, three more women entered the mansion although they were not the last to call the mansion their home. Upon the nursing home being dedicated on October 17, 1953, there were "nine guests" inside the mansion, and ten years later, the count would climb to thirty-five.[6]

Sara M. Isenberg, age 100, from Christ Church, Altoona, is greeted by Mrs. Susan May, resident supervisor, upon her admission to the Sadler Home on May 15, 1963. Her photo appeared in the 1963 issue of "Homewood Fireside".

Courtesy of Homewood Retirement Centers

GUESTS ARRIVE AT THORNWOLD HOME

Reformed Church Unit Has Capacity of 25

The first guests at the new home of the Reformed Church, the Thornwold Unit of the Homewood Church Home, arrived yesterday and three more are expected today.

The first guests to occupy the Thornwold Unit, former home of the late Dr. Horace T. Sadler, are Mrs. Elizabeth M. Rauhauser, Grace E. McElroy and Mrs. Grace Aust, all of York, and Minnie McMullen, Shippensburg.

The guests expected to arrive today are Mrs. Laura Nofsinger, Harrisburg, widow of Fred Nofsinger, late of Carlisle, and Mary M. Spangler and Ella Musser, both of York.

The home, which has been redecorated and on which fire escapes have been installed, has a capacity of 25 guests. The home is sponsored by the three synods of the Reformed Church and part of a fourth synod. They are Mercersburg, Potomac and Southern synods, and the Juniata area of the Pennsylvania Synod. The home is a unit of the Homewood Church Home, Hagerstown, Md.

Rev. Mark G. Wagner is superintendent of the home, while Mr. and Mrs. James L. DeWalt, Carlisle, are serving as caretaker and housekeeper. The local trustees, who also served as a committee in the supervision of the renovation are Glenn Todd, Crie D. Lutz and John Wentzel.

CARLISLE, PA., THURSDAY, OCTOBER 1, 1953

THE FIRST GUESTS OF THORNWOLD unit of Homewood Homes, Reformed Church, are shown here with Rev. Mark G. Wagner, the superintendent, and Mrs. James DeWalt, upper right, the housekeeper. They are left, Minnie McMullen, Shippensburg; Grace McElroy, Mrs. Elizabeth M. Rauhauser and Mrs. Grace Aust, all of York.
— Photo by Jas. F. Steinmetz Studio.

Above: Article and photograph taken from *The Evening Sentinel*, October 1, 1953. Photo by James Steinmetz.

Right: A photograph of Mrs. Elizabeth M. Rauhauser of York, which appeared in the Harrisburg *Evening News* on October 1, 1953. Rauhauser was one of the first guests inside the new Homewood Church Home. In the above photograph, she is standing next to Mrs. DeWalt, second from right.

FIRST GUEST AT NEW CHURCH HOME—About to cross the threshold of Thornwald, new unit of the Evangelical and Reformed Church home for the aged at Carlisle, is Mrs. Elizabeth M. Rauhauser, 75, of York, at left as she is greeted by Mrs. James L. DeWalt, matron.

★ ★ ★

Dedication Day

October 17, 1953

Courtesy of Homewood Retirement Centers

On the day of dedication, a bronze plaque honoring Dr. and Mrs. Horace Sadler was placed just outside what was now used as the main entrance.

The plaque read as follows:

In Appreciation To

Dr. And Mrs. Horace T. Sadler
Whose Generosity Helped Make Possible This
Sadler Unit Homewood Church Home, Inc.
Evangelical And Reformed Church

Dedicated To The Glory of God
For The Care Of The Aging

October 17, 1953

*Photos courtesy of
Homewood Retirement Centers*

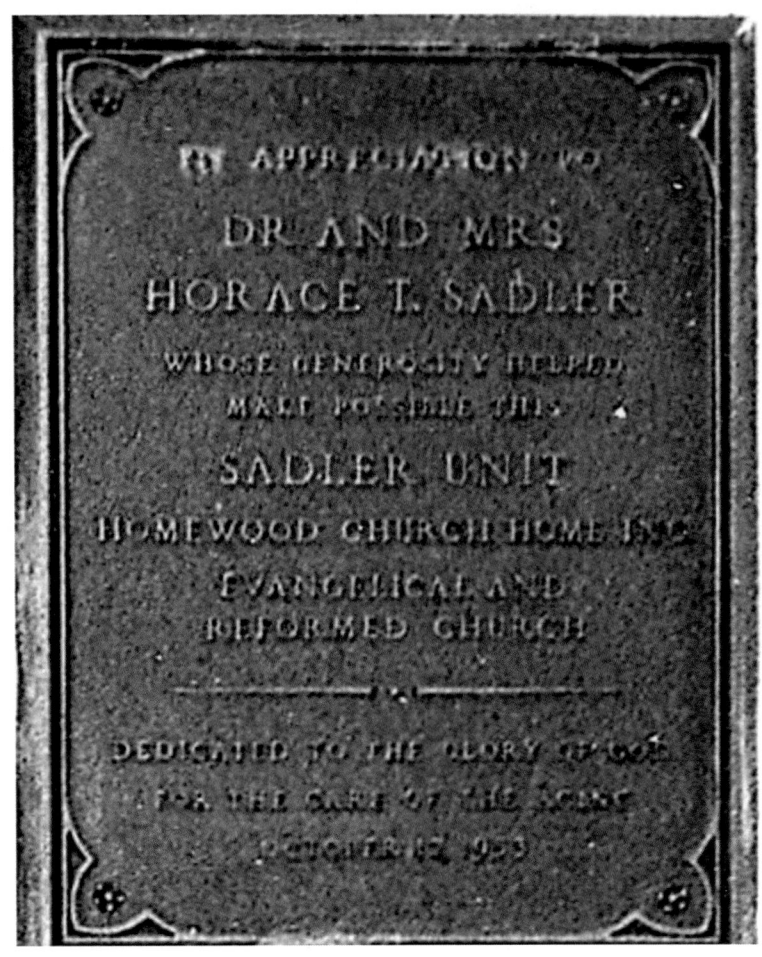

The rear entrance of Thornwald as it appeared in March 1954. Photo by James Steinmetz.

Cumberland County Historical Society, Carlisle, Pa.

The rear entrance of Thornwald as it appeared in March 1954. Note the porch located off of the kitchen and the large open porch on the second floor. By 1960, the second floor porch was renovated into an infirmary. Nearly ten years later, a small building was constructed adjacent to the kitchen along with a ramp that connected to the former conservatory. The ramp made the home handicap accessible, and was yet another step towards bringing the mansion up to code. Photo by James Steinmetz.

Cumberland County Historical Society, Carlisle, Pa.

During this time, Thornwald was once again filled with life. Like the Sadlers, who once lived at the mansion, the residents', too, dined in the dining room. Prior to arriving for their meals, they often sat in the chairs located in the main hall that where one of many pieces of Sadler heirlooms that were still in the mansion.[7]

When the residents' were not in the dining room they often spent their leisure either sitting outside, enjoying activities in the library or up on the third floor in the former billiard room and gymnasium. On occasion, they were even entertained by various clubs and organizations that came to the nursing home. Their many years inside the mansion were by far the happiest years since the Sadlers had called it their home.[8]

The residents' inside the dining room at Homewood in 1957.

Courtesy of Homewood Retirement Centers

A group of unidentified women of the Homewood Church Home washing dishes in the former butler's pantry. Photo taken by James Steinmetz on February 12, 1957.

Cumberland County Historical Society, Carlisle, Pa.

Three women of the Homewood Church Home polishing pieces of glassware inside the library.

Courtesy of Homewood Retirement Centers

Although a number of Sadler heirlooms were sold at the gigantic auction on May 27, 1953 a number of pieces still adorned the mansion. In the photographs below, the paintings on the wall along with the oriental rug were just three of the items that at one time belonged to the Sadlers.

Three unidentified women of the Homewood Church Home spending their leisure in the upstairs main hall. Photo taken by James Steinmetz on February 12, 1957. *Courtesy of Homewood Retirement Centers*

Courtesy of Thornwald Home

One of the many oriental rugs that at one time adorned the mansion.

Courtesy of Thornwald Home

Memorable Moments at Homewood

Springtime

Above left: One of two flower boxes in full bloom, which were located beside the rear entrance. Note the bronze grate, located below the flower box. The pair of bronze grates protected the basement windows of the rathskeller, and were located on either side of the rear entrance.

Courtesy of Homewood Retirement Centers.

Above: A tulip bed located outside the former conservatory.

Left: A flowering bush that was located on the rear lawn.

Courtesy of Thornwald Home

The winter of 1965

Above: The rear entrance of Homewood

Left: A birdfeeder outside the former conservatory.

Courtesy of Thornwald Home

The "Offering" statue that overlooked the main entrance of Homewood as in appeared in the winter of 1965.

Courtesy of Thornwald Home

Christmas

A Christmas tree sitting inside the former main entrance.

Courtesy of Homewood Retirement Centers

Courtesy of Thornwald Home

Christmas 1966

Courtesy of Thornwald Home

Christmas 1969
Courtesy of Thornwald Home

A table located outside the library
Courtesy of Thornwald Home

The dining room fireplace

Courtesy of Thornwald Home

The Flood of 1972

The large open lawn, which once was the site of the nine-hole golf course, looked more like a lake following the wrath of hurricane Agnes in 1972.

Courtesy of Thornwald Home

For nearly twenty years, Homewood occupied the former Thornwald Mansion until 1971, when the state deemed the mansion "unsuitable for all types of patients".[9] Therefore, a new home had to be built. According to the *Patriot-News*, the "Homewood Church Home retained 10 acres of the 45-acre plot" and established what is known today as Thornwald Home, hence deriving its name from Lewis Sadler's stately mansion in the woods.[10]

Thornwald Home
442 Walnut Bottom Road
Carlisle, PA 17013
UNITED CHURCH OF CHRIST HOMES
"Home-Like Homes Near Home"

A 1980's postcard of Thornwald Home. The address label, located above the postcard, was inscribed on the back. Note the lampposts, in the postcard above, which lined the main driveway and parking lot of the nursing home. The lampposts were reminiscent of the ones that once lined the long road that led to Thornwald.

Postcard from author

Chapter 19

Thornwald Park

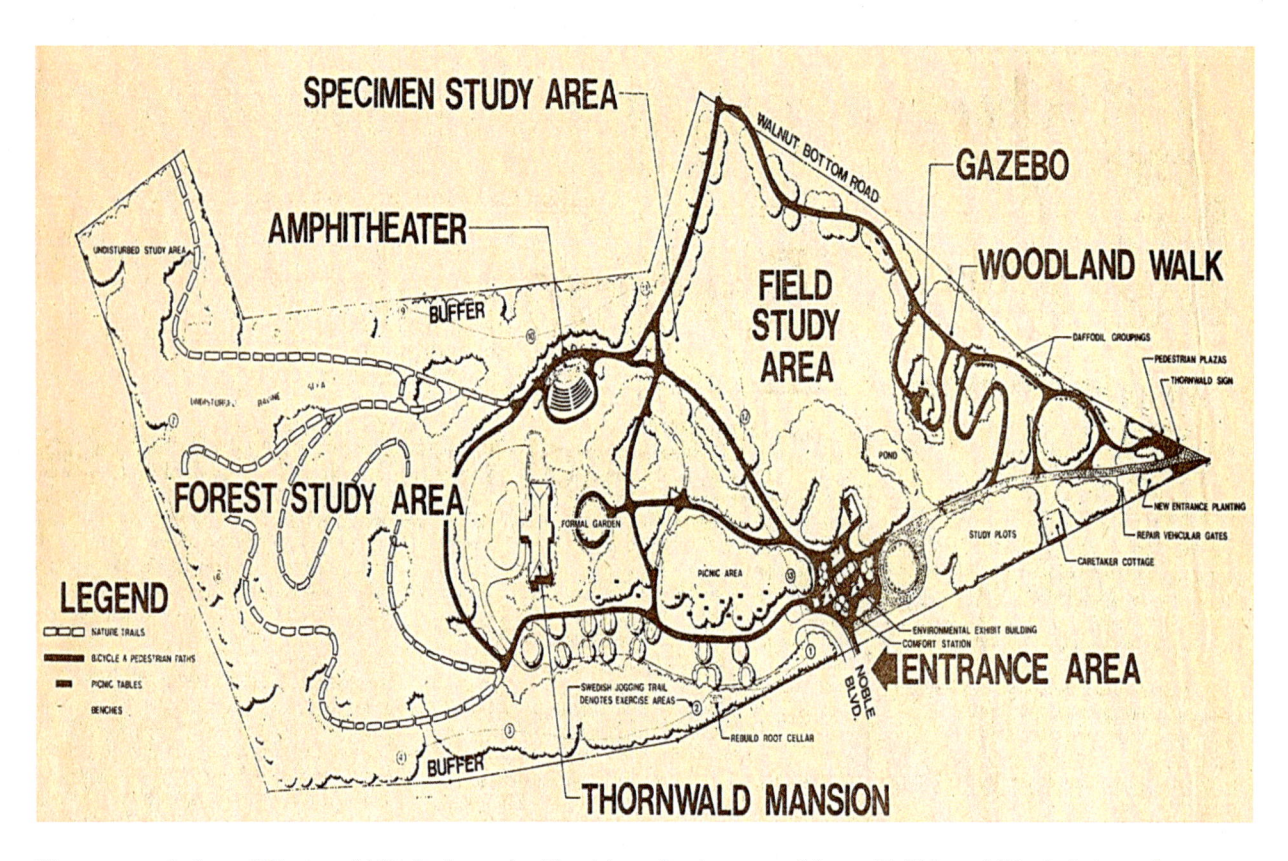

The proposed plan of Thornwald Park, drawn by Harrisburg landscape architects H. Edward Black & Associates. appeared in *The Evening Sentinel* on February 13, 1979.

On April 11, 1972, Homewood sold Thornwald and the surrounding ground to the Carlisle Area School District.[1] Despite the sale, Homewood continued to rent the mansion from the school district at $500 per month until the new facility was completed in 1974.[2] In January of that year, the residents were transferred over to the new facility although the mansion would stay vacant for another two years.

Early on, the Carlisle Area School District had plans for the Thornwald Estate, which included constructing the new middle school on the large open field that ran parallel with Walnut Bottom Road. However, such an idea caused mixed feelings in Carlisle. A number of people considered it to be the "last green space" in Carlisle and furthermore believed it could be best be used as a "recreation area".[3]

Therefore, three years later in 1975, Larry Niedlinger subdivided the grounds of the estate although it was not the first time the ground was subdivided.[4] In 1959, the Pennsylvania Department of Highways claimed nearly seven acres of ground for the construction of Interstate-81 of which only four acres was used for the highway. The remaining three-acre tract was given to the Borough of Carlisle for use as a park although the plans were never fulfilled.[5]

In November 1975, the Borough of Carlisle bought thirty-two acres of the former Thornwald Estate for $310,200 with the help of federal and state grants.[6] The ground was previously subdivided by Niedlinger, for use as a park, and was said to contain the "county's oldest, largest trees, home to a wide variety of wild flowers and a haven for birds".[7] Also, included in the sale of the ground was the gated entrance and the former automobile garage. In previous years, the tall brick wall, which once ran parallel with Walnut Bottom Road was torn down although the garage and the gated entrance still remained. In later years, the gates too were taken down leaving only the tall brick walls that made up the former entrance and pedestrian gateway.

By the following year, in August 1976, the park was officially dedicated and given the name, "Thornwald Park".[8] Thereafter, during the next few years, the former grounds of the Thornwald Estate underwent a complete transformation. Benches lined the macadamized walking paths, while picnic tables were scattered about on the former nine-hole golf course. During this time, a gazebo was added along with an amphitheater. Today the park continues with Lewis Sadler's vision in mind of "wild, natural scenery".[9]

As for the automobile garage or "caretaker's house", as it was known in later years, it was then home to Mr. and Mrs. Eugene Shearer, who had lived in the house since 1974. Upon moving into the caretaker's house, it was already fit for occupancy having two bedrooms and two bathrooms. It is likely that the garage had undergone renovations during the time that the Homewood Church Home had owned the estate and may have been used as a primary residence for the caretaker of the mansion.[10]

From 1974 until 1992, Mr. and Mrs. Eugene Shearer lived out of the caretaker's house. For a few years, the couple was in charge of maintaining the grounds of Thornwald although upon the Borough of Carlisle purchasing the lot of ground for a park the couple no longer maintained the grounds. However, the couple continued to be the caretakers of Thornwald until 1992 when in that year Mrs. Thelma Shearer passed away.[11] Thereafter, the family moved out of the house and afterwards the Borough of Carlisle rented the house out to families of the Army War College, although over the years a number of families have come to call it their home.[12]

The caretaker's house circa 1957.

Courtesy of Homewood Retirement Centers

Chapter 20

The Demise of Thornwald

The main entrance of Thornwald, as it appeared in the fall of 2006. *Photo by author*

    Nearly a week after the Borough of Carlisle had purchased the ground from the Carlisle Area School District, the district sold the mansion and the remaining two acres of ground to the Progress Foundation.[1] Despite the sale, the school district's affiliation with the mansion continued throughout the next two and a half years. During this time, the district used the mansion to house the new Alternative Learning Program.[2]
    On the inside, Thornwald still appeared the same since Homewood had left it in 1974 with the exception of the small addition and the handicap entrance, which was constructed adjacent to the kitchen and conservatory between 1966 and 1970. As for the rest of the mansion, it was still in good condition with the "heating plant" still in good working order along with the elevator that continued to service all four floors.[3]
    During the next few years, classes were held on the second floor, which was also the location of the cafeteria, where once was the location of the Sadlers master bedrooms.[4] In 1977, the first floor of the mansion became home to the Helen H. Stephens Community Mental Health Center, who occupied the mansion until 1979.[5] Afterwards, the mansion was boarded up for a short time until in 1981, when it was occupied by the New Covenant Church.[6] Five years later, in July 1986, the mansion again was sold, this time to be used as a primary residence.[7]

Up until this time, there was little work done to the mansion, since the major renovation in 1959-1960, which further brought the mansion up to code for use as a nursing home (see pages 186-191). Following the renovations, Thornwald no longer appeared the same again. While the first floor may have appeared much the same way, both the second and third floors were a far cry from how they appeared when Homewood opened in the fall of 1953. Even after the nursing home vacated the mansion in 1974, there was little done to restore the mansion back to the way it once was. Now, some twelve years later, and with the mansion slowly deteriorating from the inside out, Thornwald faced an uncertain future.

Nearly three years after the mansion was purchased in 1986, from the Progress Foundation, it still looked much the same as it did with the exception of some "cosmetic work".[8] Throughout the mansion, new light fixtures and carpet were installed along with a section of the roof replaced.[9] On the second floor, the former loggia, located adjacent to the former master bedrooms, now was renovated to accommodate a massive "14 person commercial Jacuzzi". Later the room would contain both a "eucalyptus sauna" and a "tanning booth". In later years, the first floor kitchen was upgraded to stainless steel. However, this was perhaps the last renovation to the mansion during this time.[10]

Despite the few changes that were made, the future of Thornwald began to look increasingly dim. Several years later, in 1999, both the second and third floors were now in "disrepair".[11] A number of the rooms, including the main hall along with the double grand staircase, were covered in olive green carpet. In some instances, the carpet had covered the floor where it was said to have "buckled" at different points, although these problems were small in comparison to the water damage that pervaded throughout. A number of the rooms even contained drop ceilings where the water pipes had broken, such as the large room on the second floor that once was the location of Mr. and Mrs. Lewis Sadler's master bedrooms.[12]

There was little splendor left inside Thornwald, with the exception of the first floor, which still contained its original woodwork. Despite the mansion's current appearance, both the dining room and library along with the halls of the first floor were decorated in the finest furnishings making it appear like a king's castle.

View of the library from the main hall. *Courtesy of the Borough of Carlisle*

Nearly fifteen years later, and due to financial difficulty, the mansion was put up for bankruptcy auction, which occurred in November 2001.[13] However, despite the sale, there would be no happy ending. Years seemed to tarry on without any progress, and soon even the Borough of Carlisle became concerned about the condition of the mansion because little was done since the auction. At this time, there were still no building permits or signs that work would soon begin to restore the mansion to its original condition. The massive stone columns in the front of the mansion were in need of repair, windows were broken in several places along with "holes in the fascia and soffit".[14] With the mansion in its present pitiful state, it was on the verge of being declared as "blighted" and at the same time was also an easy target for both vandals and trespassers.[15]

Even during the years that the mansion was occupied, a number of people had ignored the "no trespassing" signs and proceeded to break into the mansion.[16] However, this time in 2001, the mansion was vacant and now there was nobody around to keep watch except for the local Carlisle police who often patrolled the area. Although the owners had taken precautions and had nailed several boards over the first floor windows and doors, they did little to prevent those from breaking into the mansion.[17]

Thornwald indeed was a curiosity due to its large proportions. Those who had made their way inside the mansion posted pictures of themselves on the internet serving as proof that they had indeed stepped beyond its walls.[18] Although some had wondered into the mansion purely for curiosity sake, there were also those who had vandalized the mansion. Such as those individuals who had done nearly "$5,000 worth of damage" in the fall of 2006, although the damage was minor to what would occur nearly a year later in August 2007.[19]

Looking from the main hall into the library.

Courtesy of A. Keating

The fireplace inside the library. The painting of the 17th century gentleman, which at one time occupied the oval frame above the fireplace, was removed prior to July 1986 and afterwards became the property of the Cumberland County Historical Society.

Courtesy of A. Keating

A section of the music room

Courtesy of A. Keating

A section of the grand staircase *Courtesy of A. Keating*

This large room on the second floor was once the location of the west wing, which contained Mr. and Mrs. Lewis Sadler's master bedrooms, a bathroom, and a bedroom.
Courtesy of A. Keating

The fireplace inside the billiard room on the third floor.

Courtesy of A. Keating

A section of the upstairs billiard room.

Courtesy of A. Keating

Chapter 21

The Great Conflagration

On the evening of August 20, 2007, Carlisle area firefighters were called to put out a fire that had been started near the front entrance of the mansion. The fire was small, and therefore they were able to save the historic structure from being engulfed in flames. Upon the fire being extinguished, the crew did a thorough walk through of the mansion and seeing that everything was safe and sound they ventured home shortly after 11 pm. Although, the small fire served only as a warning sign of what was yet to come.[1]

Nearly five hours later, the individuals who may have set the first fire had returned this time to set Thornwald into a blazing inferno.[2] Across the way, an employee at Thornwald Home got a glimpse of the fire through the woods and immediately called it in, although it was already too late. Flames trailed up the steps of the mansion and made their way out the windows and through the skylights on the third floor. Carlisle area firefighters arrived on the scene, although it already was too late to save the historic structure. No one was permitted inside due to safety concerns and therefore the fire could only be fought from the outside.[3]

Hours passed, and as daybreak arrived, the fire fighters were still on the scene fighting the fire while both TV and newspaper reporters were busying about gathering the full details for the mornings news. Work continued until late into the afternoon making every effort to ensure that the fire was completely extinguished. At this time, it was reported that the fire was arson although no one was ever caught in connection with the fire.[4]

The main entrance of Thornwald as it appeared at 6:49 am on August 21, 2007
Courtesy of Andrew Henry

Courtesy of Andrew Henry

Courtesy of Andrew Henry

The photographs on the following pages were taken on August 21, 2007 between 7:30 and 9:30 a.m.

Courtesy of Andrew Henry

Courtesy of Andrew Henry

Courtesy of Andrew Henry

Courtesy of Andrew Henry

Courtesy of Andrew Henry

Courtesy of Andrew Henry

The library as it appeared during the fire. *Courtesy of Andrew Henry*

The breakfast and dining rooms fully engulfed in flames. *Courtesy of Andrew Henry*

Courtesy of Andrew Henry

Courtesy of Andrew Henry

Courtesy of Andrew Henry

    Sadly enough, Thornwald had suffered the same fate as the Boslers Cottage Hill Mansion, which was destroyed by fire in October 1925.[5] Although in comparison to Cottage Hill, Thornwald was "fire-proof". During its construction, *The Carlisle Herald* reported that it was a "modern fire-proof building, constructed of steel, stone and brick".[6] The structure itself could stand for hundreds of years and survive through the fiercest storms that came its way.

    That morning, despite the flames that ripped through the mansion, the structure still stood just as it always had for nearly a hundred years despite the concerns that it would collapse. On the inside, the thick concrete floors did not crumble nor crack while the steel reinforced walls continued to hold the mansion together.

Days and then weeks passed since the fire had occurred and many wondered what would happen to Thornwald? For a time it appeared as if it would be torn down due to the condition that it was in although just weeks later repairs were made to the roof while contractors were supporting the front portico with cinder blocks to keep it from collapsing. Also during this time, a number of men were starting the cleanup of the inside of the mansion that was now black and charred.

After the fire, there was little splendor left in the mansion. The main lobby that once boasted with oak paneling now was nothing but ashes while the double grand staircase now was only a mere memory for some. Both the library and music room were awful memories of the fire with the oak woodwork now black and charred.[7]

The main hall looking from the rear entrance. To the left, is the elevator shaft concealed by a fireproof block wall.

Courtesy of Hurley Auctions

The library. To the far right, is a section of the music room.

Courtesy of Hurley Auctions

The music room

Courtesy of Hurley Auctions

However, here and there were still evidences of how the mansion once was. On the first floor, a number of the casement windows were still present along with a few of the white shutters that survived the fire. Inside the kitchen, the English tile remained although it had turned black from the fire while the cupboards still hung on the walls. Inside the dining room, all that remained was the red marble fireplace that still contained the red marble base.[8]

The kitchen *Courtesy of Hurley Auctions*

The dining room fireplace. In the background, is a section of the conservatory.
Photo by author

A section of what once was Mr. Sadler's office. The door in the picture to the left, was part of the walk-in safe. The highlighted photo is the large walk-in safe, which at one time contained a door. At the time of the nursing home, the safe was used as a closet.

Photo by author

The window inside the office

Photo by Scott Strickler

Up on the second floor, the linen closet still was intact along with two wooden fireplace mantles inside the former guest rooms. Both Mr. and Mrs. Lewis Sadler's bedrooms were a mere memory since in prior years they were demolished and turned into one great room. Now all that was left were the two fireplaces. However, Mrs. Sadler's shower still remained along with the shelves of her wall safe. Up on the third floor, the fireplace, which once graced the billiard room, had also survived the blaze while the two deacon benches that sat on either side were now black and charred.[9]

Mr. Sadler's former master bedroom   *Photo by author*

Mrs. Sadler's wall safe

Photo by author

Mrs. Sadler's shower   *Photo by author*

The linen closet   *Photo by author*

The second floor bedroom, which overlooked the rear lawn.   *Photo by Scott Strickler*

Above: The fireplace inside the former billiard room.

Left: The elevator shaft

Bottom: The door to the elevator.

Photos by Scott Strickler

While the original splendor of the mansion was gone, the basement had been untouched by the blaze. Due to the thick reinforced concrete floors that divided the basement and the first floor, the rathskeller was spared by the blazing inferno.

The rooms in the basement still remained having been constructed entirely of brick and each was a reminder of how life was once lived. The former hot water heating plant, still contained the large compressed air tank, which forced water up to the third floor, while the large porcelain sinks inside the former laundry room were still in mint condition (see pages 97-99).

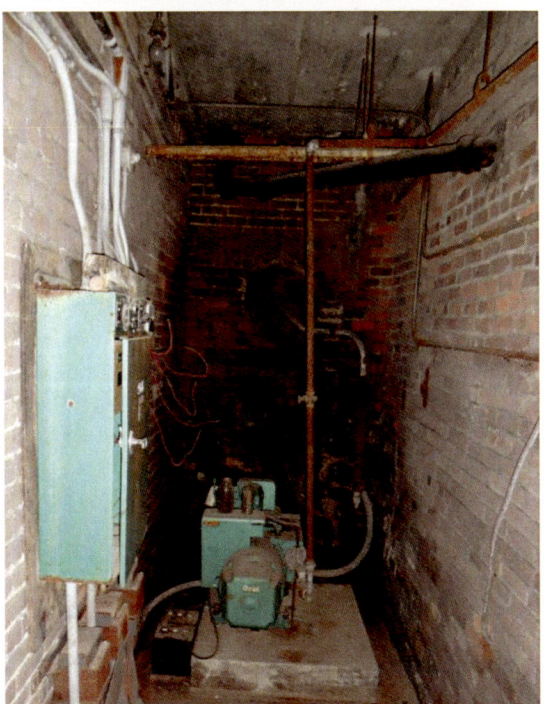

Above left: The stairs located just off the main entrance that led to the basement.

Above: The former servants' bathroom.

Left: The former coal room. In later years, the room was used to house a generator.

Photos by Scott Strickler

Down the hall, located on either end of the entrance into the wine cellar and rathskeller, were two stand-alone doorways still inset with glass panes. Inside the wine cellar, the numerous racks that once held the hundreds of bottles of wine still remained (see pages 100-101), while the rathskeller still contained its original beauty and splendor despite the years of vandalism.[10]

The rathskeller   *Courtesy of Hurley Auctions*

A view of the built-in wet bar and bathroom located inside the rathskeller.

Photo by Scott Strickler

Left: The entrance to the elevator located inside the rathskeller

Bottom Left: The orange bottle glass still intact after all these years

Bottom Right: The focal point of the rathskeller, which at one time was used as a stove.

Photos by Scott Strickler

Chapter 22

A Second Chance

The main entrance of Thornwald, as it appeared at the time of the auction, on October 28, 2010. To the right, is a section of the west wing facing the front lawn.

Photos by Scott Strickler

    Several months passed and then a year since the fire had occurred, and during this time, there was little done to restore the mansion back to the way it once was. Both the windows and doors were now boarded up with plywood while a ten-foot tall fence encircled the property keeping both vandals and trespassers alike away from the mansion. However, despite the fire and the security measures that were now in place, Thornwald still remained a curiosity. Nearly a year later, one individual attempted to break into the mansion by cutting a hole in the steel door in attempt to unlock the door from the inside although, it would be sometime until anyone would see what remained of the mansion since the fire had occurred.[1]
    Three years later and with few prospective buyers interested in purchasing the mansion, Thornwald was slated to go up for auction on October 28, 2010. Prior to the auction, the mansion was open to the public on two occasions, which drew hundreds of people from all over. Many were there as prospective buyers for the property while others wondered what all was left since the fire had occurred. Despite the number of people who had turned out to tour the property, there was little interest in purchasing the mansion. A number of people believed it was a "money pit" and therefore would cost millions of dollars to restore it back to how it once was.[2]

On the day of the auction, a number of people attended some for curiosity sake and some to get their last glimpse inside the mansion before the start of the sale that day. At two o'clock in the afternoon, the bidding war began and nearly twenty minutes later a final bid was realized bringing the mansion to be sold at $230,000 to Mrs. Rkia Hall of Carlisle whose plans are to turn it into a bed and breakfast.[3] Ironically enough, the price was not far from the $250,000 that Mr. Lewis Sadler had paid to construct the mansion in 1909.

By the following month, the sound of construction was in the air. Roofers were on the roof laying down new shingles while plans were being made to install new windows on the third floor. The total transformation from an ashen shell to a future bed and breakfast was officially under way.

Although it will never be the same as it once was, Carlisle citizens young and old await the day when they can walk into the mansion with awe and wonder similar to what Pennsylvania Governor, John Tener, may have experienced on May 7, 1911 when he stepped inside the mansion for the first time.

The rear entrance of Thornwald as it appeared in April 2011.
Note the third floor windows and new roof, which were installed by this time.
Courtesy of Maria Strickler

A view of the rear lawn as it appeared in May 2011, when the trees that engulfed the property for the past one hundred years were cut down.
Photo by Scott Strickler

The main entrance of Thornwald as it appeared in February 2012. *Photo by author*

The rear entrance of Thornwald as it appeared in February 2012. *Photo by author*

The main entrance of Thornwald as it appeared in August 2012. The concrete pad located in front of the mansion, is the base for a fountain. Both the main and rear entrance will each contain a fountain.

Photo by Scott Strickler

The rear entrance of Thornwald as it appeared on October 1, 2012, nearly two years since it was sold at auction.

Photo by author

From the Author

During researching the history behind the Sadlers and the Thornwald Mansion, I came upon an article about the Telford road that was going to be built leading to the Sadler residence. Ironically, Enos Stauffer, the man who was put in charge of superintending the work had lived at our house along North West Street from the time it was built in 1893 until his death in January 1916. At the time of discovering that he had built the road, I thought it was interesting that the man who resided at our residence had played a key role in the mansion's construction although at the time I only knew half the story.

Several months later on June 8, 2010, my husband along with his brother, were in the process of replacing the old windows of our house. One of the windows was actually an old funeral door, which at the time I was totally opposed to replacing. However, with much consideration, I allowed him to tear it out. After they had removed the funeral door, we realized that there was a gap above where the door would have slipped up inside the wall. The gap had been stuffed with insulation over the years, or at the time we thought it was insulation. However, as my husband pulled it out, we were wrong for it was not insulation but old clothes. The articles of clothing consisted of a dark blue jacket and two long underwear shirts, all which appeared to have been those of Enos Stauffer or at least belonging to the Stauffer family.

We laid out the articles of clothing on our front lawn to get a better look at them and take a few pictures. However, while I looked at the clothes I got the notion to check the pockets of the blue jacket since you never know what you will find. As I opened the right pocket of the jacket, I did not expect to find anything but much to my surprise there was a piece of paper folded neatly inside. As I gently unfolded the paper, I noticed it was blue in color. Immediately, I knew it was some sort of blueprint, but to where? I was careful not to tear it and took my time trying to decipher what it may be.

At the time, I had no idea what the blueprint could be for, that was until I saw the words written on the bottom of the page that said, "The residence for L.S. Sadler, Esqre. at Carlisle. Penn.". What we had found tucked in the wall of our house for nearly a hundred years was a blueprint for the lampposts at Thornwald. The blueprint depicted the outline of the mansion along with the location of the lampposts that were to be placed on the front lawn overlooking Walnut Bottom Road. I was awestruck and full of emotion when I saw what lay before my eyes. Never in my wildest dreams did I imagine to find a blueprint of Thornwald in the wall of our house nor have expected Enos Stauffer to have helped in building the stately mansion.

Just a few months ago, before I was about to send this book to print, my husband was in the process of renovating our bathroom. Behind our toilet, was an iron grate that had been covered up by the previous owners. The grate was connected to the chimney and was located below a built in cabinet that was located in the adjacent room.

As he removed the grate and the metal casing that was connected to the chimney, he noticed a piece of paper with writing on it. Upon closer observation, it was not a letter, but a photograph of a gentleman. As he turned the photograph over, on the back it was signed "Enos Stauffer, 2-1-1899". All this time we wanted a photograph of the Stauffer family, and now we have one along with the blueprint that Enos had tucked away in his coat pocket all this time.

A photograph of Enos Stauffer, found inside the wall
of our upstairs bathroom on March 21, 2012.
Photo from author

TELFORD ROAD

A Telford road is being built from College street on the Walnut Bottom road to the Sadler home, 3000 feet long. The foundation is of stone stood on edge. Over this will be earth, crushed stone and top dressing. Another road will be made on the west of the main driveway, which will be shorter. W. S. Yarnell is contractor, and Enos Stouffer superintendent.

*Carlisle Evening Herald,
15 August 1910*

The clothes that were found inside the wall of our house on June 8, 2010.   *Photo by author*

The pocket where the blueprint was found.

Photo by author

The blueprint unfolded.

Photo by author

The blueprint found inside the wall of our house, which depicts the location of the lampposts that were to be placed in front of the main entrance of Thornwald. Lampposts 9A and 10A, not show in photograph, were placed several feet in front of lampposts, 7A and 8A. Blueprint drawn by Hill & Stout on November 14, 1910.

Photo by author

Appendix

Thornwald Chronology

Abbreviations: CCDB: *Cumberland County Deed Book*   CEH: *Carlisle Evening Herald*
CH: *Carlisle Herald*   CV: *Carlisle Volunteer*   TES: *The Evening Sentinel*

January 8, 1872	Mary Eliza Bosler is born to Mr. and Mrs. James W. Bosler in Carlisle, Pa.
March 3, 1874	Lewis Sterrett Sadler is born to Mr. and Mrs. Wilbur Fisk Sadler in Carlisle, Pa.
June 26, 1902	Lewis Sterrett Sadler marries Mary Eliza Bosler inside the Second Presbyterian Church in Carlisle, Pa. "Sadler-Bosler," *ES* (27 June 1902)
April 28, 1909	Lewis Sadler purchases forty-six acres of Noble's Woods from Dr. Joseph Noble.
April 29, 1909	*The Evening Sentinel* becomes the first newspaper to give specific details concerning the Sadler residence.
May 15, 1909	Parker Moore and Clarence A. Bingham survey Noble's Woods and Rocky Lot.
June 7, 1909	First blueprints drawn by Hill & Stout of New York
July 3, 1909	Winfield Yarnall chosen as excavating contractor "Contract Let," *T.E.S.* (3 July 1909) 6.
July 17, 1909	Yarnall and a number of men begin to prepare the grounds for excavation. "Preparing Grounds," *CV* (17 July 1909) 1.
July 20, 1909	Yarnall breaks ground for the future Sadler residence "Start Excavations Today," *CV* (20 July 1909) 1.
September 1, 1909	Parker Moore and Clarence A. Bingham resurvey the ground. Location of the future residence, moved back several feet due to limestone rock on former building site.
September 9, 1909	Thompson–Starrett Construction Company of New York receive the contract to build the future Sadler residence. "Work Started," *CH* (9 September 1909) 1.

October 12, 1909	Foundation is completed. Also at this time, a deep trench occupies the grounds and is the location of the future water main. Foresters continue trimming trees. "That Mansion In The Forest," *CH* (12 October 1909)
October 15, 1909	Steel framework arrives *Same reference as above*
October 28, 1909	Gas and water pipes are laid for the residence. "News Notes," *CH* (28 October 1909) 1.
January 7, 1910	Work resumes on the mansion, since the winter weather had put a hold on construction. "Concrete workers are employed at their labors…" "Work at Sadler Home," *CH* (7 January 1910)
March 10, 1910	Second story is completed, and now work was to begin on constructing the roof. "The New Sadler Home," *CH* (11 March 1910)
August 1910	Third floor completed and the roof installed.
August 16, 1910	First glimpse of the inside of the mansion appears in *The Evening Sentinel* on August 16, 1910.
August 16, 1910	Yarnall and a number of men begin on constructing the Telford road, which would lead to the mansion from the Walnut Bottom Road along with a service road for "delivery wagons". *Same reference as above*
Late summer/early fall of 1910	First photograph taken of the mansion during construction.
May 5, 1911	The *Carlisle Evening Herald* announces that the mansion is completed.
May 7, 1911	The name "Thornewold" is used for the first time to identify the home of Mr. and Mrs. Lewis Sadler. "Governor at Thornewold," *CEH* (8 May 1911)
May 7, 1911	Governor Tener and a few state officials become the first guests of Mr. and Mrs. Lewis Sadler at "Thornewold". *Same reference as above*
April 29, 1912	A number of "masons" begin on constructing a "brick and concrete automobile garage" on the grounds of Thornwald. "Builders Busy Spring," *CEH* (29 April 1912)

May 22, 1912	Work begins on constructing a "commodious" garage just off the Walnut Bottom Road. "Erecting Garage," *TES* (22 May 1912)
Late August/early fall of 1912	Entrance gateway is constructed
October 3, 1914	The Sheafer brothers construct the brick wall along the Walnut Bottom Road. "50,000 for a fence at Sadler Home,"*TES* (3 October 1914)
November 23, 1915	Lewis Sadler purchases seven acres from George H. Stewart, which further enlarges his Thornwald Estate. CCDB, 8I 582
September 19, 1916	Mary Bosler Sadler passes away at the Carlisle Hospital, and three days later, the funeral takes place at Thornwald, and is the first to occur inside the mansion. "Mrs. L.S. Sadler Dies in Hospital," *TES* (19 September 1916)
December 3, 1920	Lewis Sadler hosts the largest dinner to occur at Thornwald. "Distinguished Guests at Sadler Dinner," *TES* (3 December 1920)
January 20, 1922	Lewis Sadler passes away at Thornwald. "Lewis S. Sadler, Highway Commissioner, Dies At Home," *TES* (20 January 1922)
January 8, 1923	Upon the death of Lewis Sadler, his brother, Sylvester Baker Sadler inherited Thornwald. Nearly a year later, he turned the mansion over to his youngest brother and sister-in-law, Dr. and Mrs. Horace Sadler. CCDB, 10Y 494
June 28, 1948	Old Folks home of the Potomac Synod-Reformed Church purchases Thornwald for future use as a nursing home. CCDB, 15H 477
February 27, 1953	Dr. Horace Trickett Sadler, the last surviving son of Mr. and Mrs. Wilbur Fisk Sadler, passes away inside his apartment along South Pitt Street at seventy-three years of age. "Horace T. Sadler," *TES* (28 February 1953)
May 27-28, 1953	Sadler heirlooms are auctioned off at Thornwald "Sadler Sale May Total $17,000," *TES* (28 May 1953)

September 30, 1953	First guests arrive at what was now known as the "Sadler Unit" of the Homewood Church Home. "First Four Guests Arrive at Carlisle Church Home," *TES* (1 October 1953).
1959	The Pennsylvania Department of Highways purchases ten acres of the Thornwald Estate for the future construction of Interstate-81. Three acres remained after construction, which today is owned by the Carlisle Borough. "Hear Testimony In Damage Suite," *The Evening Sentinel* (no date). Article found inside folder at Thornwald Home
April 11, 1972	Homewood sells the Thornwald Estate to the Carlisle Area School District, but retains ten acres for the construction of a future nursing home. Despite the sale, Homewood continues to occupy the mansion until 1974. CCDB 24O 653
September 30, 1953-1974	Homewood occupies the former Thornwald Mansion
November 20, 1975	The Carlisle Area School District sells thirty-two acres of the former Thornwald Estate to the Carlisle Borough for use as a park, which today is known as Thornwald Park. CCDB 26I 953
November 20, 1975	The Carlisle Area School District sells the Thornwald Mansion and two acres to the Progress Foundation. CCDB 26I 950
July 16, 1986	The Thornwald Mansion sold for use as a private residence CCDB 32C 443
November 2001	Thornwald Mansion sold at auction David Blymire, "Mansion headed for blight status," *The Sentinel* (18 August 2005)
August 21, 2007	The Thornwald Mansion is destroyed by fire Heather Stauffer, "Built for 1,000 years, dies at 100," *The Sentinel* (22 August 2007).
October 28, 2010	The Thornwald Mansion is sold at auction Observation (28 October 2010)
November 2010-present day	The Thornwald Mansion undergoes an extensive rebuild from the inside out.

Endnotes

Introduction

[1] "Mountain Springs Hotel" *Wikipedia* 18 May 2001. Wikimedia Foundation, Inc. 17 June 2011. <http://en.wiskipedia.org/wiki/Mountain_Springs_Hotel>.

[2] "That Mansion In The Forest," *Carlisle Herald* (12 October 1909) 1.

The Sadler Family

[1] Lewis Gobrecht, "The Sadler Family" *Sadler and Thornwald Information*, a notebook compiled by Gobrecht, available at the Cumberland County Historical Society, Carlisle, Pa.

[2] Richard Sadler was a descendent of Sir Ralph Sadler, who served as secretary of state under King Henry VIII. For the Sadler genealogy, see documents in "Sadler/Sterrett" folder at the Cumberland County Historical Society, Carlisle, Pa.

[3] *Biographical Annals of Cumberland County, Pennsylvania* (Chicago: The Genealogical Publishing Company, 1905) 170. See also, Wilbur Fisk Sadler's handwritten bibliography entitled "W.F. Sadler" located in "Sadler/Sterrett" folder at the Cumberland County Historical Society, Carlisle, Pa. Reference to Lycoming College, see Charles Scott Williams, *History of Lycoming College* (King Brothers, Inc., 1959) 42.

[4] "W.F. Sadler" located in "Sadler/Sterrett" folder at the Cumberland County Historical Society, Carlisle, Pa.

[5] *Ibid; Biographical Annals of Cumberland County, Pennsylvania* (Chicago: The Genealogical Publishing Company, 1905) 170.

[6] See Wilbur Sadler's handwritten bibliography entitled "W.F. Sadler" located in "Sadler/Sterrett" folder at the Cumberland County Historical Society, Carlisle, Pa. Location of first law office see "Professional Cards," *The American Volunteer* (14 September 1865) column 1, page 1.

[7] Concerning the location of Sadler's residence along South West Street see *Directory of the Borough of Carlisle* (Carlisle Herald office, 1867) 21; J.G Strong, *Map of Carlisle, Pennsylvania* .Map. Baltimore: Schmidt & Trowe, 1867; Deed from Jonas Fought to Wilbur Sadler, March 1866, Cumberland County Deed Book 2T:275-276, Recorder's Office, Carlisle, Pennsylvania. For Mrs. Harriett Stehley Sadler, see *Biographical Annals of Cumberland County, Pennsylvania* (Chicago: The Genealogical Publishing Company, 1905) 170.

[8] In reference to Sadler's early cases as a lawyer, see letter from Wilbur Fisk Sadler, Carlisle to J.D Townsend, 18 December 1868 [?], Townsend Legal Papers, Moyerman Collection, Archives and Special Collections, Dickinson College, Carlisle, Pennsylvania.

[9] James Marion Weakley as Sadler's next door neighbor, see *Directory of the Borough of Carlisle* (Carlisle Herald office, 1867) 23; for law office of "Weakley & Sadler," see Strong, J.G *Map of Carlisle, Pennsylvania* . Map. Baltimore: Schmidt & Trowe, 1867; "Professional Cards," *The American Volunteer* (3 December 1868) column 1, page 1.

[10] Secretary of law library in 1869, see *Cumberland Justice: Legal Practice in Cumberland County, 1750-2000* (Carlisle: Cumberland County Bar Foundation, 2001) 56-57. For Sadler serving as chairman of the Republican Committee see "W.F. Sadler" located in "Sadler/Sterrett" folder at the Cumberland County Historical Society, Carlisle, Pa.

[11] "W.F. Sadler" located in "Sadler/Sterrett" folder at the Cumberland County Historical Society, Carlisle, Pa.

[12] For reference to the parents of Sarah Ellen Sterrett, see letter addressed to Wilbur Sadler, Jr. from Horace Sadler, 22 April 1914, "Sadler/Sterrett" folder, Cumberland County Historical Society, Carlisle, Pa; For reference to Lawrenceville Seminary, see *Quindecennial Record: Class of Eighteen Hundred Ninety-five*, Yale College (New Haven, Connecticut, Moorehouse & Taylor Company, 1911) 221. For the wedding of Mr. and Mrs. Wilbur Fisk Sadler, see *Marriages and Deaths from the Carlisle Herald Newspapers 1866,1868-1872*, (Cumberland County Historical Society, Carlisle, Pa) 65. According to the *Directory of the Borough of Carlisle* (Carlisle Herald office, 1867), the Sterrett residence was located at 92 High Street.

[13] For information regarding Sadler's land holdings, see F.W. Beers, *Atlas of Cumberland County, Pennsylvania* (New York: F.W. Beers & Company, 1872) 43-44

[14] Deed from Mr. and Mrs. George Pettinas to Wilbur Sadler, 5 October 1867, Cumberland County Deed Book 2X 130, Recorder's Office, Carlisle, Pennsylvania.

[15] For location of homes along North College Street, see F.W. Beers, *Atlas of Cumberland County, Pennsylvania* (New York: F.W. Beers & Company, 1872) 43-44; For the future location of Judge Biddle's home along North College street, see *Insurance Maps of Carlisle, Cumberland County, Pennsylvania* (New York: Sanborn Map Company, 1902) sheet 2.

[16] For the location of Dickinson College, see F.W. Beers, *Atlas of Cumberland County, Pennsylvania* (New York: F.W. Beers & Company, 1872) 43-44.

[17] Lewis Gobrecht, "The Sadler Family" *Sadler and Thornwald Information*, a notebook compiled by Gobrecht, available at the Cumberland County Historical Society, Carlisle, Pennsylvania.

[18] For Wilbur Sadler as district attorney in 1871, see *Biographical Annals of Cumberland County, Pennsylvania* (Chicago: The Genealogical Publishing Company, 1905).

[19] *History of Cumberland and Adams Counties, Pennsylvania* (Chicago: Warner, Beers & Co., 1886) 169.

[20] U.S. Department of the Interior, Census Office, Ninth Census, 1870, Carlisle, Cumberland County, Pennsylvania, s.v. "Wilbur Saddler," *Heritage Quest,* HeritageQuestOnline.com.

[21] Location of law office at 11 W. High Street, see "Lawyers," *Sheriff & Co's Cumberland Valley Railroad Directory* (1877-78) 280. Location of law office at 8 West High Street, see *Cumberland Valley Railroad Directory,* (1907), 257.

[22] *Biographical Annals of Cumberland County, Pennsylvania* (Chicago: The Genealogical Publishing Company, 1905) 170.

[23] "W.F. Sadler" located in "Sadler/Sterrett" folder at the Cumberland County Historical Society, Carlisle, Pa.

[24] "Will Sadler Accept," *American Volunteer* (24 September 1884).

[25] Democratic Votes in Penn Township see "Second Edition," *Daily Evening Sentinel* (24 November 1884). For the judicial election of 1884, read "The Honorable Martin Christian Herman, the Election of 1884, and the Bar in 1885, " *Cumberland Justice: Legal Practice in Cumberland County, 1750-2000* (Carlisle: Cumberland County Bar Foundation, 2001) 59.

[26] "Preparatory School," *One Hundred and Sixth Annual Catalogue of Dickinson College* (1880-1890):53-54.

[27] Wilbur Sadler as trustee of Dickinson in 1882,see handwritten bibliography entitled "W.F. Sadler" located in "Sadler/Sterrett" folder at the Cumberland County Historical Society, Carlisle, Pa.

28   For Sylvester, see "Preparatory School," *One Hundred and Sixth Annual Catalogue of Dickinson College* (1880-1890):53-54. For Wilbur Sadler Jr. at Dickinson, see "Theta Delta Chi Fraternity," *Microcosm* (1890) 37.

29   Roger Tuttle, *Quarter Century Record of the Class of Ninety-Five, Yale College* (The Tuttle, Morehouse & Taylor Company, 1922), 491.

30   *Boyd's Directory of Harrisburg and Steelton* (1891) 341.

31   *Boyd's Directory of Harrisburg and Steelton* (1890) 325.

32   For Wilbur Sadler Jr., see Francis Bazley Lee, *Genealogical & Personal Memorial of Mercer County, New Jersey Vol. 1* (New York & Chicago: The Lewis Publishing, Co.,1907) 155. Accessed on June 2, 2010. Google books.

33   "Sophomore Class," *Catalogue of Yale University, 1892-93.*(Tuttle, Moorehouse & Taylor, 1893) 251. Accessed on June 16,2011. Google books.

34   For Population of New Haven, Connecticut versus Carlisle, Pennsylvania in 1890, see: *Abstract of the Twelfth Census, 1900* (Washington: Government Printing Office, 1902), 137,145. Accessed on January 13,2011. Google books.

35   "Departments of Instruction," *Catalogue of Yale University, 1893-94.*(Tuttle, Moorehouse & Taylor, 1893) 32. Accessed on November 14,2010. Google books.

36   "Sophomore Class," *Catalogue of Yale University, 1892-93.*(Tuttle, Moorehouse & Taylor, 1893) 251. Accessed on June 16,2011. Google books. For the Sadlers time at Yale and reference to 1010 Chapel St. in New Haven, see *Catalogue of Yale University, 1893-94.* (Tuttle, Moorehouse & Taylor, 1893) 270,277. Accessed on November 14,2010. Google books.

37   Roger Tuttle, *Quarter Century Record of the Class of Ninety-Five, Yale College* (The Tuttle, Morehouse & Taylor Company, 1922), 491; Clarence Day, Jr., *Decennial Record of the Class of 1896, Yale College* (New York: De Vinne Press, 1907) 548.

38   For information regarding Sylvester's time at Yale, see Clarence Day, Jr., *The 96' Half-way Book* (New Haven: Class of 1896, Yale College, 1915) 304. See also, Daniel Heisey: "A Man of Discrimination," *Pages of History: Essays on Cumberland County, Pennsylvania.* (Carlisle: New Loudon Press, 1994) 59-60.

39   "Mrs. Sarah E. Sadler: death of a most estimable woman this afternoon," *Carlisle Herald* (10 January 1895).

40   Ibid.

41   "Death of Sarah Ellen Sterrett," *The Evening Sentinel* (11 January 1895).

42   Francis Bazley Lee, *Genealogical & Personal Memorial of Mercer County, New Jersey Vol. 1* (New York & Chicago: The Lewis Publishing, Co.,1907) 155.

43   "Personal," *American Volunteer* (19 June 1897); Edward C. Kirk, D.D.S. ed. *The Dental Cosmos: a monthly record of dental science.* (Philadelphia: The S.S. White Dental Manufacturing Co., 1901) 816. Accessed on June 02, 2010. Google books.

44   "Junior Class, 96'." *Dickinson College Catalogue* (1894-1895).

"Like Father, Like Son"

[1] For history of Judge John Reed's law school, see *Cumberland Justice: Legal Practice in Cumberland County, 1750-2000* (Carlisle: Cumberland County Bar Foundation, 2001) 35.

[2] "Editorials," *Dickinsonian,* January 1890.

[3] "Junior Class, 96'." *Dickinson College Catalogue* (1894-1895): 63-68. For more information concerning the reestablished law school, see *Cumberland Justice: Legal Practice in Cumberland County, 1750-2000* (Carlisle: Cumberland County Bar Foundation, 2001) 62; Barton R. Laub, *The Dickinson School of Law: Proud and Independent* (Harrisburg: McFarland Co., 1983) 45.

[4] Ibid.

[5] "summer school, 1895" *Microcosm"* (1896): 88.

[6] "Junior Class." *Microcosm"* (1895): 80-81.

[7] "Law School Commencement," *American Volunteer* (10 June 1896) 3.

[8] For vice president of the athletic association, see "Athletic Association." *Microcosm"* (1895): 173. For the Allison Law Society, see "The Allison Law Society," *Microcosm* (1895): 84-85.

[9] Sylvester as a member of the Allison Law Society, see "The Allison Law Society," *Microcosm* (1898): 71.

[10] "Law School Commencement," *American Volunteer* (10 June 1896) 3.

[11] "Town Council," *American Volunteer* (3 March 1897).

[12] *Cumberland Valley Railroad Directory* (1902-03), *257.*

[13] "lawyers." *Johnson Lynch's Directory of Carlisle, Pa for 1896-97* (Wilmington: Johnson & Lynch, 1896) 100.

[14] *Polk's Carlisle Directory* (1926-27), 206.

[15] "law school faculty." *Microcosm* (1905): 261.

[16] For a list of books that were written by William Trickett, see "Dr. Trickett For Superior Court Judge," *American Volunteer* (15 June 1898) 2.

[17] William Trickett, *The Law of Boroughs in Pennsylvania* Vol. 2 (Philadelphia: T&J.W Johnson & Co., 1893) 5. Accessed on June 2, 2010. Google books.

[18] "The Commencement," *American Volunteer* (11 June 1898) 1.

[19] See Cumberland County Sheriff's Deed Book 4: 19-20. See also, "Sheriff's Sales," *American Volunteer* (1 February 1899) 2.

[20] For details of Martin Fry Murder trial, see Mark Podvia, "Early Years," *Cumberland Justice: Legal Practice in Cumberland County, 1750-2000* (Carlisle: Cumberland County Bar Foundation, 2001) 69.

[21] Daniel Heisey: "A Man of Discrimination," *Pages of History: Essays on Cumberland County, Pennsylvania.* (Carlisle: New Loudon Press, 1994) 63.

[22] For more information on the life of Sylvester Sadler, read Daniel Heisey: "A Man of Discrimination," *Pages of History: Essays on Cumberland County, Pennsylvania.* (Carlisle: New Loudon Press, 1994).

[23] "Attending Supreme Court," *Carlisle Herald* (27 April 1908).

The Bosler Family

[1] For Cottage Hill, see "Seven Gables Park" located in the "Seven Gables House" drop file at the Cumberland County Historical Society, Carlisle, Pa.

[2] For James W. Bosler, see *Biographical Annals of Cumberland County, Pennsylvania,* (Chicago: The Genealogical Publishing Co., 1905) 215.

[3] "James Williamson Bosler (1833-1883)" Dickinson College. Accessed on 24 November 2010. <http://chronicles.dickinson.edu/encyclo/b/ed_boslerJW.html>.

[4] *Biographical Annals of Cumberland County, Pennsylvania,*(Chicago: The Genealogical Publishing Co 1905) 215.

[5] Ibid.

[6] Birth dates of Bosler children made from observations of the Bosler and Sadler burial plots inside Ashland Cemetery in Carlisle, Pa.

[7] *Biographical Annals of Cumberland County, Pennsylvania,* (Chicago: The Genealogical Publishing Co., 1905) 216.

[8] Ibid., 217.

[9] Will of James W. Bosler see, Cumberland County Will Book 420R:256-258.

[10] *Biographical Annals of Cumberland County, Pennsylvania,*(Chicago: The Genealogical Publishing Co 1905) 216. For additional information, see also, T. De Witt Talmage, ed., "Dickinson College," *Frank Leslie's Sunday Magazine, vol. xviii- July to December, 1885.* 246. Accessed on June 15, 2010. Google books.

[11] U.S. Department of the Interior, Census Office, Tenth Census, 1880, Carlisle, Cumberland County, Pennsylvania, s.v. "James Bosler," *Heritage Quest,* HeritageQuestOnline.com.

[12] Thomas Cushing: "Catalogue," *Historical Sketch of Chauncy-Hall School, with catalogue of teachers and pupils, and appendix. 1828-1894. (*Boston: Press of David Clapp N Son , 1896) s.v. "Bosler," 92. Accessed on June 15, 2010. Google books.

[13] "Preparatory School," *One Hundred and Sixth Annual Catalogue of Dickinson College* (1880-1890):53-54.

[14] "Reminiscences of Nettie Jane Blair, August 1934," 15. Cumberland County Historical Society, Carlisle, Pa.

[15] For Dewitt Clinton Bosler, see "Record of the Class," *Harvard College: Class of 1897, Twenty-fifth Anniversary Report 1897-1922.*(Cambridge: The Riverside Press) 92. Accessed on June 18,2011. Google books. For Frank Bosler, see "Record of the Class," *Harvard College: Class of 1894, Twenty-fifth Anniversary Report 1894-1919.* (Norwood: The Plimpton Press) 42-44. Accessed on June 18,2011. Google books.

[16] Will of Helen Beltzhoover Bosler see, Cumberland County Will Book 484T:152-153.

17 Ibid, "The Inflation Calculator," 2010, S. Morgan Friedman. <http://www.westegg.com/inflation/>. 10 May 2010).

18 Ibid.

19 "Record of the Class," *Harvard College: Class of 1894, Twenty-fifth Anniversary Report 1894-1919.* (Norwood: The Plimpton Press) 43. Accessed on June 20,2011. Google books.

21 "Officers of the Alumni Association," *The Dickinson School of Law of Dickinson College* (1898-99): 80. See also, "Incorporators" *The Dickinson School of Law of Dickinson College* (1899-1900): 75.

22 "Incorporators" *The Dickinson School of Law* (1919-20): 3.

23 "Home Social News," *The Reading Eagle* (9 February 1899) 3.

The Sadler-Bosler Wedding

1 According to the will of Mrs. Helen Beltzhoover Bosler, Cumberland County Will Book 484T:152-153. upon her death her personal property, consisting of stocks, bonds, mortgages, etc. was to be divided between Frank and Mary, making them the wealthiest of her four children.
For her education, see Roger W. Tuttle, "Biographies," *Class of 1895, Quarter Century Record* (Tuttle, Moorehouse & Taylor Company, 1922) 492. For member of Carlisle Country Club see, "A Victory For Carlisle," *The Evening Volunteer* (22 June 1901) 1.

2 *Los Angeles Times* (29 May 1902). Accessed on January 10, 2012. Google books.

3 "Sadler-Bosler," *The Evening Sentinel* (27 June 1902)

4 Ibid.

5 Ibid.

6 Ibid.

7 Ibid.

8 Ibid.

9 Ibid.

10 Ibid.

11 Ibid.

Years at Cottage Hill

1 *Moore's Standard Directory and Reference Book of Carlisle* (New York City: S.H. Moore Company, 1908) 79.

2 *The Country Club of Harrisburg* (1907), 36.

3 For Sadler's membership into the Union League, see "Personals," *The Evening Sentinel* (13 July 1906) 5; *Harrisburg Club of Harrisburg, Pennsylvania* (1903), 58, 73.

4 See Cumberland County Deed Books 5L, 485 and 6A, 197.

5 "Clinton Bosler Dead," *The Evening Sentinel* (23 December 1903) 6. See also, Cumberland County Deed Books 6R, 79.

6   "Wedding Party Entertained," *Evening Sentinel* (18 June 1908).

7   "Entertained Distinguished Men," *Carlisle Daily Herald* (10 June 1908) 1.

8   Will of Helen Beltzhoover Bosler see, Cumberland County Will Book 484T:152-153. For DeWitt Clinton see, Cumberland County, Register of Wills Index A-B, Vol. 1, page 69. Inflation figure taken from "The Inflation Calculator," 2010, S. Morgan Friedman. <http://www.westegg.com/inflation/>. (10 May 2010).

Dr. and Mrs. Horace Sadler

1   Edward C. Kirk, D.D.S, ed. *The Dental Cosmos: a monthly record of dental science.* (Philadelphia: The S.S. White Dental Manufacturing Co., 1901) 816. Accessed on May 10, 2010. Google books.

2   *Directory of the Cumberland Valley Railroad* (1904-05) 300. Although his office was located at 22 West High Street, he does not show up under "Dentists" on page 485 of the directory.

3   "Chain Works to Stay Here," *Carlisle Evening Herald* (19 May 1910).

4   "Saturday Evening Wedding," *Carlisle Evening Herald* (8 March 1909). See also, "Sadler-Bosler," *The Evening Sentinel* (8 March 1909) 2.

5   "Sadler-Bosler," *The Evening Sentinel* (8 March 1909) 2.

6   Ibid., See also, "Sadler-Bosler," *The Evening Sentinel* (27 June 1902) concerning the details of Mr. and Mrs. Lewis Sadler's wedding in June 1902.

7   "Saturday Evening Wedding," *Carlisle Evening Herald* (8 March 1909).

8   "Saturday Evening Wedding," *Carlisle Evening Herald* (8 March 1909).

9   Mary O. Bradley, "Mansion predated Carlisle mall," *Patriot-News* (2 May 2003) E01.

10   Cumberland County Deed Book, 7I, 101.

11   "Will Greatly Improve Property," *Carlisle Daily Herald* (17 April 1908) 1.

12   "Saturday Evening Wedding," *Carlisle Evening Herald* (8 March 1909).

13   "Bosler Home Will Be Magnificent," *The Evening Sentinel* (27 April 1908) 4.

14   Ibid.

15   "Saturday Evening Wedding," *Carlisle Evening Herald* (8 March 1909).

16   Ann Kramer Hoffer, "Remember That" (Carlisle: Cumberland County Historical Society, 1990).

17   "Bosler Home Will Be Magnificent," *The Evening Sentinel* (27 April 1908) 4.

18   Ibid.

[19] Ann Kramer Hoffer, "Remember That " (Carlisle: Cumberland County Historical Society, 1990). See also, Mary O. Bradley, "Mansion predated Carlisle mall," *Patriot-News* (2 May 2003) E01.

[20] Mary O. Bradley, "Mansion predated Carlisle mall," *Patriot-News* (2 May 2003) E01.

[21] Ann Kramer Hoffer, 'Remember That" (Carlisle: Cumberland County Historical Society, 1990)

[22] Original spelling of Thornwald, found in *Residence and Business Directory of Carlisle, 1911-1912* (Carlisle: The Letter Shop) 92.

The Residence of L.S. Sadler

[1] "Real Estate Sale: Lewis S. Sadler, Esq. Purchases portion of the Dr. Joseph W. Noble Farm Southwest of Town." *Carlisle Daily Herald* (29 April 1909) 1.

[2] Cumberland County Deed Book, A6, 131.

[3] *Atlas of Cumberland County, Pennsylvania, 1858* (Carlisle: Cumberland County Historical Society, reprinted in 1987) 22-23).

[4] "Will of Wm. F. Noble," *American Volunteer* (22 January 1898) 3.

[5] Cumberland County Deed Book, A6, 131.

[6] "Important Real Estate Transfer," *The Evening Sentinel* (29 April 1909) 2.

[7] Cumberland County Deed Book, 7M, 321.

[8] "Important Real Estate Transfer," *The Evening Sentinel* (29 April 1909) 2; "Real Estate Sale: Lewis S. Sadler, Esq. Purchases portion of the Dr. Joseph W. Noble Farm Southwest of Town." *Carlisle Daily Herald* (29 April 1909) 1.

[9] Ibid.

[10] "Important Real Estate Transfer," *The Evening Sentinel* (29 April 1909) 2.

[11] "Personal," *Carlisle Daily Herald* (29 April 1909).

[12] "Important Real Estate Transfer," *The Evening Sentinel* (29 April 1909) 2.

[13] For trips to Europe, see "Returning Home," *American Volunteer* (27 April 1904) 2 col. 7; "Personal," *The Evening Sentinel* (13 April 1908) 4.

[14] Victor,Belcher, Richard Bond, Mike Gray, Andy Wittrick. *Sutton House: A Tudor courtier's house in Hackney*. (Swindon: English Heritage, 2004) 25.

[15] Daniel Heisey: "A Man of Discrimination," *Pages of History: Essays on Cumberland County, Pennsylvania*. (Carlisle: New Loudon Press, 1994) 70.

[16] Victor,Belcher, Richard Bond, Mike Gray, Andy Wittrick. *Sutton House: A Tudor courtier's house in Hackney*. (Swindon: English Heritage, 2004) 20-23.

17 Hill & Stout, New York, to L.S. Sadler, Esq., Carlisle, 14 August 1912, copy of letter found in "Thornwald" drop file, Cumberland County Historical Society, Carlisle, Pa. See also, H. Avary Tipping, M.A., ed., *In English Homes* (London : Office of Country Life, 1908) Vol. II. Accessed on June 02, 2010. Google books.

18 "Important Real Estate Transfer," *The Evening Sentinel* (29 April 1909) 2.

19 Ibid., For the home of Albert Boardman, see Robert B. MacKay, Anthony K. Baker, Carol A. Traynor , eds. *Long Island Country Homes and Their Architects, 1860-1940* (China: Palace Press , Ltd. 1997) 209. Accessed on Accessed on June 16, 2010. Google books.

20 Land survey found in same folder as the architectural drawings of the Thornwald Mansion. Cumberland County Historical Society, Carlisle, Pa.

21 Architectural Drawings of the Thornwald Mansion, drawn by Hill & Stout Architects, New York on June 7, 1909. Cumberland County Historical Society, Carlisle, Pa.

22 "Contract Let," *The Evening Sentinel* (3 July 1909) 6.

23 "Sadler Residence Colonial Style," *Carlisle Volunteer* (6 July 1909) 1.

24 Concerning the "building boom" of South College Street, see "More Fine Houses," *Carlisle Evening Herald* (2 May 1910) 1.

25 "Work Started," *Carlisle Herald* (9 September 1909) 1.

26 "Theodore Starrett, Dead," *The New York Times* (10 October 1917).

27 "Thompson & Starrett Co." 2000-2011, Emporis Corporation. <http://www.emporis.com/application/?nav=company&lng=3&id=102864>.(10 May 2010).

28 The name "Harry Hertzler" was inscribed on a floor board that was removed from the third floor of the mansion in the fall of 2011 during construction. Regarding the help of the Sheafer Brothers and the Italians from New York, see John Vernon Hertzler, Jr., *Thornwald* (Carlisle: The Youth Department of First Reformed Church, 1953) 4.

29 "Telford Road at New Home," *Carlisle Evening Herald* (15 August 1910) 1.

30 "That Mansion In The Forest," *Carlisle Herald* (12 October 1909) 1.

31 Ibid.

32 Ibid.

33 "Facts Concerning The Magnificent Sadler Mansion," *The Evening Sentinel* (16 August 1910) 6.

34 "That Mansion In The Forest," *Carlisle Herald* (12 October 1909) 1.

35 Ibid.

36 Jennifer Vogelsong, "Owner saves mansion," *The Sentinel Weekly* (14 December 1999) A 7.

37 "Facts Concerning The Magnificent Sadler Mansion," *The Evening Sentinel* (16 August 1910) 6.
In reference to the columns having been constructed of concrete over a wooden form, see photo album of Thornwald photographs now property of Thornwald Home, Carlisle, Pennsylvania.

38   Paul Riede, "A park in the woods," *The Evening Sentinel* (8 August 1981) C 6.

39   John Vernon Hertzler, Jr., *Thornwald* (Carlisle: The Youth Department of First Reformed Church, 1953) 3.

40   Observation, (23 October 2010).

41   Jennifer Vogelsong, "Owner saves mansion," *The Sentinel Weekly* (14 December 1999) A 7

42   Observation (1 May 2011).

43   "That Mansion In The Forest," *Carlisle Herald* (12 October 1909) 1.

44   Ibid.

45   "New Notes," *Carlisle Herald* (28 October 1909) 1.

46   "New Law Office," *Carlisle Herald* (22 November 1909) 6.

47   *Insurance Maps of Carlisle, Cumberland County, Pennsylvania* (New York: Sanborn Map Company, 1902) sheet 10.

48   "Street Grading on South Side," *Carlisle Evening Herald* (23 May 1910).

49   "Council Sent Back Ordinance Regarding Fire Co. Government," *Carlisle Evening Herald* (9 September 1910) 1.

50   "Facts Concerning The Magnificent Sadler Mansion," *The Evening Sentinel* (16 August 1910) 6.

51   Ibid.

52   Ibid.

53   Ibid.

54   Ibid.

55   "Telford Road at New Home," *Carlisle Evening Herald* (15 August 1910) 1.

56   "Facts Concerning The Magnificent Sadler Mansion," *The Evening Sentinel* (16 August 1910) 6.

"Thornwold"

1   Original spelling of Thornwald, spelled as "Thornwold", according to the *Residence and Business Directory of Carlisle, 1911-1912* (Carlisle: The Letter Shop) 92. For how Thornwald received its name, read Paul Riede, "A park in the woods," *The Evening Sentinel* (8 August 1981) C 6.

2   "Governor at Thornewold," *Carlisle Evening Herald* (8 May 1911) 4.

3   Ibid., 4.

4   Paul Riede, "A park in the woods ," *The Evening Sentinel* (8 August 1981) C 6.

[5] Victor,Belcher, Richard Bond, Mike Gray, Andy Wittrick. *Sutton House: A Tudor courtier's house in Hackney*. (Swindon: English Heritage, 2004) 7. For more information regarding English homes, read H. Avary Tipping, M.A., ed., *In English Homes* (London : Office of Country Life, 1904 - 1909) Vol. 1 - 3.

[6] Jennifer Vogelsong, "Owner saves mansion," *The Sentinel Weekly* (14 December 1999) A 7

[7] Observation, (1 May 2011).

[8] John Vernon Hertzler, Jr., *Thornwald* (Carlisle: The Youth Department of First Reformed Church, 1953) 6.

[9] Jennifer Vogelsong, "Owner saves mansion," *The Sentinel Weekly* (14 December 1999) A 7; John Vernon Hertzler, Jr., *Thornwald* (Carlisle: The Youth Department of First Reformed Church, 1953) 6. In reference to the "linen fold" pattern used in the Sutton House, see Victor,Belcher, Richard Bond, Mike Gray, Andy Wittrick. *Sutton House: A Tudor courtier's house in Hackney*. (Swindon: English Heritage, 2004) 204.

[10] See first floor blueprint, dated June 7, 1909 found in Sadler Mansion Floor Plans folder, Cumberland County Historical Society, Carlisle, Pa.

[11] Paul Riede, "A park in the woods ," *The Evening Sentinel* (8 August 1981) C 6.

[12] See first floor blueprint, dated June 7, 1909 found in Sadler Mansion Floor Plans folder, Cumberland County Historical Society, Carlisle, Pa.

[13] "Facts Concerning The Magnificent Sadler Mansion," *The Evening Sentinel* (16 August 1910) 6.

[14] Observation (1 May 2011).

[15] See first floor blueprint, dated June 7, 1909 found in Sadler Mansion Floor Plans folder, Cumberland County Historical Society, Carlisle, Pa.

[16] Ibid.

[17] Observation (23 October 2010).

[18] John Vernon Hertzler, Jr., *Thornwald* (Carlisle: The Youth Department of First Reformed Church, 1953) 5.

[19] "Personal Notes," *Carlisle Evening Herald* (7 April 1910). For the appearance of the library see, John Vernon Hertzler, Jr., *Thornwald* (Carlisle: The Youth Department of First Reformed Church, 1953) 5.

[20] Location of writing desk in library, from observation on May 1, 2011. For reference to "secret room," see, Jennifer Vogelsong, "Owner saves mansion," *The Sentinel Weekly* (14 December 1999) A 7.

[21] See first floor blueprint, dated June 7, 1909 found in Sadler Mansion Floor Plans folder, Cumberland County Historical Society, Carlisle, Pa.

[22] John Vernon Hertzler, Jr., *Thornwald* (Carlisle: The Youth Department of First Reformed Church, 1953) 6.

[23] Ibid.

[24] A tag containing the name "William Baumgarten & Co." was found underneath one of the benches that sat beside the fireplace in the upstairs billiard room in September 2011. "Hinged top" taken from third floor blueprint found in Sadler Mansion Floor Plans folder, Cumberland County Historical Society, Carlisle, Pa.

[25] "Bought Residence," *Carlisle Evening Herald* (16 May 1911) 1.

[26] U.S. Department of the Interior, Census Office, Fourteenth Census, 1920, Carlisle, Cumberland County, Pennsylvania, s.v. "Lewis Sadler," *Heritage Quest,* HeritageQuestOnline.com.

[27] In reference to the rooms which were located in the basement, see "Facts Concerning The Magnificent Sadler Mansion," *The Evening Sentinel* (16 August 1910) 6. The meaning of rathskeller as found in: Jennifer Vogelsong , "Owner saves mansion," *The Sentinel Weekly* (14 December 1999) A 7.

[28] John Vernon Hertzler, Jr., *Thornwald* (Carlisle: The Youth Department of First Reformed Church, 1953) 6.

[29] Observation (1 May 2011).

[30] The name "C.P. Biggins Co." was inscribed on a board that was found during cleanup of the mansion on August 22, 2012.

[31] Jennifer Vogelsong , "Owner saves mansion," *The Sentinel Weekly* (14 December 1999) A 7.

[32] Observation (1 May 2011).

[33] From sale of the entire contents of Thornwald on May 27, 1953 at Thornwald. Copy found in "Thornwald" drop file, Cumberland County Historical Society, Carlisle, Pa.

[34] John Vernon Hertzler, Jr., *Thornwald* (Carlisle: The Youth Department of First Reformed Church, 1953) 6.

Additions to the Thornwald Estate

[1] "A Bad One," *The Evening Sentinel* (6 December 1920) 2.

[2] "Builders' Busy Spring," *Carlisle Evening Herald* (29 April 1912) 4. For "eight-car garage" see, John Vernon Hertzler, Jr., *Thornwald* (Carlisle: The Youth Department of First Reformed Church, 1953) 3.

[3] "Erecting Garage," *The Evening Sentinel* (22 May 1912) 8; Paul Riede, "A park in the woods," *The Evening Sentinel* (8 August 1981) C 6.

[4] George M. Diffenderfer. *I Believe in Yesterday* (self-published by author, 10-25-1972), 74. Cumberland County Historical Society, Carlisle, Pa; "Jersey Bank Officials Here," *Carlisle Evening Herald* (23 September 1911) 1.

[5] Hill & Stout, New York, to L.S. Sadler, Esq., Carlisle, 14 August 1912, copy of letter found in "Thornwald" drop file at the Cumberland County Historical Society, Carlisle, Pa.

[6] Ibid., In reference to Houghton Tower, see H. Avary Tipping, M.A., ed., *In English Homes,* (London : Office of Country Life, 1908) Vol. II, 113-114, Accessed on June 02, 2010. Google books.

[7] Hill & Stout, New York, to L.S. Sadler, Esq., Carlisle, 14 August 1912, copy of letter found in "Thornwald" drop file at the Cumberland County Historical Society, Carlisle, Pa.

[8] "The Inflation Calculator," 2010, S. Morgan Friedman. <http://www.westegg.com/inflation/>. (10 May 2010).

[9] "$50,000 for a fence at Sadler Home: Magnificent Property To Be Enhanced In Beauty," *The Evening Sentinel* (3 October 1914) 6.

10   John Vernon Hertzler, Jr., *Thornwald* (Carlisle: The Youth Department of First Reformed Church, 1953) 4.

11   See, Cumberland County Deed Book, 8I 5 82.

Living in High Society

1. U.S. Department of the Interior, Census Office, Twelfth Census, 1900, Carlisle, Cumberland County, Pennsylvania, s.v. "Frank Bosler," *Heritage Quest,* HeritageQuestOnline.com. The Bosler's had two female black servants', both of whom were from Virginia. Bettie Taylor ,45, was the cook and Lusy Avington,20, was the chambermaid.

2. "Bought Residence," *Carlisle Evening Herald* (16 May 1911) 1.

3. *Residence and Business Directory of Carlisle, 1911-1912* (Carlisle: The Letter Shop) 77.

4. U.S. Department of the Interior, Census Office, Fourteenth Census, 1920, Carlisle, Cumberland County, Pennsylvania, s.v. "William McCulley," *Heritage Quest,* HeritageQuestOnline.com. At this time, McCulley (34) and his wife, Irene (34) had a one-year-old son named, William J. McCulley, Jr.

5. "People who are entertaining fresh air children," *The Evening Sentinel* (2 August 1911).

6. "Carlisle will care for 50 waifs from New York tenements," *Carlisle Evening Herald* (7 August 1912) 1.

7. "Mr. and Mrs. L.S. Sadler Observe Tenth Wedding Anniversary," *Carlisle Evening Herald* (27 June 1912) 4.

8. "Carlisle's Organizations," *Residence and Business Directory of Carlisle, 1911-1912* (Carlisle: The Letter Shop) 7.

9. "Charity Ball Brilliant Success," *The Evening Sentinel* (1 December 1914) 4.

10. "Carlislers Attend May Fete," *The Evening Sentinel* (3 May 1913) 2.

11. For the couple's trips to Europe, see "Returning Home," *American Volunteer* (27 April 1904) 2; "Personal" *The Evening Sentinel* (5 June 1906) 4; "Personal Notes," *Carlisle Evening Herald* (7 April 1910); For their two months trip to the Mediterranean, see "Personal," *The Evening Sentinel* (13 April 1908) 4.

12. "Society: Home from Europe," *Carlisle Evening Herald* (15 April 1913) 4.

13. Their trip to the Pacific Coast, see "Personal," *The Evening Sentinel* (8 April 1915) 6.

14. For Frank C. Bosler, see *Biographical Annals of Cumberland County, Pennsylvania,* (Chicago: The Genealogical Publishing Co., 1905) 217.

15. "The new president," *Carlisle Evening Herald* (5 May 1910).

16. "Charter Granted to Carlisle's New Board of Trade," *Carlisle Evening Herald* (29 March 1910).

17. "The new president," *Carlisle Evening Herald* (5 May 1910).

18. "Chain Works to Stay Here," *Carlisle Evening Herald* (19 May 1910).

19. *The Evening Sentinel* (2 November 1911) 2; For Sadler's nomination as a Republican National Delicate, see "Mr. Sadler spent $666 to run for delegate," *The Evening Sentinel* (29 April 1912) 4.

20. Ibid.

21 "Prominent Citizens Endorse the New Carlisle Hospital Project," *The Evening Sentinel* (9 July 1913) 4.

22 "Visiting Nurse Association," *The Evening Sentinel* (22 March 1913) 7.

23 "Hospital Auxiliary wants many new members," *Carlisle Evening Herald* (14 February 1919) 8.

24 "New Hospital is Completed," *The Evening Sentinel* (19 July 1916) 4; see also, Susan E. Meehan, *The Carlisle Hospital: Most Important Building in Town* (Carlisle Area Health & Wellness Foundation, 2008) 26.

25 "Personal Notes," *Carlisle Evening Herald* (15 April 1910); "Notes of interest about your friends," *The Evening Sentinel* (30 May 1913) 6.

26 Herman P. Miller and W. Harry Baker, comps. "State Institutions and Boards of Control," *Smull's Legislative Hand Book and Manual of the state of Pennsylvania* (Harrisburg: C.E. Aughinbaugh, 1912) 137.

27 "M.C. Kennedy Entertained," *Carlisle Evening Herald* (3 October 1910).

28 "Governor Tener Twills at Reception Ball Game," *Carlisle Evening Herald* (5 October 1914); For Governor Tener's visit to Thornwald, see "Governor at Thornewold," *Carlisle Evening Herald* (8 May 1911) 4.

29 "Personals," *The Evening Sentinel* (17 April 1915) 6.

30 "Entertained Justices: L.S. Sadler among notables at Governor's dinner," *The Evening Sentinel* (25 May 1915) 7.

A Black Cloud Looms Over Thornwald

1 "Mr. Kennedy gave dinner for Judge Sadler," *The Evening Sentinel* (10 January 1916).

2 "Majority & Plurality," *The Evening Sentinel* (11 November 1904) 3.

3 "Sylvester B. Sadler Elected Judge By Great Majority," *Carlisle Evening Herald* (22 September 1915) 1.

4 "Maust's Appointment Generally Expected," *The Evening Sentinel* (4 December 1920) 4.
5 Barton R. Laub, *The Dickinson School of Law: Proud and Independent* (Harrisburg: McFarland Co., 1983) 46.

6 "Personals," *The Evening Sentinel* (10 January 1916) 6.

7 "Personal Mention," *The Evening Sentinel* (3 July 1916) 4.

8 "Personals," *The Evening Sentinel* (18 September 1916) 6; "Mrs. L.S. Sadler Dies in Hospital," *The Evening Sentinel* (19 September 1916) 8. According to obituary, she was thirty-nine at the time of her death, although she was born in 1872, and not 1879, as presumed by the newspaper.

9 Ibid.

10 Ibid.

11 Cumberland County Deed Book, 8P, 298-299.

12 "Gen. W.F. Sadler Dies in Carlisle," *Star Independent* (11 November 1916). News article located in a scrapbook entitled "Press Tributes to the Late Adj. Gen. Wilbur F. Sadler, Jr." located at the Cumberland County Historical Society, Carlisle, Pa.

[13] "Sadler Burial in Carlisle Monday," *Evening Times* (11 November 1916). News article taken from "Press Tributes to the Late Adj. Gen. Wilbur F. Sadler, Jr." scrapbook; Cumberland County Historical Society, Carlisle, Pa.

[14] "Gen. W. F. Sadler, Jr.," *The Evening Sentinel* (11 November 1916) 7.

[15] "Sadler Burial in Carlisle Monday," *Evening Times* (11 November 1916). News article taken from "Press Tributes to the Late Adj. Gen. Wilbur F. Sadler, Jr." scrapbook; Cumberland County Historical Society, Carlisle, Pa.

[16] Francis Bazley Lee, *Genealogical & Personal Memorial of Mercer County, New Jersey*, Vol. I. (NY& Chicago: The Lewis Publishing Co., 1907) 155, Accessed on June 02, 2010. Google books.

[17] "Sadler Burial in Carlisle Monday," *Evening Times* (11 November 1916). News article taken from "Press Tributes to the Late Adj. Gen. Wilbur F. Sadler, Jr." scrapbook; Cumberland County Historical Society, Carlisle, Pa.

[18] Ibid; Francis Bazley Lee, *Genealogical & Personal Memorial of Mercer County, New Jersey*, Vol. I. (NY& Chicago: The Lewis Publishing Co., 1907) 155, Accessed on June 02, 2010. Google books; See also, "Gen. W. F. Sadler, Jr." *The Evening Sentinel* (11 November 1916) 7.

[19] See letter written by Wilbur Fisk Sadler, to his son, Wilbur Fisk Sadler, Jr. dated June 14, 1913 located in "Sadler/Sterrett" folder at the Cumberland County Historical Society, Carlisle, Pa. along with a number of other correspondences addressed to Wilbur Sadler, Jr. concerning Sadler/Sterrett genealogy.

[20] "Pay Tribute to General W. F. Sadler," *Star Independent* (13 November 1916); "Notable People At Sadler Burial" *Harrisburg Telegraph* (13 November 1916). News article taken from "Press Tributes to the Late Adj. Gen. Wilbur F. Sadler, Jr." scrapbook; Cumberland County Historical Society, Carlisle, Pa.

[21] "Gen. Sadler's Funeral Today," *The Evening Sentinel* (13 November 1916) 4.

[22] "Gen. Sadler leaves estate of $250,000 to 3 brothers," *The Star and Sentinel* (24 November 1916) 1. According to "The Inflation Calculator," 2010, S. Morgan Friedman. <http://www.westegg.com/inflation/> the $250,000 would be equivalent to 4.8 million today.

[23] "Masons of New Jersey unveil Memorial to General W. F. Sadler," *Carlisle Evening Herald* (28 November 1916) 1.

[24] "Wilbur Sadler's Memory Honored," *Electric Railway Journal* (2 December 1916); "Mayor Donnelly Plans Memorial To Gen. Sadler" (2 December 1916). Both news articles taken from "Press Tributes to the Late Adj. Gen. Wilbur F. Sadler, Jr." scrapbook; Cumberland County Historical Society, Carlisle, Pa.

A Man of Distinction

[1] "Mr. Sadler on Committee," *The Evening Sentinel* (22 March 1917) 7.

[2] *Philadelphia in the World War 1914-1919* (New York: Wynkoop Hallenbeck Crawford Co., 1922) 343. Accessed on October 20, 2009. Google books.

[3] "Council of National Defense and Committee of Public Safety, Executive Committee, Minutes, November 27, 1918 to October 3, 1919". Record Group-10: Records of the Office of the Governor, Pennsylvania State Archives, Harrisburg, Pa, p. 61.

[4] *Philadelphia in the World War 1914-1919* (New York: Wynkoop Hallenbeck Crawford Co., 1922) 343. Accessed on October 20, 2009. Google books.

[5] "Sadler To Join Sproul's Cabinet," *The Evening Sentinel* (16 December 1918) 4.

[6] Ibid.

[7] "Col. Sadler Sees Cunningham: Interested in State Road Through Camp Hill," *The Evening Sentinel* (5 June 1915) 2.

[8] "Sadler To Join Sproul's Cabinet," *The Evening Sentinel* (16 December 1918) 4.

[9] "Lewis S. Sadler's Distinguished Guests," *The Evening Sentinel* (20 January 1919) 6.

[10] "Governor Sproul Takes the Oath," *The Evening Sentinel* (21 January 1919) 3.

[11] "Mr. Sadler to Give Dance," *The Evening Sentinel* (21 January 1919) 4; "Attended Sadler Dance," *The Evening Sentinel* (26 January 1919) 6.

[12] "Commissioner Sadler Declines to Speak," *The Evening Sentinel* (23 January 1919).

[13] "Praise Work of Present Highway Commissioner," *Carlisle Evening Herald* (27 February 1919)1; "State Highways Being Surveyed," *Carlisle Evening Herald* (12 March 1919) 1.

[14] "Highway Work Loses One of Its Leaders," *Successful Methods: A Magazine of Construction Methods*, January 1922, 18. Accessed on October 21, 2009. Google books.

[15] "Obituary," *Highway Engineer & Contractor,* Vol. 6 (Chicago: International Trade Press, February 1922) 66. Accessed on October 21, 2009. Google books.

[16] Ibid.

[17] "Roads to Last," *Carlisle Evening Herald* (7 March 1919) 4.

[18] "Obituary," *Highway Engineer & Contractor,* Vol. 6 (Chicago: International Trade Press, February 1922) 66. Accessed on October 21, 2009. Google books.

[19] "Open to Traffic," *The Evening Sentinel* (4 June 1919) 2; "To Begin Holly Street Work Soon," *Carlisle Evening Herald* (25 March 1919) 1.

[20] "Sadler Foundation creator married into Bosler money," *The Sentinel* (2 September 1993).

[21] "$10,000 paid over for turnpike," *The Evening Sentinel* (23 July 1919) 4.

[22] "Mr. Sadler's Distinguished Guests," *The Evening Sentinel* (1 May 1919) 2.

[23] "Commissioner Fort Ill Here," *The Evening Sentinel* (17 April 1919) 4; "State Health Official Speak," *The Evening Sentinel* (17 April 1919) 6; "Ex-Governor Fort Still Here," *The Evening Sentinel* (22 April 1919) 4.

[24] "John Franklin Fort." Wikipedia 4 October 2010. Wikimedia Foundation, Inc.. 9 March 2011. <http://en.wikipedia.org/wiki/John_Franklin_Fort>.

25 "Entertained Supreme Court," *The Evening Sentinel* (21 May 1919) 2; "Presided in Gettysburg," *The Evening Sentinel* (21 May 1919) 4, in this article the paper recalled Judge McPherson having attended the dinner at Thornwald on Tuesday.

26 "Mr. Sadler to Entertain," *The Evening Sentinel* (7 June 1919) 2; "Mr. Sadler's Dinner," *The Evening Sentinel* (12 June 1919) 6.

27 "Highway Work Loses One of Its Leaders," *Successful Methods: A Magazine of Construction Methods*, January 1922, 18. Accessed on October 21, 2009. Google books.

28 "Commissioner Sadler Invited," *The Evening Sentinel* (28 February 1920) 8; "Odds & Ends," *The Evening Sentinel* (12 March 1920) 2.

29 "Ex-Judge Sadler Dead in 80th year," *The Evening Sentinel* (6 July 1920) 2.

30 Cumberland County Deed Book, J9,580.

31 "Governors This Evening," *The Evening Sentinel* (2 December 1920) 2. See also, Thomas and Beth Coolidge, "One of a Kind," a paper read before the Cumberland County Historical Society on May 26, 2010.

32 "Distinguished Guests At Sadler Dinner," *The Evening Sentinel* (3 December 1920) 4.

33 Ibid.

34 Ibid.

35 "Obituary," *Highway Engineer & Contractor,* Vol. 6 (Chicago: International Trade Press, February 1922) 66. Accessed on October 21, 2009. Google books.

36 Ibid.

37 "Is Not Candidate For Governor," *Gettysburg Times* (24 November 1919) 5.

38 "Obituary," *Highway Engineer & Contractor,* Vol. 6 (Chicago: International Trade Press, February 1922) 66. Accessed on October 21, 2009. Google books.

39 "Highway Work Loses One of Its Leaders," *Successful Methods: A Magazine of Construction Methods*, January 1922, 18. Accessed on October 21, 2009. Google books.

40 "Permanent Road Work," *The New York Times* (8 January 1922).

41 "Funeral of Lewis S. Sadler Today," *The Evening Sentinel* (23 January 1923) 2.

42 "Obituary," *Highway Engineer & Contractor,* Vol. 6 (Chicago: International Trade Press, February 1922) 68. Accessed on October 21, 2009. Google books.

43 "Funeral of Lewis S. Sadler Today," *The Evening Sentinel* (23 January 1923) 2.

44 Daniel Heisey: "A Man of Discrimination," *Pages of History: Essays on Cumberland County, Pennsylvania.* (Carlisle: New Loudon Press, 1994) 79.

45 "Lewis S. Sadler, Highway Commissioner, Dies At Home," *The Evening Sentinel* (20 January 1922) 4.

46 For Sproul's reaction to the death of Commissioner Sadler, see "Governor Sproul's Tribute," *The Evening Sentinel* (21 January 1922); In reference to Sylvester's nightmare, see Daniel Heisey, *Ghosts of Carlisle* (Carlisle: New Loudon Press, 1998) 7-8.

47 "Funeral of Lewis S. Sadler Today," *The Evening Sentinel* (23 January 1923) 2; See also, Daniel Heisey, *Ghosts of Carlisle* (Carlisle: New Loudon Press, 1998) 7-8.

48 "Lewis S. Sadler, Highway Commissioner, Dies At Home," *The Evening Sentinel* (20 January 1922) 4.

49 "Lewis S. Sadler's Sudden Death Shocks Community," *The Dickinsonian,* (21 January 1922). For Commissioner Sadler's nomination as the Governor of Pennsylvania see also, "More Senators, Like Vare, Seek Road Contracts," *Evening Public Ledger* (31 December 1921).

50 "Obituary," *Highway Engineer & Contractor,* Vol. 6 (Chicago: International Trade Press, February 1922) 68. Accessed on October 21, 2009. Google books; "More Pay for Pennsylvania Road Officials," *The Highway Magazine*, Vol. 12 (Chicago: Armco Iron Culvert Flume Manufacturers' Association, October 1921) 8. Accessed on October 21, 2009. Google books.

51 "Governor Sproul's Tribute," *The Evening Sentinel* (21 January 1922).

52 "Funeral of Lewis S. Sadler Today," *The Evening Sentinel* (23 January 1923) 2.

53 Ibid, "Hundreds at Sadler Funeral," *The Evening Sentinel* (24 January 1922).

54 "Hundreds at Sadler Funeral," *The Evening Sentinel* (24 January 1922).

55 Susan E. Meehan, *The Carlisle Hospital: Most Important Building in Town* (Carlisle Area Health & Wellness Foundation, 2008) 30.

The Inheritance

1 "Pennsylvania's Progressive Highway Policy To Be Continued," *Highway Engineer & Contractor,* Vol. 6 (Chicago: International Trade Press, February 1922) 38. Accessed on October 21, 2009. Google books.

2 "Personals," *Highway Engineer & Contractor,* Vol. 7 (Chicago: International Trade Press, November 1922) 58. Accessed on July 17, 2011. Google books.

3 Register of Wills Index R-S, vol. 1, Cumberland County Court House, Carlisle, Pennsylvania, 112.

4 Cumberland County Deed Book, 9N , 518.

5 "The New Student Activities Center," *The Dickinson Alumnus* (February 1963) 1.

6 For information on Sylvester Sadler's time serving as Justice of the Supreme Court in Philadelphia read, Daniel Heisey: "A Man of Discrimination," *Pages of History: Essays on Cumberland County, Pennsylvania.* (Carlisle: New Loudon Press, 1994) 78, 80-81.

7 "Sylvester B. Sadler Associate Justice of Supreme Court, Dies," *The Evening Sentinel* (2 March 1931) 1.

8 Cumberland County Deed Book, 10 Y, 494.

9 Cumberland County Deed Book 9T, 462.

[10] Mary O. Bradley, "Mansion predated Carlisle mall," *Patriot-News* (2 May 2003) E01.

[11] *Polk's Carlisle, Cumberland County, Pa Director, 1924-1925* (Philadelphia: R.L. Polk & Co.) 147.

[12] *Insurance Maps of Carlisle, Cumberland County, Pennsylvania* (New York: Sanborn Map Company, 1915).

[13] "Mrs. Sadler Loses Eye," *The Evening Sentinel* (20 October 1924).

[14] "Mrs. Sadler Loses Eye," *The Evening Sentinel* (20 October 1924).

[15] Henry Line, "My Memories of Thornwald, The Sadlers and the Boslers," page 3, located in "Thornwald" drop folder at the Cumberland County Historical Society, Carlisle, Pa.

[16] Cumberland County Deed Books 8Q, 127 and 8O, 24.

[17] Cumberland County Deed Book 10L, 492.

[18] For additional information on Allenberry read, Kathleen Heinze, "The Allenberry Story," *At a Place Called the Boiling Springs* (Boiling Springs Sesquicentennial Publications Committee, 1995) 197-198.

The Final Years of Justice Sylvester Sadler

[1] *Residence and Business Directory of Carlisle, 1911-1912* (Carlisle: The Letter Shop) 106; "Dr. Trickett Found Ill in Bath Room," *The Evening Sentinel* (20 April 1920) 6.

[2] Cumberland County Will Book 34:467.

[3] Mark Podvia, "Walter Harrison Hitchler," *Cumberland County History* (Summer 1999).

[4] *The Commentator* (1925) 8.

[5] *Microcosm* (1929) 12, 16-17.

[6] Mark Podvia, "Walter Harrison Hitchler," *Cumberland County History* (Summer 1999).

[7] "Sylvester Baker Sadler (1876-1931)" Dickinson College. Accessed on 24 November 2010. <http://chronicles.dickinson.edu/encyclo/s/ed_sadlerSB.htm>. For more information on the life of Sylvester Sadler, read Daniel Heisey: "A Man of Discrimination," *Pages of History: Essays on Cumberland County, Pennsylvania.* (Carlisle: New Loudon Press, 1994).

[8] "Sylvester B. Sadler Associate Justice of Supreme Court, Dies," *The Evening Sentinel* (2 March 1931) 1.

[9] "John Franklin Fort." Wikipedia 4 October 2010. Wikimedia Foundation, Inc.. 9 March 2011. <http://en.wikipedia.org/wiki/John_Franklin_Fort>.

[10] "Sylvester B. Sadler Associate Justice of Supreme Court, Dies," *The Evening Sentinel* (2 March 1931) 1. "Justice Sadler Ill of Pneumonia," *The Evening Sentinel* (24 February 1931).

[11] Ibid.

[12] "Sylvester B. Sadler Associate Justice of Supreme Court, Dies," *The Evening Sentinel* (2 March 1931) 1.

[13] Ibid.

[14] "Sadler Funeral at 2:00 tomorrow," *The Evening Sentinel* (3 March 1931) 3.

[15] "Throng in final tribute attends Sadler funeral," *The Evening Sentinel* (4 March 1931) 1.

[16] "Sadler Funeral at 2:00 tomorrow," *The Evening Sentinel* (3 March 1931) 3.

[17] "File Sadler Will, Leaving Estate of 750,000, At Carlisle," *The Gettysburg Times* (7 March 1931) 2; "The Inflation Calculator," 2010, S. Morgan Friedman. <http://www.westegg.com/inflation/>. (10 May 2010).

[18] Will of Sylvester B. Sadler see, Cumberland County Will Book 36:126.

[19] Cumberland County Deed Books 11E, 378 and 11E, 478.

[20] "American chain works now is dismantled," *Carlisle Evening Herald* (13 March 1919) 1.

[21] *Polk's Carlisle, Cumberland County, Pa Director, 1933-1934* (Philadelphia: R.L. Polk & Co.) 146.

[22] "Sadler Books for Hamilton Library," *The Evening Sentinel* (7 August 1931).

[23] "Law School to Get Four Portraits," *The Dickinson Alumnus* 9-10, (September 1931): 13; "Presents Four Portraits to Law School," *The Dickinson Alumnus* 9-10, (November 1931) 9.

The Final Years at Thornwald

[1] Interview, (27 October 2010).

[2] Henry Line, "My Memories of Thornwald, The Sadlers and the Boslers," page 5, located in "Thornwald" drop folder at the Cumberland County Historical Society, Carlisle, Pa.

[3] "Large Luncheons at Beach Club," *Palm Beach Daily News* (21 February 1935) 9.

[4] "Butler Held For Heirloom Thefts," *The Gettysburg Times* (12 January 1935) 2.

[5] U.S. Department of the Interior, Census Office, Fourteenth Census, 1920, Carlisle, Cumberland County, Pennsylvania, s.v. "Richard Grant," *Heritage Quest,* HeritageQuestOnline.com

[6] *Residence and Business Directory of Carlisle,1921-1922* (Carlisle: Carlisle Directory Co.) 74.

[7] See, the will of Sylvester B. Sadler, Cumberland County Will Book 36:126.

[8] See, will of Sylvester B. Sadler, Cumberland County Will Book 36:126; "The Inflation Calculator," 2010, S. Morgan Friedman. <http://www.westegg.com/inflation/>. (10 May 2010).

[9] "Butler Held For Heirloom Thefts," *The Gettysburg Times* (12 January 1935) 2; "The Inflation Calculator," 2010, S. Morgan Friedman. <http://www.westegg.com/inflation/>. (10 May 2010).

[10] "Butler Held For Heirloom Thefts," *The Gettysburg Times* (12 January 1935) 2; "Dealer Accused with Negro Butler," *The Evening Sentinel* (14 January 1935) 5.

[11] "Sadlers Host to Dignitaries," *The Evening Sentinel* (2 March 1935) 3.

[12] Henry Line, "My Memories of Thornwald, The Sadlers and the Boslers," 3, located in "Thornwald" drop folder at the Cumberland County Historical Society, Carlisle, Pa.

[13] Ibid, 3.

[14] Ibid, 4.

[15] Ibid.

[16] Kathleen Heinze, "The Allenberry Story," *At a Place Called the Boiling Springs* (Boiling Springs Sesquicentennial Publications Committee, 1995) 198.

[17] Henry Line, "My Memories of Thornwald, The Sadlers and the Boslers," 8.

[18] See page copied from the *Historical Encyclopedia of Wyoming* located in James W. Bosler's student drop file at the Dickinson College Archives and Special Collections, Carlisle, Pa.

[19] Cumberland County Deed Book 15H, 477; "Three Synods Buy Estate As Home For the Aged," *Huntington Daily News* (13 July 1948) 5.

[20] "Deaths," *The Evening Sentinel* (18 May 1950) 2.

The End of an Era

[1] Henry Line, "My Memories of Thornwald, The Sadlers and the Boslers," 5.

[2] Observation from a photograph of "Stence" Miller, also known as John X. Miller, taken at Thornwald in 1953 by James Steinmetz. Photograph located at the Cumberland County Historical Society, Carlisle, Pa.

[3] *Residence and Business Directory of Carlisle, 1911-1912* (Carlisle: The Letter Shop) 85.

[4] *Polk's Carlisle, (Cumberland County, PA), vol. 1951-52.* (Philadelphia: R.L. Polk & Co., Inc., 1952). 260, 440.

[5] "To Dedicate Law School Dorm At Commencement," *The Dickinson Alumnus* (May 1952).

[6] John Vernon Hertzler, Jr., *Thornwald* (Carlisle: The Youth Department of First Reformed Church, 1953) 3.

[7] Ibid, 7.

[8] Ibid, 3.

[9] Ibid, 5.

[10] Ibid.

[11] Ibid.

[12] Henry Line, "My Memories of Thornwald, The Sadlers and the Boslers," 4.

[13] John Vernon Hertzler, Jr., *Thornwald* (Carlisle: The Youth Department of First Reformed Church, 1953) 6.

[14] See, auction bill dated May 27, 1953 containing an exhaustive list of items sold out of Thornwald. Copy of the auction bill can be found inside the "Thornwald" drop file located at the Cumberland County Historical Society, Carlisle, Pa.

[15] Ibid.

[16] John Vernon Hertzler, Jr., *Thornwald* (Carlisle: The Youth Department of First Reformed Church, 1953) 6.

[17] Ibid.

[18] See, auction bill dated May 27, 1953 containing an exhaustive list of items sold out of Thornwald. Copy of the auction bill can be found inside the "Thornwald" drop file located at the Cumberland County Historical Society, Carlisle, Pa.

[19] John Vernon Hertzler, Jr., *Thornwald* (Carlisle: The Youth Department of First Reformed Church, 1953) 6-7.

[20] "Horace T. Sadler," *The Evening Sentinel* (28 February 1953) 4.

[21] "Dr. H.T. Sadler, Carlisle, Dies," *The Star and Sentinel* (7 March 1953) 3.

[22] "Sadler Will Creates Foundation To Pay Income To Hospital," *The Evening Sentinel* (6 March 1953) 1.

[23] Ibid.

[24] For the will of Sylvester Sadler, see Cumberland County Will Book 36:126-127.

[25] "Sadler Will Creates Foundation To Pay Income To Hospital," *The Evening Sentinel* (6 March 1953) 1.

[26] "News From Neighboring Counties: Plan Addition to Hospital Annex," *Gettysburg Times* (12 September 1934).

[27] Susan E. Meehan, *The Carlisle Hospital: Most Important Building in Town* (Carlisle Area Health & Wellness Foundation, 2008) 35.

[28] "Sadler Will Creates Foundation To Pay Income To Hospital," *The Evening Sentinel* (6 March 1953) 1.

[29] "Rare Antiques to Go on Block At 52-Acre Carlisle Mansion," *The Patriot News* (26 May 1953); See also, Susan E. Meehan, *The Carlisle Hospital: Most Important Building in Town* (Carlisle Area Health & Wellness Foundation, 2008) 44.

[30] "Rare Antiques to Go on Block At 52-Acre Carlisle Mansion," *The Patriot News* (26 May 1953).

[31] Interview, (27 October 2010).

The Sale of the Sadler Heirlooms

[1] For the will of Horace T. Sadler, see Cumberland County Will Book 48:93-99

[3] "Rare Antiques to Go on Block At 52-Acre Carlisle Mansion," *The Patriot News* (26 May 1953).

[4] Ibid.

[5] "Sadler Sale May Total $17,000," *The Evening Sentinel* (28 May 1953)

[6] Ibid., Prices in parentheses, taken from "The Inflation Calculator," 2010, S. Morgan Friedman. <http://www.westegg.com/inflation/>. (10 May 2010).

[7] Ibid.

[8] "Sadler Sale May Total $17,000," *The Evening Sentinel* (28 May 1953).

[9] See , auction bill dated June 8, 1974 containing a list of items sold at the new Homewood Retirement Center now known as Thornwald Home. Copy of the auction bill found inside the "Thornwald" drop file located at the Cumberland County Historical Society, Carlisle, Pa.

10   Deb Cline, "Books of old Sadler estate provide 'reading' of family," *The Evening Sentinel* (7 June 1977).

11   Ibid.

12   See, "Carlisle Area School District Library Books- Sadler Estate" found in the "Thornwald" drop file located at the Cumberland County Historical Society, Carlisle, Pa.

13   See, January 1, 1983 auction bill entitled "Public Auction-New Years Day" found in "Thornwald" drop file located at the Cumberland County Historical Society, Carlisle, Pa.

Homewood

1   "First Four Guests Arrive at Carlisle Church Home," *The Evening News* (1 October 1954) 1.

2   See blueprints drawn by E.G. Dempwolf of York in January 1953, entitled "Alterations to Sadler Unit Homewood Church Home for The Evangelical & Reformed Church, Carlisle, Pa.". Blueprints located at the Cumberland County Historical Society, Carlisle, Pa.

3   For reference to the infirmary see, "Hear Testimony In Damage Suit," *The Evening Sentinel* article taken from folder containing miscellaneous newspaper clippings concerning Homewood, property of Thornwald Home, Carlisle, PA.

4   Paul Ried, "A park in the woods," *The Evening Sentinel* (8 August 1981) C 6.

5   "Guests Arrive At Thornwold Home," *The Evening Sentinel* (1 October 1953) 1; "First Four Guests Arrive at Carlisle Church Home," *The Evening News* (1 October 1954) 1.

6   "Church Synods Dedicate Home," *The Evening Sentinel*, (19 October 1953) 2, "Sadler Home Residents," *Homewood Fireside,* (1963) p. 8, located in "Thornwald" drop file at the Cumberland County Historical Society, Carlisle, Pa.

7   Paul Ried, "A park in the woods," *The Evening Sentinel* (8 August 1981) C 6.

8   Ibid.

9   "Decision to Buy Sadler Estate Controversial in Carlisle," *Sunday Patriot News* (26 September 1971) A 2.

10   Ibid.

Thornwald Park

1   Cumberland County Deed Book 24O, 653.

2   "350,000 for Sadler Home," *Homewood Fireside,* vol. 23 (1972).

3   Interview with Harold North, (01 November 2010); See also, "Decision to Buy Sadler Estate Controversial in Carlisle," *Sunday Patriot News* (26 September 1971) A 2.

4   See, Cumberland County Deed Book, 26I, 953.

5   "Hear Testimony In Damage Suit," *The Evening Sentinel* article taken from folder containing miscellaneous newspaper clippings concerning Homewood, property of Thornwald Home, Carlisle, PA; See also, "Decision to Buy Sadler Estate Controversial in Carlisle," *Sunday Patriot News* (26 September 1971), which makes

[6] reference to the three acre tract which at the time still was not developed. See, Cumberland County Deed Book, 26I, 953.

[7] For more information regarding the beginnings of Thornwald Park, read "Thornwald Park: History Plans Purpose," a brochure located in folder entitled "Carlisle, *Sentinel*, Cumb. Co.," Cumberland County Historical Society, Carlisle, Pa.

[8] " Town's newest park, Thornwald, dedicated," *The Evening Sentinel* (16 August 1976) 6.

[9] "That Mansion In The Forest," *Carlisle Herald* (12 October 1909) 1.

[10] Interview with Ron Shearer, (29 March 2011).

[11] Ibid.

[12] From Andrea Crouse, (2 February 2011).

The Demise of Thornwald

[1] See, Cumberland County Deed Book 26I, 950.

[2] "Alternative Learning Program Moved to Homewood Mansion," *The Evening Sentinel* (21 November 1975).

[3] Interview with Lester Wallis, (28 March 2011).

[4] Ibid.

[5] Paul Ried, "A park in the woods," *The Evening Sentinel* (8 August 1981) C 6.

[6] Ibid.; Pastor Francis L. Kurtansky to Dwayne McLaughlin, 21 September 1981, letter located in folder entitled, "Thornwald Mansion-850 Bicentennial Drive" at the Carlisle Borough office, Carlisle, Pa.

[7] See, Cumberland County Deed Book 32C, 443.

[8] Dwainto Ben, "Memorandum,"(25 January 1989), located in folder entitled "850 Bicentennial Drive" at the Carlisle Borough office, Carlisle, Pa.

[9] Ibid.

[10] Jennifer Vogelsong, "Owner saves mansion," *The Sentinel Weekly* (14 December 1999) A 7

[11] Ibid.

[12] David Blymire, "Thornwald Mansion goes up for auction," *The Sentinel* (5 December 1999) B 11.

[13] David Blymire, "Mansion headed for blight status," *The Sentinel* (18 August 2005).

[14] Ibid.; See also letter, from Michael Landis to Kenneth Womack, 1 December 2004, located in folder, "850 Bicentennial Drive," at the Carlisle Borough office, Carlisle, Pa.

[15] Ibid.

[16] From handwritten note, entitled "Vandalism" located in folder, "850 Bicentennial Drive," at the Carlisle

17 Borough office, Carlisle, Pa.
Letter from Michael Landis to Kenneth Womack, 1 December 2004, located in folder, "850 Bicentennial Drive," at the Carlisle Borough office, Carlisle, Pa.

18 Joseph Cress, "Police probe online photos of Thornwald intruders," *The Sentinel* (24 August 2007) 1.

19 The Sentinel staff, "Vandals damage Thornwald Mansion inside," *The Sentinel* (2 October 2006).

The Great Conflagration

1 Heather Stauffer, "House probably destroyed, officials say," *The Sentinel* (21 August 2007) 1.

2 Ibid.

3 Heather Stauffer, "Built for 1,000 years, dies at 100," *The Sentinel* (22 August 2007) 1.

4 Joseph Cress, "Future of Thornwald Mansion unknown," *The Sentinel* (17 August 2008) 1.

5 "Bosler Stables and Garage are Burned," *The Evening Sentinel* (13 October 1925).

6 "That Mansion In The Forest," *Carlisle Herald* (12 October 1909) 1.

7 Observation (23 October 2010).

8 Ibid.

9 Ibid.

10 Ibid.

A Second Chance

1 Police report from Harrisburg Area police reported by McCoy Brothers (1 July 2009), located in folder, "850 Bicentennial Drive," at the Carlisle Borough office, Carlisle, Pa.

2 Joseph Cress, "More curious than serious at Thornwald," (16 October 2010) 1.

3 Observation (28 October 2010).

Select Bibliography

Letters/Unpublished Documents

Blueprints of Thornwald drawn by Hill & Stout of New York in 1909 located at the Cumberland County Historical Society, Carlisle, Pa.

Blueprints drawn for the Homewood Church Home in August 1959 by Paul Reed, located at the Cumberland County Historical Society, Carlisle, Pa.

"Council of National Defense and Committee of Public Safety, Executive Committee, Minutes, November 27, 1918 to October 3, 1919". Record Group-10: Records of the Office of the Governor, Pennsylvania State Archives, Harrisburg, Pa.

Diffenderfer, George M. *I Believe in Yesterday* (self-published by author, 10-25-1972). Cumberland County Historical Society, Carlisle, Pa.

Gobrecht, Lewis "The Sadler Family" *Sadler and Thornwald Information*, a notebook, Cumberland County Historical Society, Carlisle, Pennsylvania.

"James W. Bosler" student drop file, Archives and Special Collections, Dickinson College, Carlisle, Pa.

Letters and documents located in folder "850 Bicentennial Drive," property of the Borough of Carlisle, Pa.

Letter from Hill & Stout, New York, to L.S. Sadler, Esq., Carlisle, 14 August 1912, copy of letter found in "Thornwald" drop file at the Cumberland County Historical Society, Carlisle, Pa.

Letter from Wilbur Fisk Sadler, Carlisle to J.D Townsend, 18 December 1868 [?], Townsend Legal Papers, Moyerman Collection, Archives and Special Collections, Dickinson College , Carlisle, Pennsylvania.

Letter from Wilbur Fisk Sadler, to his son, Wilbur Fisk Sadler, Jr. dated June 14, 1913 located in "Sadler/Sterrett" folder at the Cumberland County Historical Society, Carlisle, Pa.

"Lewis S. Sadler" student drop file, Archives and Special Collections, Dickinson College, Carlisle, Pa.

Line, Henry "My Memories of Thornwald, The Sadlers and the Boslers," located in "Thornwald" drop folder at the Cumberland County Historical Society, Carlisle, Pa.

"Press Tributes to the Late Adj. Gen. Wilbur F. Sadler, Jr.," a scrapbook, Cumberland County Historical Society, Carlisle, Pa.

"Reminiscences of Nettie Jane Blair, August 1934". Cumberland County Historical Society, Carlisle, Pa.

"Seven Gables House" drop file, Cumberland County Historical Society, Carlisle, Pa.

"Thornwald" drop file, Cumberland County Historical Society, Carlisle, Pa.

"Thornwald Park: History Plans Purpose," a brochure located in folder entitled "Carlisle, *Sentinel*, Cumb. Co.," Cumberland County Historical Society, Carlisle, Pa.

Wilbur Fisk Sadler's handwritten bibliography entitled "W.F. Sadler" located in "Sadler/Sterrett" folder at the Cumberland County Historical Society, Carlisle, Pa.

Newsletters/Newspapers

American Volunteer(Carlisle)
Dickinsonian (Carlisle, Dickinson College)
Daily Evening Sentinel (Carlisle)
Gettysburg Times(Gettysburg)
Huntington Daily News
Palm Beach Daily News
The Carlisle Evening Herald(Carlisle)
The Carlisle Herald(Carlisle)
The Evening Sentinel (Carlisle)
The Evening Volunteer(Carlisle)
The Homewood Fireside
The New York Times
The Patriot-News (Harrisburg)
The Reading Eagle (Reading)
The Sentinel (Carlisle)
The Star and Sentinel (Gettysburg)

Maps/Atlases

Atlas of Cumberland County, Pennsylvania, 1858 (Carlisle: Cumberland County Historical Society, reprinted in 1987).

Beers, F.W. *Atlas of Cumberland County, Pennsylvania* (New York: F.W. Beers & Company, 1872).

Insurance Maps of Carlisle, Cumberland County, Pennsylvania (New York: Sanborn Map Company, 1902).

Insurance Maps of Carlisle, Cumberland County, Pennsylvania (New York: Sanborn Map Company, 1915).

Strong, J.G. *Map of Carlisle, Pennsylvania* (Baltimore: Schmidt & Trowe, 1867).

Books/Catalogues/Magazines

Abstract of the Twelfth Census, 1900 .Washington: Government Printing Office, 1902.

Belcher, Victor, Richard Bond, Mike Gray, Andy Wittrick. *Sutton House: A Tudor courtier's house in Hackney*. Swindon: English Heritage, 2004.

Biographical Annals of Cumberland County, Pennsylvania. Chicago: The Genealogical Publishing Company, 1905.

Boyd's Directory of Harrisburg and Steelton .1890-1891.

*Catalogue of Yale University, 1892-93.*Tuttle, Moorehouse & Taylor, 1893.

*Catalogue of Yale University, 1893-94.*Tuttle, Moorehouse & Taylor, 1893.

Coolidge, Beth, Thomas Coolidge. "One of a Kind," 2010.

*Cumberland County, Pennsylvania Cemetery Records.*Bowie: Heritage Books, Inc., 1994.

Cumberland Justice: Legal Practice in Cumberland County, 1750-2000 .Carlisle: Cumberland County Bar Foundation, 2001.

Cumberland Valley Railroad Directory, 1902-1907.

Cushing Thomas. "Catalogue". *Historical Sketch of Chauncy-Hall School, with catalogue of teachers and pupils, and appendix. 1828-1894.* Boston: Press of David Clapp N Son , 1896.

Davidson, Marshall B. *The American Heritage: History of Notable American Houses.* New York: American Heritage Publishing Co., 1971.

Day, Clarence Jr., *Decennial Record of the Class of 1896, Yale College.* New York: De Vinne Press, 1907.

Day, Clarence Jr. *The 96' Half-way Book .* New Haven: Class of 1896, Yale College, 1915.

Dickinson College Catalogue, 1894-1895.

Directory of the Borough of Carlisle . Carlisle Herald office, 1867.

Harrisburg Club of Harrisburg, Pennsylvania. 1903.

Harvard College: Class of 1894, Twenty-fifth Anniversary Report 1894-1919. Norwood: The Plimpton Press.

Harvard College: Class of 1897, Twenty-fifth Anniversary Report 1897-1922. Cambridge: The Riverside Press.

Heinze, Kathleen "The Allenberry Story," *At a Place Called the Boiling Springs.* Boiling Springs Sesquicentennial Publications Committee, 1995.

Heisey, Daniel. "A Man of Discrimination," *Pages of History: Essays on Cumberland County, Pennsylvania.* Carlisle: New Loudon Press, 1994.

Heisey, Daniel. *Ghosts of Carlisle.* Carlisle: New Loudon Press, 1998.

Hertzler, John Vernon Jr., *Thornwald .* Carlisle: The Youth Department of First Reformed Church, 1953.

History of Cumberland and Adams Counties, Pennsylvania. Chicago: Warner, Beers & Co., 1886.

Highway Engineer & Contractor, Vol. 6. Chicago: International Trade Press, February 1922.

Highway Engineer & Contractor, Vol. 7. Chicago: International Trade Press, November 1922.

Hoffer, Ann Kramer. "Remember That". Carlisle: Cumberland County Historical Society, 1990.

Johnson Lynch's Directory of Carlisle, Pa for 1896-97. Wilmington: Johnson & Lynch, 1896.

Kirk, Edward C. D.D.S, ed. *The Dental Cosmos: a monthly record of dental science.* Philadelphia: The S.S. White Dental Manufacturing Co., 1901.

Laub, Barton R. *The Dickinson School of Law: Proud and Independent.* Harrisburg: McFarland Co., 1983.

Lee, Francis Bazley *Genealogical & Personal Memorial of Mercer County, New Jersey Vol. 1.* New York & Chicago: The Lewis Publishing, Co., 1907.

MacKay, Robert B., Anthony K. Baker, Carol A. Traynor , eds. *Long Island Country Homes and Their Architects, 1860-1940.* China: Palace Press , Ltd. 1997.

Marriages and Deaths from the Carlisle Herald Newspapers 1866, 1868-1872. Cumberland County Historical Society, Carlisle, Pa.

Meehan, Susan E. *The Carlisle Hospital: Most Important Building in Town* .Carlisle Area Health & Wellness Foundation, 2008.

Microcosm (Dickinson College yearbook).1890-1905.

Miller, Henry P. and W. Harry Baker, comps. "State Institutions and Boards of Control," *Smull's Legislative Hand Book and Manual of the state of Pennsylvania.* Harrisburg: C.E. Aughinbaugh, 1912.

Moore's Standard Directory and Reference Book of Carlisle. New York City: S.H. Moore Company, 1908.

One Hundred and Sixth Annual Catalogue of Dickinson College. 1880-1890.

Philadelphia in the World War 1914-1919. New York: Wynkoop Hallenbeck Crawford Co., 1922.

Podvia, Mark. "Walter Harrison Hitchler". *Cumberland County History.* Summer 1999.

Polk's Carlisle, Cumberland County, Pa Directory. 1924-1925; 1926-27; 1933-34; 1951-52.

Polk's Philadelphia City Directory, 1925 Part II (M-Z).

Quindecennial Record: Class of Eighteen Hundred Ninety-five. Yale College .New Haven, Connecticut, Moorehouse & Taylor Company, 1911.

Reed, George Liffingwell A.B. *Alumni Record of Dickinson College.* Carlisle: Dickinson College, 1905.

Residence and Business Directory of Carlisle, 1911-1912.

Sheriff & Co's Cumberland Valley Railroad Directory. 1877-78.

Successful Methods: A Magazine of Construction Methods, January 1922.

Talmage, T. De Witt ed. "Dickinson College," *Frank Leslie's Sunday Magazine, vol. xviii- July to December, 1885.*

The Commentator (Dickinson Law School yearbook) 1929.

The Country Club of Harrisburg, 1907.

The Dickinson Alumnus September 1931, November 1931; May 1952; February 1963.

The Dickinson School of Law of Dickinson College, a college catalogue. 1898-99, 1899-1900, 1919-20.

The Highway Magazine, Vol. 12. Chicago: Armco Iron Culvert Flume Manufacturers' Association, October 1921.

Trickett, William. *The Law of Boroughs in Pennsylvania Vol. 2.* Philadelphia: T&J.W Johnson & Co., 1893.

Tuttle, Roger. *Quarter Century Record of the Class of Ninety-Five, Yale College.* The Tuttle, Morehouse & Taylor Company, 1922.

Williams, Charles Scott. *History of Lycoming College.* King Brothers, Inc., 1959.

Young, Henry J. *Abstracts of the Inscriptions in Ashland Cemetery, Carlisle, Cumberland County, Pennsylvania.* 1976.

Select Index

Page numbers in **bold** denote illustrations

A

Ahl family 27-28
Albion Point 10, 12, **27-32**, 36, 37, 71, 92, **139**
Allenberry 25, 140-**141**, 144, 148, 152
Ashland Cemetery 14, 121-122, **123**, 131, 137, 142, 144, 152, 170
Atterbury, William W. 132-**133**
auction
    1953 170, **172-178**
    2010 240

B

basement 46, 52, 64, 76, 93, **95-106**, 121, 139, **237-239**
Biles, George H. **126**, 137-138
billiard room 28, 36, 48, **92**, 107, 169, 194, 202, **221**, 234, **236**
Bingham, Clarence A. 34-35, 37
Boardman, Albert B. 37
Borough of Carlisle 214-215, 216, 218
Bosler, Elizabeth 152
Bosler, Frank 16, 21, 25, 116, 121
Bosler, Frank Jr. 152
Bosler, Helen B. 19-20
Bosler-Sadler, Helen 19-20, 21, 23, 24-**26**, 27-28, 114, 117, **140**, 149, 152, 168
Bosler, James W. 18, **19**, 20
Bosler-Sadler, Mary 19, 21, **22**, 23-27, 114-115, 117, **121**, 152
Bosler Memorial Library **20**
Brown, Harry G. 28
Brumbaugh, Gov. Martin 119, 124
butler's pantry 74, **76**, 107, 168, 170, **203**

C

Carlisle Area School District 178, 214, 216
Carlisle Armory 114-115
Carlisle Deposit Bank 9, 19
Carlisle Hospital **117**, 121, 130, 136-137, 152, 170
conservatory 48, 58, **66**, 71, 74, 80, 216, **232**
Corson, Fred 149
Cottage Hill **18**-21, 23-**24**, 25-28, 32, 36, 114-115, 229

D

dedication
    Homewood 196, **198**-199
    Thornwald Park 215
Dickinson College 10-**12**, 13, 15, 19-20, 25, 47, 149
Dickinson Law School **145**, 156
Dickinson Preparatory School 11-12, 20
dining room
    Albion Point 28, **30**
    Thornwald 36, **71-72**, 73-74, 168, 192, 196, **202**, 217, **232**
Dysert, John 142, 144

E

east wing **88**, 93, 193
Ege-Bucher Mansion 23, **28**, 36
Emory Chapel **15**-16, 120
entrance gateway 36, **53**, **109-112**, 113, **162**
Europe 12, 36, 114-115, 169

F

Farmers Trust Company 25, 113-114, **115-116**, 124, 137-138, 144, 149, 170
fire **222-229**
Fort, John Franklin 14, 25, **130**

G

garage
    Albion Point **31**
    Thornwald 36, **108**, 215
Gleim, Frank 139, 144, **147** - 148, 170
Grant, Richard 144, 148-149
gymnasium 48, **91**- 92, 169, 172, 194

H

Hall, Rkia 71, 240
Harrisburg
    Chestnut Street Hall 115
    Moser, Sadler, Musselman 12
Helen Stephens Mental Health Center 216
Herman, Judge Martin 11
Hertzler, Harry 42
Hertzler Jr., John Vernon 45, **156**-157, 168-170
Hill & Stout 37, **67, 74-76, 91, 93, 245**
Holland Union building 138
Homewood **5**, **168-169**, 177-178, **184-214**, 215-217

K

Kennedy, Moorhead 23,25,**118**,132
kitchen 48, 70, **74-75**, 76, 216-217, **232**

L

library 36, 48, 62, 71, 73, 78, **80-83**, 107, 137, 144, 149, **150-151**, **168-169**, **176**-178, **182**, **192**, 196-**197**, 202-**203**, **217-218**, 230-**231**
Line, Henry 149, 152
loggia 58, **62**, 73, 86, 88, **161**, 193, 217

M

main entrance 28, **50-51,58-61**, 64, 68, 70-71, 109, **147**, 157, **159-160, 209, 222, 228, 240, 242-243**
main hall
  Albion Point **29**
  Thornwald 58, **68**, **70**, 80, 168, **178**, 192, 202, **204**, 217, **230**
Mansion House 141
McCormick, Vance 23
McCulley, William 93,114,136,139
Miller, John X. "Stence" 154-**155**,170
Moore, Parker M. 34-35,37,121
Mooreland 9, 47
music room **78**-79, 168- 169, 230, **231**

N

New Covenant Church 216
Noble, Dr. Joseph **32**,48,154
Noble, William 32
Noble's woods 32, **34-35**, 36, 43, 47, 48
North College Street 9, **10**, 13-14, 16-17, 24, 26, 86, 124, 131, 138

P

PA Commission of Public Safety & Defense 124
PA Council of National Defense 124, 136
Pershing, Gen. John J. 132-**133**
porte-cochere 44, **64-65**
portico 44, 58, **61**, 64, 121, 172, 230
Potomac Synod-Reformed Church 152

Q

Quigley, J. Earl 144

R

Ragged Edge **118**,120,124
rathskeller 36, 96, 100, **102-105**, 106, 152, 169, 170, 237, **238-239**
rear entrance **55-57**, 58, **64-65**, 68, **70**, 106, **147**, **157-158**, 177, **200-201, 206-207, 223-224, 229, 241-243**
reception room 36, 71, **78-79**, 80, 168-169, **231**
Rose Balcony 24-**25**, 121, 129, 140-141

S

Sadler
  book collection 80, **82**, 144, 178
  Curtilage 156
  family 9-14, **13**
  heirlooms **168-169, 172-183, 192, 204-205**
  master bedrooms 48, 86, 88, 107, 169, 192-193, 216-217, **220, 234**
  Mausoleum 121, **123**, 137, 142, 144, 152, 170
  paintings **145**
  residence (N. College Street) **10**, 138
Sadler, Dr. Horace 11-**13**, 14, 23, 25-**26**, 34, 45, 114-117, 121-122, 136-**150**, **151**-152, 154, **155**-156,170,**171**
  dog 149
Sadler, Lewis **8**, 9, 11-**13**, 14, **16**, 21, **22-28**, 32, 36, 47-48, 54, 80, 86, 93, 108, 114-121, 124-**125**, **126**-137, 144
Sadler-Sterrett, Sarah E 9, 11, 14
Sadler, Sir Ralph 36
Sadler, Sylvester 9, 11-**13**, 14, 16-**17**, 21, 23, **138**, 142-**143**, 144-**145**
Sadler, Wilbur **8**, 9-**13**, 14- 17, 19, 21, 25, 115, 117-118, 120, 122, **131**, 142, 145-146, 156
Sadler Jr., Wilbur 11-**13**, 14, **121**-124, 137
Sadler & Sadler 16, 24, 47, 115, 147
secret room (office) 80, **83**, **233**
servants' dining room 36, **76-77**, 88, 95, 192
servants' quarters 36, 88, **93**, 114, 139, 148, 169
Sheafer brothers 42, 113
Sigma Phi Fraternity 138
South College Street 32, 42, **47**, 120, 129, 137
Sproul, Gov. William 120, 124, 126, **127**, 129-131, 135, 136-138
Standard Chain Works 116, 144
Stauffer, Enos 42, 52, 244-**245**
Supreme Court 17, 119-120, 131, 136-138, 142, 144
Sutton House 36, 68, 71

T

Telford road 53, 111
Tener, Gov. John **54**, 115, 117-118, 24
Thompson-Starrett **42**, 48
Thornwald
  funerals **121-123**, 136-137, 142-144, 152
  golfing accident **140**
  guests **54**, 114, 126-**127**, **130**, 131, **132-133**, 149, **150-151**, 152
  robbery **148**
Thornwald Home **178-182**, 213
Thornwald Park **214-215**
Thornwold **107**, 54, 146
Trickett, William **11**, 15-17, 120, 142, 144, **145**
Trickett Hall **120**, 145

W

wall **113**, 215
Weakley, James 9, 11, 15-16
Weakley & Sadler 11
Wertz, Peter 115-116
west wing **86-87**, 88, **93**, **193**, **220**, **240**
wine cellar 96, **100-101**, 106, 238

Y

Yarnall, Winfield S. 37, 42, 52

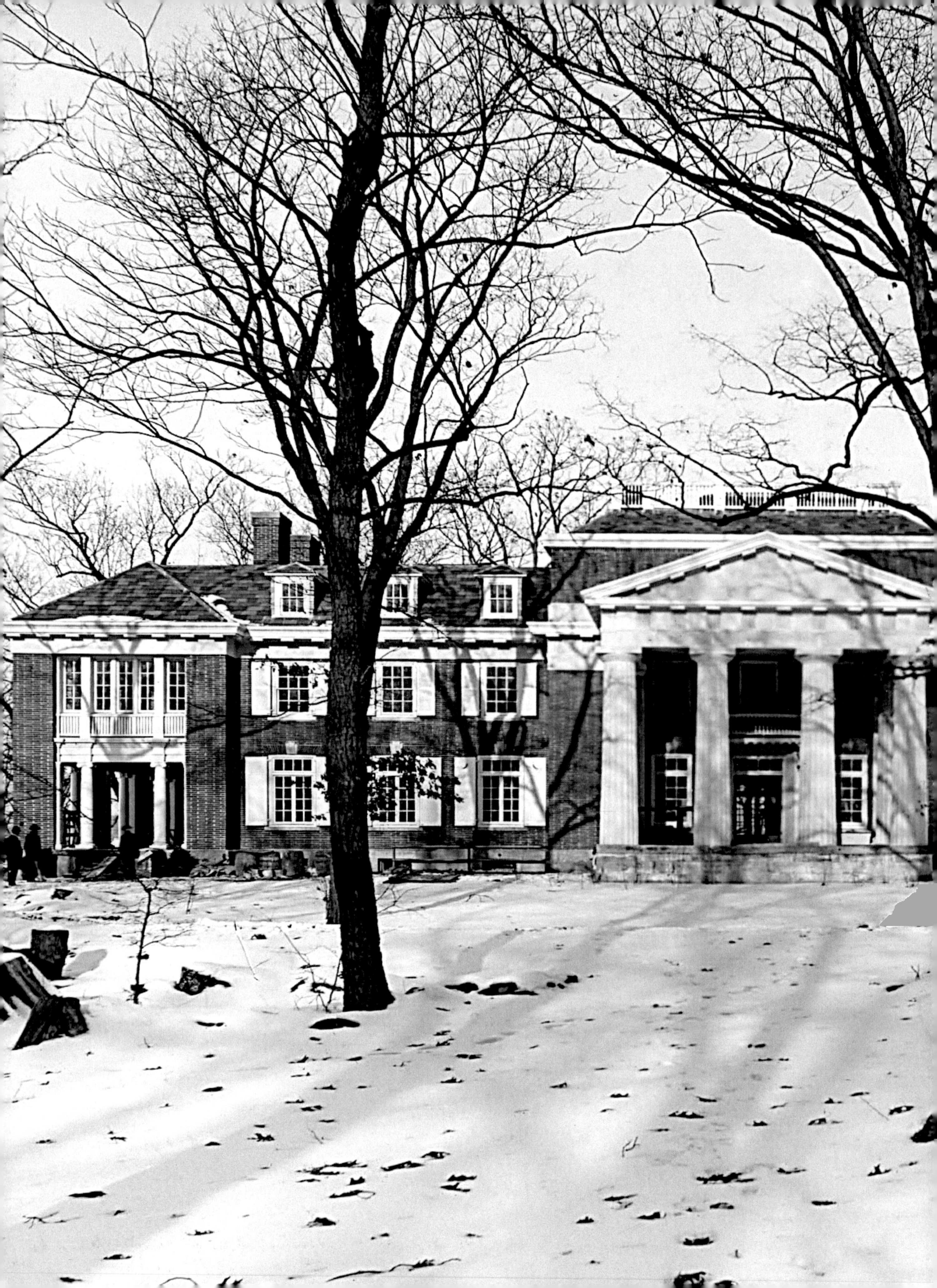